Authentic
Patriotism

Authentic Patriotism

HOW TO RESTORE AMERICA'S IDEALS—WITHOUT LOSING OUR TEMPERS OR OUR MINDS

Stephen P. Kiernan

ST. MARTIN'S GRIFFIN
NEW YORK

www.stmartins.com

Grateful acknowledgment is given for permission to reprint the song lyric "Strange Fruit" by Lewis Allen. Copyright 1939 (renewed) by Music Sales Corporation. International Copyright Secured. All Rights Reserved. Used by permission.

Book design by Meryl Sussman Levavi

The Library of Congress has cataloged the hardcover edition as follows:

Kiernan, Stephen P.
    Authentic patriotism : restoring America's founding ideals through selfless action / Stephen P. Kiernan.—1st ed.
      p. cm.
    ISBN 978-0-312-37911-7
    1. Patriotism—United States. 2. Citizenship—United States. 3. Political participation—United States. 4. Progressivism (United States politics) 5. United States—Politics and government. 6. United States—Social conditions. I. Title.
    JK1759.K54 2010
    323.60973—dc22

2009045701

ISBN 978-0-312-57340-9 (trade paperback)

First St. Martin's Griffin Edition: June 2011

P1

For my amazing sons
and the nation I hope they inherit

Contents

PART ONE

A Nation Adrift

I

A Human Benefit

The only principles of public conduct that are worthy of
a gentleman . . . are to sacrifice estate, ease, health and
applause, and even life, to the sacred calls of his country.
These manly sentiments, in private life, make the good
citizen; in public life, the patriot and the hero.

—JAMES OTIS JR., 1725–83

THE YOUNG DOCTOR ARRIVED at Harlem Hospital with as
much idealism as expertise. After college, medical school, and
a surgical residency in Washington, D.C., plus three more years of
training at Memorial Sloan-Kettering Cancer Center in New York
City, Harold Freeman, M.D., had precise ambitions.

"I was going to cut cancer out of Harlem," he said. "I thought like
a surgeon, you see. And I came there with enthusiasm. It was like I
had a knife in my hand."

He had good reasons for his ambitions. The women of Harlem
contracted breast cancer at rates similar to women in the rest of the city,
but they died at double the rate. Freeman thought the problem could be
solved by medicine, by surgeons like himself. The real cause, though,
and the limited impact his skills could have, became plain after only a
few patient examinations.

"Women would come in for the first visit, and you would ask
them to disrobe. But then you couldn't see the breast. The breasts
would be replaced by cancer, completely replaced. All you could see

was an ulcerated, bleeding mass. I thought, how in the world can this happen in America?"

Dr. Freeman is now a nationally recognized authority on the links between cancer, poverty, and race. But in those days he was a newly minted surgeon, thirty-four years old. He had turned down opportunities at major medical centers and in private practice, because instead of enriching himself he wanted to help the African American community. He was accustomed to treating one patient at a time, a tactic that in Harlem too often proved futile. Breast cancer is a beatable disease, but success hinges on how early treatment begins. The cases he saw were all advanced. "Cancer would not yield to the knife," he said. "It was too late."

Over time Freeman pieced together the problem. Low-income women did not have health insurance, and thus no primary care doctors to give them regular examinations. They would show up at the emergency room with worries, complaints, or lumps. Freeman recalled, "They would be told, 'Your condition is not an emergency. Go to the Medicaid office on Thirty-fourth Street.'"

But these women could not afford transportation, nor spare the hours the trip would take. They might also be intimidated by the bureaucracy. So they would simply go without care until the cancer had indeed become an emergency—by which time it was far beyond the reach of medicine.

"These women were all poor," Dr. Freeman observed. "They were all black too. I wondered: How can we disentangle poverty and race from their medical condition? It is a complex question. They led me to my life's work."

The first step was to screen women for cancer earlier. Harlem Hospital clinics operated Monday through Friday, which meant some medical units were idle on weekends. "I adopted an area," Dr. Freeman said, "and set up a Saturday clinic without administrative approval." He chuckles at the memory. "I was very diplomatic about being rebellious."

The clinic was tiny: one nurse, one doctor, and a clerk, providing examinations for free. Optimism came easily. "Fairly soon, we were beginning to get some cases where the masses were small," Freeman said.

When hospital management found out about the clinic, they ordered that it be shut down. "But then we had a stroke of luck, because the administrator assigned to closing it got fired." Soon the city agency that oversees public hospitals decided to support the clinic, found a path through the Medicaid bureaucracy, and made the whole operation legal.

"We had now established several ways for women to be screened," Freeman recalls, "even mammography, and even if they couldn't pay. That was in 1979. The clinic has been open every Saturday from then till now."

Over the following decade the rate at which Harlem women died of breast cancer slowed, but the decline was nowhere near as dramatic as Freeman had expected. He applied a surgeon's logic: "If you recognize that there is a problem, you want to do something about it, and you want to complete the entire task. If I'm operating on a person with cancer of the right colon, for example, I make an incision, I observe the mass, I remove the mass, and I close the incision. The case is not over until the entire task is done. With the clinic, women were getting the test results, but that only opens the problem. It doesn't close it. These women need biopsies, they need treatment."

That would take more than a weekly clinic. It would require resources, money, a new attitude about caring for the poor. To win friends to his ideas, Freeman began writing. His *Cancer in the Economically Disadvantaged* (1989) remains a landmark in connecting disease to income and race. Among the new friends he won to his cause, the American Cancer Society brought him onto its board, later making him president. Freeman used that position to hold hearings on poverty and disease across the country.

"We wanted to hear the views of the poor people. In Saint Louis, Phoenix, northern New Jersey, Sacramento, they all said the same thing. 'We meet barriers when we attempt to access care.' For me, looking through the lens of Harlem, they enabled me to see that it was a national problem—for poor people, of any race, anywhere."

Freeman found four kinds of obstacles that kept poor women from receiving decent breast care. Financial barriers came first, from lack of health insurance to inability to pay for medicines or transportation. Communication was second, because patients often did not understand what doctors told them. More and more of them did not speak

English. Fear came third, because in addition to their terrifying illness, poor people do not trust caregivers and are highly skeptical of large institutions. Last was complexity. Cancer care involves a Byzantine maze of oncologists, radiologists, surgeons, paperwork, referrals, moving around hospital clinics, and more. "In a fragmented system," Freeman said, "people get lost."

His idea was to create a new kind of caregiver, a nonmedical guide and advocate for the patient: a navigator. "They would be put on the case the moment the doctor said something must be done. They would listen, then ask the patient, 'Did you understand? Let me show you where you need to go now.' The navigator takes the burden from the patient."

Navigators were inexpensive compared to the rest of health care, initially costing about $40,000 a year. And they dramatically shortened the time from diagnosis to resolution of a case. Cancer mortality in Harlem fell so fast, other health institutions noticed. They began coming to observe the navigator model.

"We are about to have six people here from the Cleveland Clinic, a huge and prestigious hospital system." He smiles and shakes his head. "Yes, they are coming to Harlem—to learn from us."

The man and his idea became better known. When the head of Sloan-Kettering asked the designer Ralph Lauren if he would contribute to their research, Lauren replied that he wanted to help people directly. So the hospital referred him to Freeman.

"This was six years ago," the doctor recalled. "We met, and he asked me, 'What is your vision?' I told him. He thanked me. I thanked him. And two weeks later I received a check for five million dollars." Then the Livestrong Foundation, founded by bike racing legend and cancer survivor Lance Armstrong, also made generous donations.

This funding made possible the creation of the Ralph Lauren Center for Cancer Care and Prevention in East Harlem—an organization developing new community-based models for cancer prevention and treatment. The money also financed research, which led to more publications, which meant that more hospitals heard about navigators.

As the concept spread, Freeman became famous in medical circles. The Institute of Medicine recognized him, as did the National Academy of Sciences. The Robin Hood Foundation—a group of hugely successful New Yorkers who underwrite programs proven most effective at reducing poverty-related problems—gave Freeman their Hero Award. He also won the Mary Woodard Lasker Public Service Award, from a foundation named for that prestigious medical research advocate. The citation read:

> Dr. Freeman has shifted the paradigm for understanding disease in poor communities and among minority populations. Caring for the voiceless in our society, Dr. Freeman's humanitarian efforts have increased survival rates for thousands of people. Uncommon zeal in the pursuit of his goal, devotion to patients, and a diplomatic, sensitive approach to change characterize his advocacy. Dr. Freeman exemplifies the highest qualities of a public servant on behalf of the underserved.

Gradually Freeman became adept at speaking to large audiences. Picture him: a tall black man, wearing brown-framed glasses, his voice so soft it compels the entire room to hush, hands before him held fingertip to fingertip, somewhere between grasping a ball and folding in prayer. He developed powerful sound bites: "I believe poverty is a condition that should not be punishable by death."

He also began speaking about himself, his journey and motivations. The topic starts with his father, who died at forty-eight, when Freeman was thirteen, from the same cancer that Lance Armstrong survived. No wonder the young Harold chose the path that he did. His mother did not let the challenge of raising her sons alone diminish her ambitions for them. When a school counselor told Freeman and his classmates they would be foolish to set their sights on becoming doctors or lawyers, and should content themselves with a lesser station in life, "She went down there, she was very angry, she went to the school and confronted this person."

Moving backward in time, he tells about his great-granduncle, who went to Harvard and in 1869 became the nation's first black dentist. But if there is an ultimate model for Freeman, his dignity and determination, it is his great-great-grandfather, Walter. "He did not have a last name," Freeman said, "because he was a slave."

Walter's slave master was George Badger, a judge in Raleigh, North Carolina, who allowed Walter to hire himself out as a carpenter when his plantation work was finished. "He allowed Walter to keep half of his earnings, until he had saved three thousand dollars, at which point he bought his freedom. It was 1839. Then he continued to work four more years, until he had purchased the freedom of his wife, Eliza, and five children."

In 2006, Freeman went in search of his family's archives. Raleigh historians had no documents to guide him. But the University of North Carolina at Chapel Hill maintained voluminous records, because Badger had later become a U.S. senator.

"They kept the materials behind locked, closed glass doors. But there was a folder with all of the records. George Badger had purchased Walter for three hundred and eighty-eight dollars; I saw the bill of sale: one human, Walter. The writing was beautiful. Really remarkable penmanship. A year after the purchase the slave master had married; the girl was from a prosperous family, and their wedding gift was fourteen slaves. I went through the names, and one of them was named Eliza. That was my great-great-grandmother."

The family moved to the Washington, D.C., area, where Robert, the future dentist, was born. When the next census came, the official asked Walter if he had a last name.

"'I am a *free man*,'" the doctor recounted Walter replying. He smiled slightly. "And that is how I came by my last name: Freeman."

EVENTUALLY ENOUGH TIME had passed since the birth of the navigator concept for Freeman to conduct research on its impact. "First we studied a twenty-two-year period ending in 1986. So this was before we had intervened. In that time, six hundred and six patients were treated for breast cancer at Harlem Hospital. They were one hundred percent black, and all poor. Half had later-stage cancer when they came in. Five years after diagnosis, thirty-nine percent of the six hundred and six were alive.

"Then we studied a six-year period ending in 2000. This group was also all minorities—seventy-five percent black and twenty-five percent Hispanic—and all poor. In those six years there were three hundred and twenty-five patients at Harlem Hospital with breast cancer. But by then we had assured that anyone could get a mammogram. And if there was a finding, everyone received navigation. This time the five-year survival rate was seventy percent.

"We had not changed the conditions, demographics, poverty, or percent uninsured. All we had changed were the screening and the navigator. And all those women continued to live."

DR. FREEMAN'S STORY bears telling because it reveals how the world may be continuously improved. It demonstrates how compassion can save lives. It shows how a person can decide all by himself to expand the range of life's possibilities. It reminds us that the arc of lives in America can run from the depths of slavery to the pinnacle of public service, because opportunity still exists here. It proves how ambition on behalf of others is an unstoppable force for change.

In America, cancer is the second leading cause of mortality, killing 550,000 people a year. In America, having the world's strongest economy has not been sufficient to prevent millions of people from remaining poor. Yet one man was willing—even eager—to take on both of these challenges at once. Two decades into the government's war on poverty, he found a battlefield where victories were scarce. Decades into government's and the free market's war on cancer, he found a critical area that had been entirely neglected. So here he was, a highly trained physician, granted—yet still only one individual, one determined person, seeking to make a difference. He would do it not for his own benefit, but because he saw a need and wanted to help.

"Each one of us is gifted," Freeman said. "I am gifted. So are you. We each need to find our gift, whatever it may be, and we have to develop it so we can create a human benefit from within ourselves. I believe this is the only way to achieve satisfaction and happiness in this life."

There is a name for a person with such courage, such commitment, such a sense of being part of something larger than the himself. There is a name for a person who sees a problem and declares that it cannot be allowed to persist in a country as great as ours. There is a name for a person who exercises independence as a means of working for the common good.

This is an authentic patriot.

2

No Longer the Fringe

The money changers have fled from their high seats in the temple of our civilization. We may now restore that temple to the ancient truths.

The measure of the restoration lies in the extent to which we apply social values more noble than monetary profit. . . . These dark days will be worth all they cost if they teach us that our true destiny is not to be ministered unto but to minister to ourselves and to our fellow men.

If I read the temper of our people correctly, we now realize as we have never before our interdependence on each other; that we cannot merely take, but we must give as well; that if we are to go forward we must move as a trained and loyal army willing to sacrifice for the good of a common discipline, because without such discipline, no progress is made, no leadership becomes effective.

We are, I know, ready and willing to submit our lives and property to such discipline because it makes possible a leadership which aims at a larger good.

— FRANKLIN DELANO ROOSEVELT, MARCH 4, 1933

ONE HUNDRED YEARS AGO, the sun never set on the British Empire. The majestic enterprise of the United Kingdom, her colonies and businesses, literally spanned the globe. Yet today Great Britain, while an important actor on the international stage, is far from being the world's preeminent force in commerce, military might, or diplomacy. The supremacy of nations through time is never assured.

That lesson bears directly on the United States today. While this country has never held the vast colonies of imperial Britain, barely two decades ago America did possess international preeminence and unrivaled influence. The twentieth century could well be called "the American century," because it witnessed the emergence of this nation as a global leader: the strongest economy, the font of innovation, the mightiest armed forces, the source of prosperity, the defender of great ideals from liberty at home to victory abroad, the living manifestation of all the potential contained in a capitalist democracy. With the collapse of the Soviet Union, America stood alone as the world's sole superpower.

The United States still possesses all the potential for greatness that it ever did. Yet today America is a nation adrift.

Some would blame the wars in Iraq and Afghanistan, calling them drains on the federal budget, distractions from domestic concerns, and operations of questionable purpose. Others attribute the nation's woes to the economy, arguing that jobs lost to other nations, unscrupulous lending, excessive consumerism, and corporate greed have undermined America's well-being.

Whatever their merit, these arguments confuse cause with effect. War and the economy are not the reasons for America's problems; rather, they are symptoms of the underlying illness. The fighting continues without clear goals for the same reason the economy stumbles along without a clear course.

Even if both problems were solved, that reason would remain. Indeed, by the time you hold this book, the battles in Iraq and Afghanistan may be ended, thanks to massive American investments in blood and coin, with the troops hopefully basking in public gratitude. Likewise the economy shows signs of turning toward recovery, if only by inches: Foreclosures, layoffs, and bankruptcies have slowed, while investment markets are stumbling northward. But do you think the soldiers' return will mean the end of America's drift? Do you believe a wave of hiring or new records for the Dow Jones Industrial Average will restore the nation's greatness? Of course not. The deeper issues will remain. The challenges that confront America today are larger than the primary foreign and domestic turmoils of the moment. They have developed over the span of a generation, flourishing in peace as in war, worsening in good economic times and bad. If anything, the invasion of Iraq and the deep recession are symptomatic of the disconnection and alienation that ails our country. You cannot successfully prosecute a war without involving the citizenry at home. You cannot build sustainable economic growth unless the benefits reach more than a fraction of the populace.

The problem, in its essence, is one of *engagement*. The American people are no longer fully engaged in the task of building a more perfect union. Their involvement in improving the condition of the country has waned, one person at a time, until most of the population considers that mission somebody else's business.

Civic passivity might work in some other country, under some other system—a military dictatorship, for example, in which the generals and their armies protect their interests while the public fends for itself and hopes to avoid trouble. But passivity under a political system like America's is a potentially fatal shortcoming. A democracy without the active efforts of engaged citizens is like a monarchy without a king.

Yet that is what America has become. What is the proper way to measure a country's drift? There are many: Among the developed nations, for example, the United States stands highest in energy use per person and highest in contribution to global warming. It also ranks worst in teen pregnancy, worst in obesity, worst in the rate of sexually transmitted diseases, highest in the percentage of the population in jail, highest in tons of trash produced per person, nearly worst in infant mortality, highest in divorce, worst in violent crimes from sexual assault to murder, highest in the percentage of children born to unwed mothers, highest in bankruptcy, highest in the production and consumption of pornography, greatest in time lost to passive entertainments such as TV and video games, and highest in the number of people without adequate health care.

Over the past twenty years the U.S. economy has relied increasingly—and too heavily—on people consuming things, instead of people making things. The results are indebtedness, risk, over-emphasis on material comforts, and isolation instead of community.

These ailments have created a culture of need whose volume is stunning. Today there are about 320 million people in the United States. Forty million of them live in poverty, with another 25 million teetering on the edge. Forty-six million people have no health insurance, with 25 million more underinsured. Some 38 million people are living with a disability. About 3.5 million Americans each year experience homelessness.

If you add these numbers up, there is only one possible conclusion: Need is not a fringe issue. Not anymore. Hunger, illness that worsens by going untreated, housing that is shabby or overpriced or nonexistent—these troubles are rapidly becoming the norm. They are woven into the fabric of this country. The longer these needs go un-met, the greater they become.

Each of the domestic problems cited above is a call to action. Each is also trending in the wrong direction.

Meanwhile the immediate international concern of our time, the potential for terrorist attacks on America and her friends, ought to unite us against a shared threat and a common foe. Instead this issue has been used to create political wedges, to feed worry, to divide us.

The other urgent global concern, the planet's health, is a life-threatening problem government has too long denied. The free market, meanwhile, has remained anchored in place by advocates for the status quo. As a consequence the great engine for innovation, America's economy, has instead protected obsolete cars, factories, and sources of energy.

This country is not an island. While America founders, the rest of the world is busy charting a forward course. Twenty-seven nations put aside ancient economic and political differences, surrendered their currencies, and formed the powerful European Union. China continues its rapid rise out of Third World conditions to become a globally competitive economy; there are now more people who speak English in China than in the United States. Moreover, China's government shows few qualms about displacing people or destroying the environment to reach its goals.

Oil-rich nations from Russia to the Persian Gulf to Venezuela continue to enjoy disproportionate political and economic clout— as well as enough hubris to insult the United States—especially when petroleum prices remain high. India has capitalized on U.S. firms' interest in lower labor costs, winning millions of our service industry jobs.

Groups not aligned with any nation are also flourishing at America's expense. Al Qaeda trains, equips, and finances terrorists whose declared enemy is Western culture in general, and the United States in particular. Lawlessness in Somalia has led to modern-day piracy in the shipping lanes of the Indian Ocean.

On one continent after another, the world sees nations and groups with new political powers, new financial might, new global influence, while the economic and diplomatic influence of the United States are both in decline.

The journalist Thomas Friedman describes a trip he and his wife took from John F. Kennedy International Airport in New York. "In J.F.K.'s waiting lounge we could barely find a place to sit. Eighteen hours later we landed at Singapore's ultramodern airport, with free Internet portals and children's play zones throughout. We felt like we had just flown from the Flintstones to the Jetsons."

Such disparity exists among mature Western democracies too. "If all Americans could compare Berlin's luxurious central train station with the grimy, decrepit Penn Station in New York City," Friedman wrote, "they would swear we were the ones who lost World War II."

Simultaneously with America's growing problems, in other words, has come the undeniable rise of the rest of the world. As Fareed Zakaria, international editor of *Newsweek,* has written:

> The world's tallest building is in Taipei, and will soon be in Dubai. Its largest publicly traded company is in Beijing. Its biggest refinery is being constructed in India. Its largest passenger aircraft is built in Europe. The largest investment fund on the planet is in Abu Dhabi; the biggest movie industry is Bollywood, not Hollywood.

Once quintessentially American icons have been usurped by the natives. The largest Ferris wheel is in Singapore. The largest casino is in Macao, which overtook Las Vegas in gambling revenues last year [2007]. America no longer dominates even its favorite sport, shopping. The Mall of America in Minnesota once boasted that it was the largest shopping mall in the world. Today it wouldn't make the top ten. In the most recent rankings, only two of the world's richest ten people are American.

These lists are arbitrary and a bit silly, but consider that only ten years ago, the United States would have serenely topped almost every one of these categories.

The greatest expression of the situation is not in symbols like these, however, nor in the worst-of list above. It is in people's own experience of living in the United States today. When New Orleans was underwater, did you feel disbelief? When you saw photos of U.S. soldiers torturing naked prisoners, did you have a taste of shame? When another house in your community sprouts a FOR SALE sign due to foreclosure, do you feel your own security weakening? When you hear about schoolyard shootings and workplace killings, do you wonder about your own safety? When you watch your retirement funds dwindle, do you lose confidence in the future? When you observe the soaring costs of college, do you worry about educating your kids? When you see the breathtaking expense of health care, do you fret about what might happen if you should become sick?

Do you feel, in other words, like the distance between your life and the lives of those people in need is shrinking? Do you believe that the responses of government are too little, too late? Do you sense that the free market is indifferent to whether things turn out well for you and your family? Does the news often fill you with anger, frustration, or fear? Do you tire of politicians who behave as though all the nation's problems are simply the other party's fault? When you pause to contemplate how much America has to cherish, how much is at stake, and how much decay the country is seeing, do you experience sadness?

Do you feel like your nation is adrift?

These emotions are not mere nostalgia. The United States has faced its challenges in the past too, of course. But the range and depth of the problems today, and the public's disengagement from the task of solving them, make the past seem genuinely rosier.

For years now, polls have found that a majority of Americans believe their country is headed in the wrong direction. This high level of discontent derives from the political climate, to be sure, but it also reflects broader cultural concerns. This country simply does not feel as strong as it once did.

The irony is that America's resources—in people, ingenuity, and spirit—are as muscular as ever. You would think when a nation so wealthy, so powerful, so blessed with potential becomes adrift, that her people would join hands, build bridges, raise barns, and share sacrifices on her behalf.

Instead most Americans are not engaged, and do not consider the well-being of their nation an issue meriting their attention. The public stands on the sidelines, worried but passive, disenfranchised but hoping someone will come along and fix everything.

Maybe the rescue will come from Wall Street. People follow the financial news, hoping stocks will rise—as in time they assuredly will. But the public is purely a spectator in the mayhem of investing; people are no more masters of their stocks' fates than the passengers on an airplane are making it land safely. Moreover, the financial industry contributed so much to the economy's collapse, it seems like the realm that least deserves public trust.

Maybe the answer could be President Barack Obama. His call to unity of national spirit, his urgings toward service, have galvanized millions of people. Even those who voted for John McCain acknowledged the charismatic appeal of Obama's message. But he arrived at the White House with two wars under way, an economy in crisis, and global mayhem, from the nuclear ambitions of North Korea to the contested election in Iran. Moreover, government is too sluggish, and too divided by partisanship, to lead the way to a stronger America. The best government can do is follow. Waiting for Washington to solve our problems only exacerbates our passivity.

And that is the main problem, underlying all of the others: We

Americans today are not agents of our own salvation. We see problems, but do not participate in solving them. What we experience, therefore, is what anyone experiences who observes a problem but does not contribute to its solution: anxiety. When we stop to think about the nation's future, we have a bad feeling in our guts.

Fortunately, anxiety and inaction are not omnipresent—not even close—as most of this book will attest. Many Americans are lifting their communities and their nation in ways never before imagined. Their stories, their methods, their achievements, and their satisfactions offer lessons to the rest of the country: that an individual can make a meaningful difference. That the freedoms America confers on its citizens nourish that potential for change. That every person who contributes to the common purpose also helps to renew the nation. That the humanitarian gains from civic engagement make economic sense. That working on behalf of a larger purpose *feels good.*

The people who know these things, and act on them, they are the authentic patriots. Part two of this book is about them: how they started, what they learned, how their energy and ideas can spread.

This book chooses not to address needs in other nations, but not out of any denial of problems elsewhere, nor with a blind eye to the increase in global interconnection. Many authentic patriots devote their energies to commendable projects in other lands. But the capacity of this nation to help others depends in large measure on its own well-being; we cannot lift the world as well as we might until we are taking better care of ourselves. We need to get our house in order first.

Moreover, the unique combination of American pioneer spirit, American liberty to pursue whatever goals a person chooses, American ingenuity in a society that is constantly improvised, and American ability to sidestep obstacles when doing so enables things to get done faster—these attributes are easier to see if the projects are closer to home.

But this book is also about you. Part three is about the opportunity for every American to participate in national rejuvenation. It explains what the elements of authentic patriots' successes have been, so their gains can be replicated and their attitude spread. It offers examples of people from all walks of life solving all kinds of problems—and along the way discovering how good it feels to make a difference.

The need for more people who understand this discovery, the need for an America whose people are engaged in restoring our nation's well-being, is urgent. Simply project current trends a few years forward. At some point, the mechanisms that balance our society will break. Will it happen when 60 million Americans lack health insurance? Or when 50 million live in poverty? Or when 3 million are in jail? What happens when another city is ravaged by environmental disaster like New Orleans, or another terrorist strike occurs, or the economy dips too far to rescue? These are all plausible possibilities.

They do not account, either, for the day when this is a nation of 500 million people, sharing a globe with 9 billion. Or the inevitable time when there is no more oil. When nuclear threats from terrorists or rogue states make the Cold War look like old men playing chess. When climate change irrevocably alters sea levels and shorelines, seasons and crops, air quality and the survival of species. When something as completely predictable as the aging of the baby boomers creates massive new demands on government services.

Today there are far too many people who behave as if addressing these needs—of anticipating and meeting them, of sustaining the country's well-being—is not their job. The result has been a disconnection of people from one another, and a loss of common purpose.

The central question of our time, therefore, is how we remedy the situation. The answer will not be determined by people a hundred years in the future. Rather, it is being written by what we do here, now, today. In a democracy, people only receive the nation they earn for themselves. What resources are there for reversing the decay? How will we cope? Who will restore this nation adrift?

3

The Need for a New Way

There is a great tradition of warning in presidential farewells, and I've got one that's been on my mind for some time. But oddly enough it starts with one of the things I'm proudest of in the past eight years: the resurgence of national pride that I called the new patriotism. This national feeling is good, but it won't count for much, and it won't last, unless it's grounded in thoughtfulness and knowledge. An informed patriotism is what we want. . . . Those of us who are over thirty-five or so years of age grew up in a different America. We were taught, very directly, what it means to be an American. And we absorbed, almost from the air, a love of country and an appreciation of its institutions. . . .

Some things have changed. Younger parents aren't sure that an unambivalent appreciation of America is the right thing to teach modern children. And as for those who create the popular culture, well-grounded patriotism is no longer the style. . . . If we forget what we did, we won't know who we are. I'm warning of an eradication of the American memory that could result, ultimately, in an erosion of the American spirit.

— RONALD REAGAN, JANUARY 11, 1989

THROUGHOUT HISTORY, AMERICANS HAVE embraced two ways of solving the country's most serious problems. The first means is through government, which liberals have embraced as the well-intentioned expression of the people's collective will. Government will help people when they cannot help themselves, through spending, regulation, litigation, and legislation. The second mechanism is the free market, which is the preferred solution of conservatives. Capitalism will energize ideas, reward merit, cultivate creativity, and thereby spread prosperity.

Each approach has its own devotees. Each served the nation well in addressing the challenges of the twentieth century. And neither is remotely capable of responding to today's problems with the swiftness, energy, initiative, sacrifice, and resolve that these difficult moments demand.

The old ways will no longer work. If you contrast the societal impact of government and free markets two generations ago with their current condition, it is clear that they have become sharks with no teeth.

ON THE DAY before his inauguration, Franklin Roosevelt visited the White House for the traditional courtesy tour by the outgoing president. Instead of the usual pleasantries, however, Herbert Hoover had something more substantive planned. He'd arranged for the Secretary of the Treasury and the head of the Federal Reserve Bank to join him and Roosevelt for an Oval Office meeting on the economic crisis sweeping the nation. Already 6,350 banks had failed or closed. Five million people were unemployed. The president urged an immediate response by the president-elect.

Roosevelt ignored the alarm, and took office the next day. But he swiftly became aware that the nation was entering unprecedented economic difficulties. Following the stock market crash in September 1929, access to capital vanished and confidence in the currency crumbled. The number of unemployed people eventually reached 11 million. The economy stalled as never before. Meanwhile a combination of antiquated agricultural techniques and a prolonged drought had devastated thousands of farms—and in that era agriculture was a much larger segment of the economy than it is today.

This combination of urban and rural devastation was unlike any economic downturn that the nation had experienced before. No one employer could solve the myriad problems. No industry had a reach so wide that it could employ all the surplus workers. No financial institution had the resources sufficient to underwrite a nationwide recovery. Above all, no individual had the means to inspire an economic revival.

The only solution was for government to take the lead, and in an unprecedented way. While relief took many forms, the primary approach was fiscal policy: spending.

Using the Reconstruction Finance Corporation, which Hoover had created, Roosevelt led the federal government to spend billions of dollars essentially employing people. The RFC loaned money to states for public works projects, to railroads to keep freight moving, and to banks for loans to farmers and home builders.

As the financial system stabilized, spending by Roosevelt's RFC leapt to greater heights: $1.5 billion (in 1930s dollars) for relief grants, almost $250 million for rural electrification, $200 million to the Export-Import Bank, $35 million for disaster relief, and more. Meanwhile the Works Progress Administration and the Civilian Conservation Corps put thousands of men and women to work. Some people logged, others taught, others played in orchestras, and they all drew a wage.

These federal agencies built things: bridges, roads, schools, and courthouses. And so, brick by brick, the nation crept out of poverty first and dependency next. For many people on the political left, this degree of government involvement set the standard.

To be sure, many of the best ideas of government in the past century have endured because of this belief: Social Security unquestionably reduces poverty among the elderly. Medicare without doubt enables seniors to receive health care. Head Start continues to provide youngsters with a safe place to prepare for school, while their low-income parents work to better their lives. Land conservation certainly protects species, valuable habitat, and pristine wilderness. Foreign aid wins America friends while reaffirming this nation's importance to the world.

President Lyndon Johnson's War on Poverty has been widely criticized, but its impact was nonetheless profound: The portion of U.S. children living in poverty fell from 23 percent in 1963 to 14 percent in 1969.

Not surprisingly, many liberals therefore continue to see government as central to solving new or newly pressing public concerns. If a people are discriminated against, government can enforce equality. If an individual is suffering, a combination of training and handouts will restore him. If an industry is guilty of excess, regulation will curb it.

But here is the brutal reality: This model no longer works. Government no longer responds sufficiently to the most difficult issues facing the nation. Despite dire and urgent national problems, any progress government provides today is small, the gains difficult if not impossible to quantify. The response is not nearly the equal of the challenge.

How is this possible? How did the long-proven might of government become feckless? The reasons are many; here we will consider four.

First, no discussion of contemporary governing can overlook the force of lobbying. In their efforts to influence Congress, the various special interests now collectively spend $16 million *per day*. While the right of people to petition their government is guaranteed in the Constitution, still it is fair to ask on whose behalf that daily fortune is spent. In health care, do the voices on behalf of the uninsured sound equally to those of health insurers, hospitals, physicians, nurses, medical schools, pharmaceutical companies, and medical technology manufacturers? In housing, do those who speak on behalf of the homeless reach as many ears as advocates for the construction industry, real estate, or household financial services? Do those who petition government on behalf of the unemployed and underpaid experience the same access as groups that oppose a higher minimum wage or expanded job training programs?

The power of lobbyists to persuade has a definite influence on policy. Presidents of both parties have been known to support legislation actually written by lobbyists. But there is another, less well known way that lobbyists gain power: through campaign funding. If the widget manufacturers' association sees a potential ally in a candidate, its lobbyists are swift to contact individual widget makers with calls to support that candidate financially. Should that politician win, his indebtedness will be repaid with the association's access to his office. Thus the founding principle of government as the representation of the people's will is no longer certain.

The second reason government cannot solve the great problems of our time is that its influence has been dramatically diminished. The economic collapse that began in 2008 illustrates the point: When Congress injected $850 *billion* into the financial system to restore the banking industry, the markets did not even pause for breath before continuing their downward spiral. When the bailout spending reached $1.3 trillion in 2009—that's $3,600 for every man, woman, and child within the nation's borders—the economy responded by continuing to shed six hundred thousand jobs each month.

Granted, the bailout funds probably prevented the collapse from being worse. But the resulting economic conditions and persistent uncertainty prove that government simply lacks the clout of a generation ago.

And when government does aim high, the public has reason for skepticism. Too often a grand enterprise shirks its obligations. Medicare, for example, pays only about 60 percent of the costs of its beneficiaries' care. Likewise Congress's well-meaning mandates for special education at local schools have never been provided with federal funding as the legislation promised.

Some of government's diminished influence is also the result of self-inflicted wounds. Congress provides a steady supply of justifications for the public's loss of confidence in its members: One has a refrigerator stuffed with cash, another seeks a homosexual tryst in an airport bathroom. One is convicted of concealing lavish gifts, another of emailing young congressional pages with hopes of seduction. These personal peccadilloes are nothing, though, compared with partisanship. In 2009, while the United States endured the worst economy since the Great Depression, bleeding more than twenty thousand jobs a day, several governors said they would refuse federal stimulus money. Forget the acute needs of the people of their states, forget the fragility of the national economy, forget the Depression era's proof of fiscal policy as an economic balm—scoring political points mattered more.

Still, the problem is greater than the misdeeds of these disappointing few. The triviality of contemporary politics, the perpetual animosities and petty symbolisms, the sound and fury over tiny steps and small ambitions, they are rendered in full view on C-SPAN every day. There the cameras show representatives and senators delivering speech after speech in the House and Senate chambers—to rooms that are otherwise empty. In what was once called the world's greatest deliberative body, no one is debating; no one is even listening.

The third reason government responds too little to today's urgent needs is the increasing complexity of legislating. Once upon a time Congress could behave in a dramatic way, enacting powerful changes to policy and spending. But today the pressure of partisanship kills most bold ideas. One need only observe the rituals of character attack that both parties commit the moment anyone is nominated to the Supreme Court: Denouncements of the president's candidate begin literally within minutes. That is what passes for policy debate today.

No wonder the public routinely ranks the ethics of Congress below those of lawyers and journalists. No wonder Congress rarely rises above a 50 percent approval rating. Try to recall a piece of lawmaking that transformed government or redirected society in the past twenty-five years. Like the health care reform under debate at the time of this writing, there are examples—but they are as rare as parking spots outside the Capitol.

The business of Congress used to be the well-being of the nation. Today its members focus instead on the home district, and serve their constituents with the earmark. An earmark is a modest addition to a large, must-pass bill—for example, one that funds a major arm of government. The bill's particulars may be as ugly as a dog's breakfast, but if each member of Congress can add something to placate voters back home, the proposal will pass. Thus, for example, instead of a national housing initiative to respond to the rapid increase in homeless families all over the country, a representative or senator will earmark funds for a housing project in his or her district.

Often pundits criticize these earmarks as benefiting too few people, and being too lavish with the public's money. Often that criticism is fair too; government is capable of breathtaking waste. But frequently, earmarks represent a frank pragmatism on the part of members of Congress, a you-scratch-my-back realism, to achieve the little that is possible in an era of partisanship and small accomplishments. You do what you can, and hope the folks at home are happy enough to re-elect you.

But if one martini is delicious, twenty martinis are toxic. Earmarks have reached an absurd volume. The federal budget passed in December 2007 contained nine thousand of them. They cost billions.

That profligacy leads directly to the fourth reason government can no longer serve as the primary force for answering human needs: lack of money. Washington is simply too saddled with debt to entertain novel ideas or new initiatives. As of late October 2009, the federal treasury was indebted by $11,910,626,411,014.95. That's $11.9 *trillion*. If you divide that liability by the nation's population, the obligation stands at $38,774.30 per American.

At the time of this writing, a debate is under way about reforming health care financing. Over a decade, the Obama administration's plan would cost nearly a trillion dollars more. Yet even this prediction is based on an assumption of cutting costs that have not yet been identified. The need for a more rational system of paying for health care is so great, it's probable that some portion of the current proposals could become law. Depending on the result, that reform may provide a welcome exception to the last several decades of legislative history. But it will also intensify the extent to which government's capacity to address other urgent needs is constrained by overspending in the past.

Think of it as simply as this: Today, wholly apart from health care financing reform, the nation's debt is climbing at a rate of $3.8 billion per day. The rate may accelerate too. Current projections anticipate the federal government will spend $980 billion more than its tax revenues in fiscal 2009. Then there are the war and reconstruction in Iraq, expected to fly north of $1 trillion. The 2008 bailout of the Fannie Mae and Freddie Mac mortgage finance agencies included $5 trillion in loan guarantees; much of that money will be recovered, because the buildings in question are still standing, but not all. Some additional drain on federal coffers is certain.

The immediate temptation is to blame the national debt increase on President George W. Bush. Certainly he deserves to be held accountable. His tax cuts reduced federal revenues at the same time spending was soaring both with massive outlays and with the expenses of a prolonged war he advocated and prosecuted.

But Bush is not solely to blame, not nearly. His budgets passed one Congress after another, eight times, regardless of whether Democrats or Republicans held the majority. War funding consistently remained outside of the budget process, a shared denial of fiscal reality that drew almost no resistance. In other words, Congress went along for the ride.

Here's an interesting challenge: Try to name one person on Capitol Hill—any senator, any representative—with a reputation for frugality. While you were drawing a blank, the national debt continued to rise at the rate of $44,000 per second.

Even so, the blame does not lie entirely along Washington's Pennsylvania Avenue. Some accountability belongs with Main Street too. After all, the spending plans that Congress passed and Bush signed drew practically zero outcry from the American people. White House fiscal policy provoked no civil disobedience, either. As recently as 1992, the federal debt was a central presidential campaign issue; in 2004, by contrast, Bush's record deficits did not prevent him from winning re-election by a solid margin. Even in his second term, with Bush's approval ratings in the basement, the voice of public protest rarely sounded more than a whisper. So the American public is also complicit in the nation's soaring debt.

The Obama administration appears willing to continue the pattern, with more than $1.5 trillion in new outlays in the president's first budget year—spending based not on revenue forecasts but on hopes for a sunnier economy in some future time.

At this point the debt defies comprehension: What is a trillion? What is 10 trillion? The numbers are too huge to grasp. But their weight is nonetheless both certain and growing. All told, red ink appears to be one of Washington's few bipartisan accomplishments.

With responsibility for creating the problem shared so broadly, then, and with no national politician emphasizing—much less offering to solve—the debt problem, the result is predictable: This is not a government that can afford new ideas. It cannot even afford to meet its existing obligations.

And those demands are growing like kudzu. Aging baby boomers expect to receive the Medicare health coverage promised them. They plan to collect the Social Security retirement support toward which they have contributed during all their working years. The strain of these programs on federal coffers will only increase.

Satisfying those expectations will not eliminate the government's other responsibilities too. Children still need education. Critical infrastructure needs—roads, bridges, electric transmission systems, rail, and more—require trillions in investment. National defense continues to be a priority; it may even grow in importance. In today's interconnected and unstable world, a prosperous nation undefended is like a woman strolling through a bad neighborhood wearing diamonds. It is an invitation to danger.

For the next generation at least, government simply will not have the wherewithal to embark on grand new initiatives. Even if we could somehow create the political will to restore electoral integrity, even if we could broadcast the people's voices as loudly as the lobbyists', even if we could cultivate an attitude of responsibility in the public that would lead it to pressure government to think in the longer term, even then the nation will not have enough cash to act on that potential.

America's human needs are acute and urgent, but the traditional liberal mechanism of government response is simply not available to help.

WHAT OF THE marketplace, then? If conservatives crow at the insufficiency of government, to what extent does capitalism address the nation's needs? As with government's dwindling role compared with the 1930s, the answer for capitalism lies in history. What the free market could achieve years ago is vastly greater than what it contributes today.

On December 7, 1941, Japanese aircraft attacked the U.S. base at

Pearl Harbor in Hawaii, and in a matter of minutes inflicted devastating damage on the American military. The central tragedy was the loss of more than twenty-four hundred lives. In the aftermath, however, there arose challenges that rivaled the nation's grief. The United States would now be compelled to fight two wars, on two continents, half a world apart. Lacking today's communication and information management tools, this task would tax the capacity of every system: manufacturing, distribution, research, education, and more. It would require the effort of every citizen: to serve in the armed forces, to buy war bonds, to accept rationing, to recycle metals, to go without luxuries and some necessities—and above everything else, to build the tools and weapons needed to wage the greatest military undertaking in human history.

That effort prevailed because virtually everyone took part. Evidence of the greatest sacrifices remain visible to anyone who visits Arlington National Cemetery, travels to the watery memorial in Pearl Harbor, or stands mute before the rows of white crosses in the fields of France.

The success of those ultimate contributions was primarily due to valor. But it also resulted from the nation's unprecedented reliance on enterprise. American capitalism—the economic engines, the financial services, the extractors of raw materials, the engineers, inventors, and fabricators, the manufacturing system—performed as never before. It is plausible to argue that Allied soldiers might not have won, had America's capitalists not outperformed their adversaries in building tanks, planes, ships, shells, jeeps, bombs, boots, helmets, guns, bullets.

Since that victory, Americans on the right have maintained a belief that the solutions to the nation's problems exist foremost in the marketplace. Capitalism, with its focus on competition to benefit the consumer, and with its nose ever in the wind to sniff opportunity, offers an appealing idea as the cause of national well-being. After all, there is no government program better than a decent job. And when a person prospers, he spends his wages and thus make possible the prosperity of those who manufacture the goods and perform the services he buys. One person's gain does not come at another's expense. A rising tide lifts all boats.

Unfortunately, that reasoning no longer holds true. Links in the economic chain are no longer connected. The globalization of labor, capital, and markets means that the prosperous person's spending is far less likely to affect his neighbors' circumstances at all. The successful capitalist may in fact be making his money on another continent, and spending it elsewhere too.

Consider two manifestations of this change: who gains from economic growth and where new jobs arise. Each shows how capitalism has evolved in ways that make it a diminishing force for societal good.

The first major alteration is in how economic gains are shared—or more accurately, not shared. Since the founding of the American labor movement, gains in prosperity among the richest Americans have roughly paralleled those of people at lower income levels. That is, if the boss had a good year, then the workers did too. Sometimes lower-wage earners actually did better. In the thirty years following World War II, incomes in the lower 90 percent of households rose more than those of the top 1 percent.

That pattern no longer applies. Since 1976, the lower 90 percent has enjoyed only a 20 percent gain in income, while the top 1 percent has seen growth of 232 percent. A man in his thirties today, if you adjust for inflation, actually earns 12 percent less than a man the same age thirty years ago.

During the 1990s the gap grew slowly, in part because so many Americans shared in the booming stock market. But at the turn of the twenty-first century, this trend had vanished. Between 1998 and 2001, the distance between the top tenth of earners and the lowest tenth grew by 70 percent. The bottom tenth took home $10,300 a year, on average, while the top tenth received $833,600.

The smaller the income slice you consider, the worse the disparity. By 2005 the top 10 percent of wage earners, those making more than $100,000 a year, took home 48.5 percent of total national income. The highest 1 percent—whose average annual earnings were $1.1 million—received 21.8 percent of the national total. And in 2006 the fifteen thousand families in the top 0.01 percent of the population (that's one one-hundredth of 1 percent)—received 5.5 percent of the nation's total income. For their pains, these high earners received an income tax reduction.

A similar divergence has occurred in corporate compensation. In 1983, the ratio of the top bosses' pay to that of entry-level workers, among the five hundred companies in the Standard & Poor's stock index, was 42 to 1. That is, the CEO made forty-two dollars for every dollar that the mailroom clerk earned.

Today that ratio stands at 431 to 1. Even in the chilly economic climate of 2006 to 2008, the median pay of S&P top executives' pay rose by $280,000, to a cozy $8.4 million per year.

In 2008, John Thain ranked first among U.S. CEOs, receiving $83 million that year as head of Merrill Lynch. Over at General Motors, Rick Wagoner presided over 2007 losses of $39 billion, a 19 percent fall in his company's stock value, and the closing of four plants in 2008. Yet his pay rose by 64 percent, to $15.7 million. Merrill Lynch subsequently sold itself to survive, and General Motors needed government bailout funds (and Wagoner's forced departure) to continue operating—which makes their pay all the more galling.

But these headline cases are not such a rarity. As a group, the ten highest-paid U.S. CEOs of 2007 made more than half a billion dollars.

Income trends that favored relatively few people have had a simultaneously caustic impact on the other end of the financial spectrum. Today 19 percent of American children grow up in impoverished homes. In Colorado, where 180,000 children live in poverty, the rate has increased by 73 percent since 2000. In New Hampshire the rate of children in poverty has leapt 47 percent in that period. In Delaware the increase is 45 percent—just since the turn of the century.

The effects are not limited to children. The poverty rate among men over seventy-five has leapt by 29 percent since 2000. Among older women the rate has risen nearly 20 percent. Between 1991 and 2007 bankruptcy filings for people aged sixty-five to seventy-four increased 178 percent. For people over seventy-five, bankruptcies in that period grew 567 percent.

Since the new century began, Americans of all ages have declared bankruptcy by the millions. Hundreds of thousands have lost their homes. Millions more have lost their health benefits at work.

The gap between capitalism's rewards and societal good is not merely a rich-get-richer situation. In fact, a smaller portion of economic gains today make it into *anyone's* wallet. Instead growth in corporate earnings has vastly outpaced wages. Since 2001, people's salaries have increased 1.9 percent a year, while corporate profits grew 12.8 percent annually. These trends compound one another, so that in 2006 the U.S. economy set several records of dubious merit: The portion of the nation's total income going to salaries was the smallest since 1929. The percentage captured in corporate profits was the highest since just before the Great Depression. The share flowing to the top 1 percent of households was the largest since 1929. And the overall wage inequality gap grew the widest since just before the Great Depression.

If history does not repeat itself, then it rhymes. In retrospect, these records were portents of the economic collapse that followed, in both 1929 and 2008. An economy cannot survive solely on the enrichment of a few; it must create opportunities for many.

For some people, the polarization of wealth and poverty is morally evil; affluence is unjust while others starve. It's an appealing argument—for about five seconds. After all, if a society agrees to function with a capitalist economy in order to cultivate the highest prosperity for the most people, should success be punished? Does it make sense to set a ceiling on achievement? And if so, how can that limit be anything but arbitrary? And if it is arbitrary, how can it be moral?

The stronger case against such a great disparity in wealth is practical. If you and three friends and Bill Gates are sitting in a room, your average net worth runs somewhere around $17 billion. If Bill makes $1 billion more, average worth in the room jumps by $200 million—but four of you have actually not advanced one nickel.

Likewise, if 90 percent of workers are not sharing in capitalism's good times, then the economy has no ballast should a storm strike its sails. That's one reason why the collapse of 2008 struck so severely: Too many people were living at the limits of their means, while too few were benefiting from the economy's growth. When credit markets weakened, the economy lacked the resilience to absorb that problem and continue growing.

At this writing, more than 13 million Americans are out of work. Another 11 million are underemployed, working part-time.

The economy continues to shed more than six hundred thousand jobs a month; on a single day in early 2009, two hundred thousand people lost their jobs.

In October 2009 the public outcry over executive pay led regulators to establish limits at corporations that had received federal bailouts. But these few companies will not materially alter the trends in income disparity. Thus this obstacle to capitalism's fostering a stronger society will remain intact for the foreseeable future. Mc-Mansions will continue to rise in open fields, on average one-third larger than homes built in 1976. Meanwhile 37 million Americans will continue to spend more than one-third of their income on housing. And the number of homeless people—currently 3.5 million a year—will continue to rise.

It is hard to fathom that as recently as 1980, homelessness was a rarity. The National Coalition for the Homeless was not even founded until 1984. Now the lack of affordable housing is commonplace, in communities large and small. The problem has evolved too in ways that confirm the income trends discussed above. In the 1980s and '90s, the nation's homeless population consisted primarily of drug addicts and alcoholics, people unmoored by de-institutionalization, disabled veterans. Today the fastest-growing homeless population is children—whose parents work in retail or entry-level service jobs. These families' financial circumstances are so tenuous, their safety nets so frail, all it takes is one unexpected car repair or one unforeseen medical bill, and they are out on the street. Each year about 1.35 million of America's homeless people, therefore, are children.

Forget the image of the grizzled drunkard snoring on a subway grate, the tattooed snarler pushing a shopping cart filled with all his worldly possessions, or the wild-haired madwoman living by the train tracks in a house of cardboard. The average homeless person in America today is nine years old.

The second reason capitalism no longer serves its prior role is globalization. The world's economy today is interconnected in many growing ways: in financial markets, in the markets for many goods and services, in capital flows, and in the availability of labor. That is welcome news for U.S. businesses that make goods desired abroad.

But it is bad news for many kinds of U.S. workers. As long as large portions of the earth are populated by people desperate for even subsistence wages, globalization will hurt the incomes of workers in more prosperous countries.

Put another way, jobs go where labor costs are cheapest. The U.S. economy is anemic, but not when it comes to outsourcing. The Forrester Research consulting firm has estimated that service jobs are leaving the United States at the rate of twenty thousand per month. By 2015, Forrester predicts, 3.3 million service jobs will have moved offshore.

Certain industries lead the way. In a 2003 survey of information technology chief executives, 68 percent said their outsourcing contracts would grow. Deloitte Research predicted in 2004 that 2 million financial jobs—payroll processing, accounting—would move overseas by 2009. McKinsey & Company estimated that $18.4 billion in information technology and $11.4 billion in business services had already moved offshore—and this sum represents only one-tenth of the potential.

Defenders of outsourcing argue that the losses are insignificant compared with the total of 130 million jobs in the U.S. economy. But that reasoning overlooks simple rules of supply and demand: If there are fewer opportunities to work in the United States, wages will fall. The federal Bureau of Labor Statistics found that only 36 percent of manufacturing workers displaced by outsourcing found jobs that paid the same or better. Instead 31 percent of them did not find themselves fully reemployed. Twenty-five percent of them took pay cuts of about one-third.

But here's the toughest thing about outsourcing: Some people try to portray it as wrong, or paint the companies who do it as somehow evil or immoral. They are forgetting that this is precisely how capitalism is supposed to work. The job of a corporation is to find the cheapest way to make its goods or provide its services. Outsourcing clearly lowers labor costs. That is how the corporation endures; it is how the system lives.

The same argument holds for CEOs' wages. According to capitalist theory, executives' wages should not be established by some societal benchmark or external force. Their compensation should be determined solely by what someone is willing to pay for a top executive.

There's the rub: Capitalism is an excellent system for fostering individual gain and economic growth. But the economy is only a subset of society. Many social concerns have no standing in capitalism, because no profit can be made from solving them. Why should capitalism care about racial injustice? Why pay any heed to diseases that afflict people too poor to pay hospital bills? Why educate students with special needs?

To a true capitalist, the answer is that these people and their problems are significant only to the extent that money can be made in solving them. Otherwise employers should find competent workers at the lowest wage, investors should seek the highest returns, and chief executives should receive whatever compensation the market will bear.

With the globalization of labor and finance, capitalism will simultaneously grow more effective as an economic mechanism for owners, and increasingly indifferent to human needs. Is a prisoner a life wasted, or an impediment removed from the paths of commerce? What is a homeless person but an inefficiency wrung out of the system?

So THERE YOU have it, the unfortunate confluence of two failures: Government cannot solve today's toughest problems. The free market cannot fix them either. And thus does the most powerful nation on earth founder.

The clearest evidence of the limitations of both government and capitalism may have been revealed on October 9, 2007. On that day, the Dow Jones Industrial Average reached its all-time high of 14,164. The Standard & Poor's average soon attained its record high too. In other words, investor confidence in the free market reached its zenith.

That month also marked the pinnacle of U.S. federal government spending. The federal budget was the largest ever; the deficit at a record level too (a peak it has since surpassed). So government's fiscal exertions on the people's behalf had reached an all-time high.

. And yet October 2007 also saw a record number of homeless children in the United States, a record number of people living with daily hunger, record numbers of teens dropping out of school, record demand at food pantries, and record numbers of people in jail.

In other words, there is no longer any connection between the prosperity of the marketplace and the extent of the nation's need. There is a dwindling link between government outlays and America's human condition. Rising tides do not lift all boats; some vessels get swamped.

If the best economic system on earth, operating in what is arguably the wealthiest nation on earth—and with all the energy and innovation of capitalism—cannot address the myriad social ills that afflict the United States, who or what will? Likewise, if political bickering, partisanship, and excessive debt prevent government from leading the way to a stronger country, who will?

Who is going to solve today's problems? Who is going to help raise those babies out of poverty? Who is going to help their parents finish school so they can earn a decent wage? Who is going to feed those senior citizens? Who is going to repair America's troubled race relations? Who is going to see the toughest problems and not look away, but instead get involved and find answers? Whose job will it be?

There is an answer to these questions. It is a singular force, capable of restoring this nation beyond anything government or the marketplace could accomplish. It is, in fact, the original animating energy of the American idea. To understand its potential today, and the acute need for it at this very moment, requires a brief history lesson. It is the story of one of the most sublime ideas humanity has yet conceived.

4

Founding Principles

We have too many high-sounding words, and too few actions that correspond with them.

— ABIGAIL ADAMS

A slender acquaintance with the world must convince every man that actions, not words, are the true criterion of the attachment of friends.

— GEORGE WASHINGTON

WHEN THE SETTLERS OF the Thirteen Colonies began agitating for independence in the 1700s, their immediate motive was to be free of a tyrannical king. But they had a larger purpose too. They wanted to embrace a new idea about what a person was. This idea led to rebellion in 1776, shaped the methods of warfare that won the conflict, formed the national character over two centuries, and, above all, fuels the best ideas for renewing America today.

In this nation's origins lie the essential elements for its renewal.

Consider for a moment what life was like in the years leading up to the American Revolution. The peak of the British power pyramid was the king, below whom stood two hundred or so ranked peers: dukes, earls, and barons. The next echelon included knights and esquires, then gentlemen—wealthy but not titled landowners. It was a small club. Four hundred families owned one-fifth of all the land in Great Britain, while 60 percent of the population owned no house or property of any kind. The aristocracy comprised about 5 percent of the population. Everyone else was a commoner.

The law fully recognized these two classes of humanity. Gentlemen could hold rank in the army and navy, but not commoners—regardless of their talent, intellect, or strength. Gentlemen captured in war could be paroled, while commoners went to prison. Gentlemen did not receive physical punishment for misdeeds, while commoners might have their ears cut or their backs flogged. In prerevolutionary Massachusetts, courts openly debated whether plaintiffs or defendants were gentlemen, because the law treated these classes differently.

Such rigid social divisions had visible implications in the economy and politics. British land was rarely purchased or sold, but rather handed down within families. Governing was a hobby of the peers and gentry, who prided themselves on what they considered the virtue of having no personal interest in the outcome of issues and debates. Judges, magistrates, and governors received their positions from the king and served at his pleasure.

Laboring men, by contrast, were considered bred to their occupations like beasts of burden, whether the work was coopering, blacksmithing, printing, or any other trade in which a person might possibly sweat. To give political power to such a being—ignorant, perhaps illiterate, and of course the opposite of disinterested in the outcomes of governing—was so unthinkable as to be comic.

Moreover, the upper classes believed that this social stratification worked to everyone's benefit. The hardship of commoners was a desirable thing, for example, because it spurred them out of laziness. Massachusetts Lieutenant Governor Thomas Hutchinson, who sided with the Loyalists during the Revolution, wrote in 1761, "Poverty will produce industry and frugality."

Similarly, the excesses of the peers and gentry sustained commoners like so much trickle-down economics. As Montesquieu, one of the great political theorists of the Enlightenment, wrote, "If the rich do not spend so lavishly, the poor would die."

Spiritual life was equally hierarchical. The primary religious entity was the Church of England. Setting aside for a moment the faith of that congregation, which some people of good conscience follow still today, at the time it may as well have been called the Church of George III. People were required to pay taxes specifically to finance the church. In the southern American colonies, the gentry entered church only after commoners were seated. At Sunday services, there were special prayers for the king and other royalty. Anyone who wished to practice another faith must apply for permission, which might or might not be granted. In the early days of the Virginia colony, a person could be arrested for preaching without a permit. Quakers were deported, Catholics prohibited from holding public office. It was a crime to deny belief in the Holy Trinity, and speaking ill of Scripture could be punishable by death.

Whether in church, court, business, or society, the rules were not subtle. Colonists, who nearly all fell in the nonaristocrat category, understood them well. John Adams once described which class of people—if he had to choose between the greats and the commoners of Massachusetts—he personally identified with: "the multitude, the million, the populace, the vulgar, the mob, the herd, the rabble."

Likewise Benjamin Franklin opened his autobiography with the observation that he was "the youngest son of the youngest son for five generations back." He was, in other words, a living example of why rights of inheritance were unfair.

But the social norms were so entrenched, the mother country so assured in its dominion, that any resistance was treated as impudence and ingratitude. In 1773, for example, Parliament passed a punitive tax through the Tea Act, even though the colonists had no representation in Parliament. They responded, as every schoolchild knows, by throwing the Boston Tea Party. But Parliament's next actions were equally clear: The Administration of Justice Act effectively eliminated colonial courts; trials for crimes committed in Massachusetts would now be conducted in England. The Massachusetts Government Act overthrew local democracy, placing the powers of juries and town meetings in an executive officer answering to the king. The Boston Port Act aimed to sap the city's financial vitality by placing it under economic blockade.

Such edicts were only part of the problem; the hierarchy they reinforced was equally offensive. Thus the immediate cause for rebellion was that the colonists desired representation in government and liberation from the arbitrary whims of their monarch. These reasons have been repeated so often, in the ears of modern Americans the words have become almost platitudes.

But there was another motive as well, larger than the economy of Boston, deeper than the question of where trials took place, and in the end vastly more significant and enduring than the reign of any king.

The colonists rebelled not only to free themselves from the yoke of British rule but also in order to reject the stratification of British society. They fought to bring to life one of the Enlightenment's highest ideals: a new and nobler definition of what a human being is.

According to progressive thinkers of the eighteenth century, people did not need to bow to someone whose sole claim to superiority over them was birth. They considered the people intelligent and informed enough to govern themselves. Some of them might even be smarter than royalty. Likewise people did not need to profess the king's faith in order to gain the grace of God. Each person was endowed with sufficient moral and spiritual insight to choose his own path to redemption. Some might even be more devout than the king.

Bosh, said the ruling class. As late as 1775, the royally appointed governor of Georgia sniffed in disdain when he learned who the leaders of the revolutionary cause in Savannah were: "a parcel of the lowest people, chiefly carpenters, shoemakers, blacksmiths, etc. with a Jew at their head."

By contrast the Virginia Declaration of Rights, written by George Mason the following year, declared outright:

> No man or set of men are entitled to exclusive or separate emoluments or privileges from the community, but in consideration of public services. . . . The ideal of man being born a magistrate, a legislator or a judge is unnatural and absurd.

In the New World, in other words, merit alone would count. A man should advance not because of which family he was born into but by virtue of his intellect, character, exertion, and luck.

What gall. His Majesty was mindful of how much he stood to lose if the colonies should sever themselves from his domain. They were a source of ready revenue. They provided abundant raw materials, from tobacco to trees tall enough to serve as masts for the British navy. The New World, its extent and resources promising beyond imagination, was a fitting extension of the crown's reach, a rich addition to the empire.

All the more reason to smother insurrection and remind the upstarts of their lowly status. New edicts represented only one form of this condescending attitude. A more terrifying illustration came in the spring of 1776, in New York Harbor. There George Washington and the fledgling colonial army had gathered after an unexpected victory in Boston. At the time the colonies did not possess a navy, not even a single ship. To demonstrate his power, the king sent warships to New York that May and June, foremost among them the sixty-four-gun HMS *Asia*. Soon the British added two fifty-gun ships, the *Centurion* and *Chatham*, then the *Phoenix* with its forty guns, next the thirty-gun *Greyhound* with an army general aboard. These ships also bore tens of thousands of troops. The king then added the *Rose*, as well as the *Eagle*—another sixty-four-gun ship, this one commanded by the fearsome Admiral Lord Richard Howe. Colonists spied five more ships arriving one day, eight another, twenty another. By late June the harbor and its outer reaches were crammed with some four hundred ships, including seventy-three warships and eight ships of the line with fifty or more guns each. It was the largest military force ever dispatched by any nation on earth.

And what did the colonists do that July? How did they reply to this terrifying display of power and glory?

They declared their independence. They cataloged their grievances, explained their reasons, and announced their permanent separation from Great Britain. The bonds were dissolved, the ropes that tied the colonists to the monarchy permanently cut.

It was not mere impudence that this act of rebellion displayed. It was character. It was determination. The king had failed to realize that every step he took to suppress the colonists, to intimidate them, to reinforce their inferiority, only invigorated their growing conception of what a human being is.

Today these ideas are strong threads in the American fabric, but in the 1700s they were as radical as anyone could imagine. It was an act of breathtaking audacity to declare that all people were endowed with inalienable rights. It constituted a rejection of an ancient social and political order to suggest that all people are created equal.

Granted, it has taken centuries for some of the promises in these concepts to be kept—for example, conferring voting rights to men who did not own property, then to African Americans, and then to women. Some of the promises remain unfulfilled to this day. But the fact that these goals take so long to achieve only reinforces how ambitious they are.

Sometimes a clash between cultures can be captured in language, when the words each side uses reveal the deep differences between them. So it is with this moment in history, in the terms the British and the colonists each used to describe common people.

To the throne, they were known as subjects. They were subject to the king's whims, they were subject to his laws, and they were at all times subjected to his will.

The colonists, by contrast, called one another *citizen*. In 1776, *citizen* was one of the most revolutionary nouns you could use. The difference between a subject and a citizen "is immense," wrote South Carolina historian David Ramsay:

> Subject . . . means one who is under the power of another; but a citizen is a unit of a mass of free people who, collectively, possess sovereignty. Subjects look up to a master, but citizens are so far equal, that none have hereditary rights superior to others. Each citizen of a free state contains, within himself, by nature and the constitution, as much of the common sovereignty as another.

When the Founders rejected the status of subjects and embraced citizenship, *that* was the real moment of revolution. It constituted a new understanding of who they were.

That difference shaped the warfare to come. Instead of a conscripted professional army marching in red-uniformed rank and file, the colonists assembled a volunteer citizens' army and fought in ordinary clothes, using their knowledge of the local landscape as a weapon. The British hired Hessian mercenaries to do their fighting;

colonial soldiers battled often without pay. When these methods won the citizens their independence, the idea of the nobility of an individual was validated for all time.

If the concept seems obvious now, it was not so clear then. Consider what happened in France. After the people of that nation had stormed the Bastille in the name of liberty, toppled a king in the name of fraternity, and guillotined off thirteen thousand heads in the name of equality, Napoleon took power and installed himself as emperor. Thus the French made a journey from monarch to monarch. It would take more than a century and several more republics for the democratic promise of the French Revolution to be fulfilled.

The infant America went in a radically different direction. As the new Congress deliberated about what form of government to take, it called on General George Washington to appear and offer advice. Some representatives were concerned that he might seize power; others were hoping that he would. Washington fretted, dodged, delayed, and ultimately arrived on December 23, 1783. The war was over, the peace treaty signed, Britain's acceptance of the colonies' independence formalized.

Instead of appearing in uniform, Washington came before Congress in an ordinary suit of clothes. He urged the nation's soldiers "to return to our private stations in the bosom of a peaceful, free and happy country." For himself, Washington declared his plan to retire to his farm on Mount Vernon. And then he gave Congress his sword.

It stunned the globe. His duty as a soldier completed, Washington was returning to the life of a citizen. No one was more amazed than the British. "'Tis a conduct so novel," wrote the painter John Turnbull in London, "so unconceivable to people who, far from giving up powers they possess, are willing to convulse the empire to acquire more." Even George III reportedly remarked that if Washington relinquished this opportunity for power, "he will be the greatest man in the world."

What Washington had done, however, was not intended to enlarge his reputation. Rather, to the new nation his deed declared that a general was no loftier than a farmer. All were citizens.

Political leaders of the time were not fools about human nature. They knew what temptation is, and how power can corrupt. That is why they created a government with checks and balances. What the Founders designed was based less on curbing potential abuses, though, than on affirming the inherent worth and dignity of every human being.

Once they embraced that idea, they lived it. They even seemed to take pleasure in belaboring it. When the U.S. Senate convened for the first time, for example, it held a long debate about what to call the president. Too many proposed titles hewed too closely to how a monarch might be addressed: "Excellency" or "His Majesty the President." The Senate appointed a committee to resolve the issue. Its proposal— "His Highness the President of the United States of America and Protector of the Rights of the Same"—demonstrates once again the merits of committees.

Still, this was not a trivial matter. The real question was what relation the top elected official would have with the people, and no nation had dealt with such an issue before. Eventually James Madison proposed a title representing the balance of respect and reserve that Congress embraced, Washington himself preferred, and America's commanders in chief have answered to ever since: "Mister President."

The man was not a king, any more than his farmer neighbors were subjects. They were all endowed with rights and responsibilities equally, from the moment of their birth.

THIS NOBLE IDEA of a citizen had one component that was essential in 1783 and remains so now. Indeed, its absence in contemporary life is a major cause of America's present-day drift. That component is *patriotism*.

Now: If ever a word has been diminished, manipulated, co-opted, distorted, and treated as if it were a possession, *patriotism* is it. The time has come, in honor of the Founders who defined this word's true meaning and intent, defended it with their lives, and honored it in their conduct, to return to that proper usage.

It will not happen easily. For too many people, *patriotism* is defined as an unwavering faith in traditional values. It is expressed by flying the flag, by buying a bumper sticker that pledges support for the troops, by a love-it-or-leave-it mentality.

That is not patriotism. Not even close. The flag is an important symbol, and the men and women who defend America's interests do deserve backing during strife and gratitude afterward. But self-righteous expressions of conservative opinion are far too shallow to be called the real thing.

For too many other people, patriotism is scorned as weak or simple or compliant with outdated norms. These views are expressed by protest, by ridicule of power, by buying a bumper sticker that mocks leaders or questions authority.

This is not patriotism either. Not even close. Free speech is essential to a healthy democracy, and dissent an important manifestation of liberty. But these expressions of liberal perspectives are far too superficial to be called the real thing.

True patriotism—not some divisive shadow, not insistence on being in the right about an issue, not a bludgeon to hammer those with whom you disagree, but the honest emotion, the *authentic* thing—is love of country. Not love of self, nor love of one set of ideas, but genuine love for the common purpose and shared values within a geographic boundary.

In other words, authentic patriotism is not about you, what you believe or what you think is right. Authentic patriotism is about the United States of America, its well-being, its future, its adherence to founding principles. Authentic patriotism is not an opinion. It is an action.

So a bumper sticker for or against on any issue? That is no more a proof of patriotism than the antiroyalist rantings of a Boston drunkard in a 1770s pub. Authentic patriotism is what the colonists demonstrated when they stopped having opinions and started taking steps.

The Founders understood this distinction. They knew that winning the people their freedom was only half of the equation. The other half entailed cultivating common purpose. The good of the individual would endure over time only with equal attention to the good of the whole, the full society, the nation. *E pluribus unum*: From many, one.

This notion in the United States today is almost entirely gone. Our society currently is characterized by isolation, separation, the diminishment of community, the electronic virtualization of friendships and contact, the loss of mutuality, the disappearance of common purpose. Emphasis on the individual has flourished; regard for the whole has withered.

The Founders warned against the dangers of such a state of affairs. Thomas Jefferson explained it in a letter to his daughter Polly:

> I am convinced that our own happiness requires that we should continue to mix with the world, and to keep pace with it. . . .
>
> I can speak from experience on the subject. From 1793 to 1797, I remained closely at home, saw none but those who came there, and at length became very sensible of the ill effect it had upon my own mind, and of its direct and irresistible tendency to render me unfit for society, and uneasy when necessarily engaged in it.
>
> I felt enough of the effect of withdrawing from the world then to see that it led to an anti-social and misanthropic state of mind, which severely punishes him who gives into it; and it is a lesson I shall never forget.

That instruction brings us back to today. Here is that same nation, still possessed of lofty ideals, still striving to realize those goals, still a work in progress. But today it is a nation adrift: The government's capacity to respond to urgent problems is constrained as never before. Capitalism's access to global labor, global capital, and global markets has created a creature of growing indifference to domestic issues. Above all, the people are increasingly alienated from the formidable powers that they as citizens wield.

What will solve the problems of today? A renewed embrace of the power of an individual, a recommitment to the revolutionary idea of what a person is, a return to patriotism's original, authentic meaning—with a fervor that is unapologetic and unabashed. There is no *them*, no distant entity that will solve the nation's problems. In a democracy, there is only *us*, the people who elect the government, who live in our neighborhoods, who worship in our faith communities. Each one of us contains the same potential that the nation's Founders not only believed in but spent their lives demonstrating—the noble power of every individual to effect change. What the Founders knew, Americans must rediscover.

There are signs that this thinking is taking hold once again—new initiatives with a new energy, new kinds of people who are not waiting for government to act, who are not willing to trust the free market for answers, but are committed to restoring this nation adrift.

These people are not just old-fashioned do-gooders. They are living manifestations of the Founders' original principles. They are making a visible difference addressing some of the toughest challenges this country faces. Despite setbacks and frustrations, their stories are uplifting—even inspirational. Like the Founders, these authentic patriots have not only embraced the idea of the nobility of every human being, they are living it.

Their work offers three immediate lessons about how a democracy can thrive in the century ahead. First, if they can make a difference, starting with no more than a good idea and the determination to help, then anyone can. Second, if this kind of involvement is essential to renewing the nation, then everyone is needed. Third, if the challenges America faces today are less fundamental than breaking free of a tyrant king, then they are vastly more complicated. If the people can rise to the challenge, as they have before, time after time, and if they are joined by millions of others who also see the importance of working toward a common purpose, then the best chapter of the American story may yet lie ahead.

ONE LAST HISTORY lesson, in that regard. The tale may be apocryphal, but it has endured sufficiently through the ages to bear repeating.

In June 1776, Philadelphia was swelteringly hot. It was also experiencing a pestilent invasion of black flies. Thomas Jefferson sat in his apartment, using a lap desk he had invented, writing draft after draft of a document. Periodically he would present his work to a gathering of men for suggestions and debate. They were not merely editing his writing, however; the delegates were divided over its conclusions. Were the colonies truly ready to cast off British rule?

Picture these gentlemen, in their heavy suits: twenty-four lawyers, eleven merchants, nine farmers, a dozen men of other occupations. The doors are closed because their discussion is treasonous. The windows are shut as well, against the black flies. While they debate the future of liberty, then, they sweat. Even amid this lofty endeavor, asserting that humanity possesses inherent nobility sufficient to create and govern a nation, they remain people of the common realm.

On July 2 they sit before a finished document. Much of it catalogs their grievances against the king, almost as an indictment. But it also contains several phrases whose assertions are so grand, they have remained part of the national spirit ever since:

> We hold these truths to be self-evident: that all men are created equal, that they are endowed by their Creator with certain unalienable rights; that among these are life, liberty and the pursuit of happiness.

When it comes time to sign, they understand the potential consequences. In fact, nine of them will die in the Revolutionary War. Twelve will see their homes ransacked and burned. Five will be captured as traitors and tortured before they die.

So it is a sober moment indeed when the quills are dipped in ink. In a moment, John Adams will place his name with the rest of the Massachusetts delegation. Thomas Jefferson will likewise sign beside his fellow Virginians.

But first, with the large blank space before him, comes John Hancock. One of the wealthiest men in New England, he is a man of substance and means. Of everyone in that room, Hancock is arguably the person with the most to lose. Yet he signs in huge letters, with flourishes beneath. Later asked why, he replies that he did it so the king "can read that name without spectacles."

His gesture represented more than mere bravado. It was a manifestation of what remain the best and most reliable attributes of Americans from that day to this: undaunted courage, determination to build a nation worthy of its people, and above all a willingness to sacrifice in common purpose for the sake of the greater whole.

To restore a nation adrift, America needs many, many men and women of this spirit. You will meet six authentic patriots in detail in part two, and dozens more in part three. Their work is praiseworthy, but their example matters even more. They demonstrate what every person in this nation is capable of accomplishing. And those deeds, should they become as widespread as the need for them, deserve to be written in letters as large and indelible as John Hancock's signature.

PART TWO

Authentic Patriots

5

Seven Steps to a Cure

Alone we can do so little. Together we can do so much.

— HELEN KELLER

We are social creatures. The worst punishment we can
inflict, short of the death penalty, is solitary confinement.

— ALISON HAWTHORNE DEMING

JENIFER ESTESS WAS AN angel. Before she became a research
activist, before she testified in Congress, before she revealed how
society had ignored a terrible illness, before she inspired medical scientists, before she became a model of courage for her friends and
family, before she epitomized the waste that occurs when a person
dies young, before she accomplished any of those things, Jenifer Estess
was an angel—a Naked Angel.

That was the name of the New York theater group where she was
a producer: the Naked Angels. Broadway in the late 1980s was not a
booming enterprise; Forty-second Street was in transition, to put it
charitably. The city itself was chaotic too: Drivers who stopped at a
traffic light could expect squeegee men to descend, clean the windshield without invitation, and demand payment. The Giuliani administration, which sought to sweep the city of crime like a squeegee
cleaning a windshield, remained years away. So too was the revival of
Times Square that would replace peep shows with Disney spectacles.

Opportunities for new actors, playwrights, and directors, always rare, at that time were minimal. Some of the more energetic of these artists responded by founding Naked Angels.

Virtually any enterprise in the dramatic arts represents foremost an act of love. There's practically no money in it. Fame is a fickle friend, arriving more often by chance than due to talent. The work must be its own reward.

And it was work. In a downtown office/rehearsal room/performance space, this fledgling company offered original plays that intended to say something new and in a new way. Employing what later became known as guerilla marketing, Naked Angels used no advertising; the company relied instead on word of mouth, good reviews, and the cachet of being in on something unique.

As an actor and producer, Jenifer was at the heart of it. She was a classic beauty: raven hair, bright lipstick, a brilliant smile, quick with her booming, hearty laugh, and so fashion conscious that when she went to the beach she wore black jeans. She was also all theater. Years later, speaking to an interviewer about the nature of hope, Jenifer quoted *West Side Story*: "'Could it be? Yes it could. Something's coming, something good.'"

The Naked Angels worked endless hours, and a few company members launched major careers. But those breakouts were not the immediate goal. In a theatrical start-up, there is a nearly familial camaraderie, a we're-in-this-together spirit. Building sets, printing playbills, acting, directing, designing lighting effects, learning cues, raising funds, developing characters—all of these endeavors build deep bonds, spark fierce rivalries, and sometimes ignite inspiration.

For Jenifer, this atmosphere was important for reasons that only became clear years later: She was building an expertise in idealism. In the first step of the journey that awaited, she was developing a vast capacity to exert herself on behalf of a larger purpose.

Soon she would come up against one of the toughest problems the American medical system faces. She would learn that government's efforts have been wholly inadequate. She would likewise discover that the free market had dismissed solving the problem as insufficiently profitable. She would conclude that the only way to achieve progress is for individuals to exercise their freedom to pursue their passions, and to claim the rights and powers given to them by the nation's Founders. She would, in other words, become an authentic patriot.

Jenifer's original plan, however, foresaw nothing of the sort. She expected to exert her skills in a wider theatrical way. She left Naked Angels for a day job in publicity, with the longer-term goal of making movies with her sisters.

The sisters. Growing up in the suburbs of New York City, Jenifer had four siblings, but she became especially close to Valerie and Meredith.

"She was my best friend," Meredith recalls. "But I hate that term. It is so inadequate. We were completely in each other's lives."

They were no-nonsense women in many ways, a trait they attribute to their father's abrupt departure as they were entering adolescence. But the sisters were dreamers too, imagining a feature film production company that would rely on each woman's unique strengths. It was all the stuff of someday, of furtive planning, of lunchtime imagine-out-loud sessions.

"I always dreamed of writing plays for her to produce, and then movies," recalls Valerie Estess. "And then Meredith has the business savvy. She has a sense of how to run things."

The only odd thing, though, was Jenifer's energy. Most days she remained as charged as ever, but sometimes she crashed with fatigue. One day the sisters went to the store for a nephew's birthday party, and Jenifer "had trouble getting out of the car," Meredith recalls.

Jenifer was hardly an urban sluggard. At thirty-five, she worked out regularly. She kept precise track of her progress on cardio equipment. She took yoga classes. She hoofed it all over New York City.

"One day she and I went to the gym," Meredith says, "and she was definitely behind on the treadmill. She was just not able to keep up at all."

All of a sudden Jenifer had a hard time lifting her sisters' toddlers for her usual fierce hugs. Sometimes she broke into heavy sweats for no reason. She started stumbling when she crossed the street. One weekend, while working at a film festival on Nantucket, she called Meredith.

"She said, 'The weirdest thing is happening,'" Meredith remembers. "'The muscles in my leg are rippling. It's like a twitch in your eye, but it doesn't stop. And you can see it. It's very freaky. Very scary.'"

Then came March 17, 1997. For most city residents it was Saint Patrick's Day, a time to wear green, catch the parade, raise a song, and maybe hoist a few pints. For Jenifer, though, March 17 was the day she nearly lost a battle with the wind.

Early that morning she'd worked out, and the abdominal exercises had felt especially tough. Afterward she bent down in her closet for some soap and became stuck in that crouch. It took time, and real effort, to straighten herself. Even the towel felt heavy after her shower. But the wind, that was the truly scary thing. As she walked to work on Amsterdam Avenue, it pushed against her with every step.

"I sweated and slowed down on the sidewalk just as I had in the shower," Jenifer writes in *Tales from the Bed*, a book she later co-wrote with Valerie. "I tried to fight the wind. I tried accelerating on the human highway of tourists walking to the Saint Patrick's Day parade, but there was nothing in my tank. I was alone in a sea of Kelly green. . . . Did I mention the wind? It was really blowing. It had a personality now—it wanted me dead."

Jenifer felt huge relief on reaching her West Side office, where she worked at a public relations job twenty floors up. She put her feet on the desk and caught her breath. Better still, that was a day with one of those dream lunches, Jenifer and Meredith meeting to discuss a new movie treatment Valerie had written. By noon, the wind was history and the sisters huddled in Jenifer's office with the door closed. Jenifer was just reaching for a tuna sandwich when Meredith noticed her sister's legs twitching. All three women had observed these jumping muscles, ever since Nantucket. But now they were more intense. Meredith insisted that Jenifer stop and look at herself. It was happening in her arms too. It looked as though she had snakes under her skin, writhing. There was no more denying it. She was in trouble.

So BEGAN THE second phase of Jenifer's odyssey, the diagnostic portion. Sometimes the process was comical, like the day she went to a doctor who was too short to examine her ears without climbing on a stool. Sometimes the process was absurdly obscure—one doctor called Jenifer's twitches "benign fasciculations," as if everyone knows what that means. More often, Jenifer's treatment was callous. Examining rooms were filthy. Doctors misspoke or avoided bad news. They joked at inappropriate times, they were cold, they were glib.

Finally one physician told Jenifer that she had a motor neuron disease. Motor neurons are oddly shaped cells, with a small nucleus and long vinelike tendrils. Their function is to carry the electrical signal from the brain to the muscles, telling them when to move and how. Motor neurons enable our legs to run, voices to sing, and hands to clasp. Others sustain our ability to swallow, digest, and even breathe.

This biology was unknown to Jenifer as she went from doctor to doctor. What she and her sisters did know was that something scary was happening, and that tests intended to rule out certain grim possibilities were failing to do so. In April, a neurologist at Columbia University put a hand on her knee and gave her problem a name. "You probably have ALS, Jenifer."

ALS stands for amyotrophic lateral sclerosis. It is more commonly known as Lou Gehrig's disease, after the New York Yankees legend diagnosed with ALS when he was thirty-five—the same age as Jenifer.

When a person has ALS, the motor neurons die back like vines withering. The brain's link with its body is broken. People gradually lose the ability to control their muscles. The symptoms typically start in the extremities and inch inward. Afflicted people stumble, then can't walk without help, then can't move their legs. They can't play the piano, then can't button their shirts, then can't move their fingers. They can't swallow, and then they can't speak. They can't eat, and then they can't breathe.

Worst, all through this process of physical decay the cognitive capacity of the brain remains perfectly intact. The patient knows exactly what is going on, experiences each loss of function as a harbinger of the eventual ultimate loss, and undergoes increasing isolation as the ability to move and then to communicate dwindles away. The diseased body becomes a cage for a still healthy mind. While there are no good ways to die, ALS is among the most merciless.

There is no known treatment. There is no known cure. There is one medicine to slow the disease but it is expensive, has negative side effects, and buys months at most. Decades of research have brought negligible results.

The brutal truth is that no one diagnosed with ALS escapes its ravages. Lou Gehrig didn't. The hundreds of thousands of people identified since ALS was discovered two hundred years ago haven't. The roughly fifty-six hundred people diagnosed with ALS every year don't. Whether the course of the disease takes two years or five, or in rare cases somewhat longer, an ALS diagnosis is a death sentence.

But try telling that to a Naked Angel.

YOU MIGHT THINK an illness that is catastrophic for the patient, in every case, would inspire government to leap into action, to make a priority of understanding the cause and finding a cure. Government's role as a catalyst—funding research, or creating incentives for new medicines and treatments—is ideally suited for a problem as complex and devastating as ALS.

Yet government has given ALS wholly inadequate attention. As Jenifer and her sisters would soon learn—in step three of her odyssey, the bad-to-worse phase—this disease has simply not been a priority. In many ways, actually, government has been an obstacle.

First, consider research funding. While fifty-six hundred diagnoses a year sounds like many people—about one in eight hundred American males will die of ALS—the big research money goes to illnesses such as cancer and heart disease (which each cause about six hundred thousand U.S. deaths each year). Funding also goes to diseases whose numbers are not yet so high but which, if unchecked, could become epidemic (for example, HIV).

Federal support of ALS research has, by comparison, been wholly insufficient. Labs at Johns Hopkins University, the Jonas Salk Institute, Harvard University, Columbia University, and elsewhere compete for funding. But the total in many years is $15 million or less. By contrast, government support for cystic fibrosis—which afflicts roughly the same number of people as ALS—runs $80 million a year.

One reason may be that ALS is just too difficult, compared with other diseases. Cancer research has brought marvels: new medicines, new tests, earlier detection, less invasive surgeries, and best of all, people living longer. Heart disease research has borne similar fruit: medicines that lower cholesterol and blood pressure, preventive screenings, public awareness about nutrition and exercise, improvements in emergency medicine, bypass surgeries, and stents—a menu of interventions that result in longer lives. In other words, the money has been well spent.

With ALS, by contrast, research has yielded little. Yes, scientists have identified one genetic indicator for the disease, which fires if some unknown trigger somehow should be pulled. But that is miles from a cure. People with ALS keep right on dying, as steadily and brutally as ever.

"I remember going to the library," Meredith says. "I went by myself, on a Saturday, just started looking it up. 'Always fatal,' one book said. 'Always fatal,' said the next one. Just like that: Always fatal, always fatal."

"Initially we felt very intimidated," Valerie adds. "You are given a diagnosis, and you're expected to go home and live with it. 'There's nothing we can do for you, not one thing, you're going to die.'"

Despite that certainty, politics have presented an impediment to curing ALS. One of the most promising avenues of research has involved stem cells, and Washington has repeatedly constrained use of these cells.

This issue bears brief explanation. When a child is conceived, the initial sperm and egg combine to make a single cell that divides and grows as new cells are produced. At first these cells have no specified function; they have not yet differentiated. They possess the capacity to develop into any kind of cell in the future body—lung or liver, brain or bladder, heart or heel.

One of the challenges with ALS (and other neuron diseases such as Parkinson's and Alzheimer's) is that most nerve tissue, once it has died, does not grow back. Unlike skin or bone or blood, it does not regenerate. The thinking of researchers working on ALS and those other diseases is that stem cells could be doctored into developing into new nerve tissue.

What may be scientifically appealing, however, is not always

ethically welcome. The most promising stem cells are those derived
from human fertility programs. When a couple has difficulty conceiv-
ing, doctors join sperm and egg outside the womb, make many embryos, then plant several in the mother's womb. Extra embryos remain
frozen, and potentially viable. Removing stem cells means the embryos cannot develop into a baby.

For some people of conscience, these manufactured embryos represent human life every bit as worthy of protection as a living child.
For other people of conscience, the imperatives for treating already
living people who are afflicted by neural diseases outweigh the embryos' potential to become human—especially if the mother and father have no intention of defrosting the embryos for use in fertility
therapy.

The debate has been more than philosophical. President George
W. Bush sided with those concerned about the embryos' potential vi-
ability, constraining research funding and leaning on scientists who
opposed his view. In 2004 the Bush administration removed a leading
cell biologist and a prominent physician ethicist from the President's
Council on Bioethics. The consensus in the scientific community was
that the two failed to hold sufficiently to the president's view on bio-
medical research. Their replacements aligned themselves more closely
with the administration's position. The eleven thousand scientists of
the American Society for Cell Biology issued a statement criticizing
the president for placing politics ahead of science, and 170 researchers
signed an open letter to Bush protesting the decision. In a 2007 compromise, the Bush administration declared that stem cell research
could continue, but only using certain existing cell lines.

Whatever the merits of either side of the argument, the political
debate has had an undeniable practical effect: Federal policy limits
research using embryonic stem cells, funding goes elsewhere, and
people with ALS keep on dying. Government is not part of the
solution.

Optimists like the Estess sisters therefore might think that capitalism would ride to the rescue. After all, given the unavoidable outcome of an ALS diagnosis, and thus the understandable desperation
of patients, the free market ought to find treatments in a hurry—if

only because people will pay practically anything to avoid certain death.

Not so. The cost of developing drugs is so high, the expense of winning regulatory approval for a new medicine so great, and the demands of drug company stockholders for returns on their investment so relentless, all of these forces combine to make ALS an orphan disease.

The word *orphan* may have even worse connotations for illness than the usual meaning of a parentless child. An orphan disease, in clinical terms, is one that affects fewer than two hundred thousand Americans at a time. What the name *orphan* really means, though, is that the disease strikes too few people to justify the cost of finding a cure. Yet these illnesses inflict considerable suffering. The National Organization for Rare Disorders keeps a tally of six thousand orphan diseases, collectively afflicting 25 million Americans. About thirty thousand of them have ALS.

Critics of the pharmaceutical industry argue that motor neuron disease matters more than such maladies as erectile dysfunction, for example, and thus deserve greater exertion in research. Of course these voices speak the truth. But the unfortunate reality is that the actions of drug companies completely align with the incentives and rewards of the market. Corporations must turn a profit to survive, and that is easier done by remedying insufficient erections than it is by treating dying motor neurons.

Generally the profit motive works too. In recent years the drug industry has made huge advances in treatment—from high blood pressure to cholesterol, digestive problems to glaucoma. But market incentives have proven tragically insufficient for ALS and other orphan diseases.

"I hate that term anyway," Meredith Estess says, her voice rising in indignation. "*Orphan disease* sounds like something abandoned, doesn't it? *Orphan*. Excuse me, but we are talking about actual people, and actual suffering, with their families right by their side suffering too. And there is nothing 'orphan' about that at all."

Regardless of which word best describes Jenifer's situation, the result was the same. Neither government nor private enterprise offered comfort—or even hope—to the Estess family. The message was clear: Take your diagnosis and live with it, as well and as long as you can. Fortunately, Jenifer's hope came from within. So her journey began its fourth step, leadership.

THINGS HAD TO get worse first. Jenifer had to start using a cane. She needed to admit that she could not live alone. She had to stop work. She sought a second opinion, though the doctor merely confirmed the bad news, then advised her either to go to Paris or to max out her credit cards.

Her sisters provided better remedies. Meredith offered housing, while Valerie scoured the Internet for clinical options. As winter turned to spring, they helped Jenifer try alternative treatments: nutritional supplements, electric muscle stimulation, sage incense, even a psychic healer. Meanwhile the cane was proving inadequate. A nurse, with offhand indifference, suggested that Jenifer start using a wheelchair before she fell.

Slowly Jenifer's attitude began to change. As she later wrote, "I started taking the whole thing personally—and politically. I felt that my country had let me and millions of sick people down. If you had ALS, Alzheimer's or Parkinson's, you weren't a citizen of the United States. You were strictly Third World. Why wasn't America declaring war on disease? It seemed to me we could be more efficient and aggressive in fighting brain disease, and not just by throwing money at it. Where was the game plan?"

There was none. Over Thanksgiving dinner, the sisters sat with Jenifer's friend Julianne Hoffenberg and groused about the glacial pace of progress against ALS. Doctors and researchers did not work together, did not show much passion for finding a cure, did not feel a strong enough sense of urgency. That was when Julianne spoke the perfect words: "Those doctors need to collaborate like we did at Naked Angels, don't you think, Jen?"

There was a long silence. And in that void, a new idea was born.

Where government was an obstacle, the marketplace indifferent, and a cure imperative if Jenifer were to survive, private leadership would step into the void. The leadership would be called Project ALS.

This new foundation would raise money, fund research, and accelerate work on the disease in time to save Jenifer's life.

Years before, when their father had run for the local school board, Valerie rode her bike around town putting campaign fliers in mailboxes. "I really drank the Kool-Aid at that age," she says. "As a girl, I believed you could make a difference."

For starters, the sisters decided to throw a fund-raising bash. A friend of Jenifer's from childhood and theater days, the movie star Ben Stiller, agreed to be the host. Jenifer tapped more theater pals for supporting roles. The sisters worked the phones, sent invitations, sought corporate underwriters. *InStyle* magazine stepped in as an early lead sponsor. Celebrities' involvement sparked media attention and the event sold out quickly.

On a June night in 1997, nine hundred people crowded into the Roseland Ballroom in Manhattan for the inaugural Project ALS dinner. They laughed, they danced, they learned sobering information about the disease. Then they bid on auction items, pledged their financial support, and launched Project ALS as a force that would change the course of medical research.

The event netted $800,000—and Project ALS was not even legally incorporated yet. Jenifer moved back to the city, into a West Twelfth Street apartment that instantly became Project ALS headquarters. The sisters approached a doctor Jenifer had seen early in her illness, convincing him to serve as a research advisor. Applicants for funding were eager to tap this new source. Within days, Project ALS was writing checks.

SO FAR, JENIFER'S initiative resembled those of many people who advocate for curing a disease. Many organizations hold fund-raising events, support research, and raise public awareness. But the urgency of Jenifer's illness led to a novel approach. In the interests of time, anyone who received money from Project ALS would have to follow an innovative path.

To understand just how innovative, consider how most medical research funding occurs: A researcher completes a lengthy and detailed grant application; some run to fifty pages. That task can take weeks or even months. The evaluation and decision process takes nine more months. Then grant winners wait to receive their money. From the birth of an idea to the start of research, it is not uncommon for a year to pass. Only then can labs be equipped, staff hired and trained, and the studies commence. All of these processes are competitive too, as researchers vie against one another for funds. Thus each phase in the process is proprietary, and deeply secretive. When studies conclude, the results remain confidential until they appear as an article in a scientific journal—a process that requires prolonged editorial review and thus entails further delay. Only upon publication of a study's results do colleagues learn in detail what their peers are discovering. Only then can they challenge the assumptions, poke holes in the findings, or add their own wisdom. This method has been the norm for decades. It offers the benefits of thoughtfulness, thorough vetting of new ideas, competitive energy among researchers, and cautious embracing of new concepts.

The Estess sisters, however, did not have the luxury of this time-consuming approach. They could also see how little fruit this slow method had borne for people with Jenifer's disease. So they created a different process.

Project ALS applicants write a general description of their research idea and what it could contribute, usually just a few pages. The advisory board—which now includes not only the sisters but also a veritable *Who's Who* of neuron and stem cell research in America—decides in a single meeting whether a proposed project sounds worthwhile. If the board approves, Project ALS cuts the check almost immediately. One 2008 applicant submitted a four-page proposal and had the grant money in hand ten days later.

Researchers clearly understand the degree of trust Project ALS bestows upon them. In the eleven years since the first grants, there have been no disasters, no studies that proved to be a waste of money, no projects whose funding was stopped for any reason.

"We were complete amateurs," Valerie says. "But in a way, that made us more useful. We weren't bound by the usual rules. We just wanted to save our sister's life."

Shortening the grant application process was not the most unorthodox aspect of the Project ALS approach. The sisters devised something additional that, for science, was rather revolutionary. Instead of keeping study results secret until publication, researchers with Project ALS grants meet quarterly to share with one another what they're finding—completely in the open. Hailing from places as diverse and high powered as the Motor Neuron Center at Columbia University, the Memorial Sloan-Kettering Cancer Center in New York, the Harvard Stem Cell Institute, the Robert Packard Center for ALS Research at Johns Hopkins, the Salk Institute in San Diego, and others, leading researchers share insights, ask questions, offer advice, and celebrate successes. Competition is replaced by collaboration.

"Remember in the college library, when everyone worked by themselves in those separate carrels?" Valerie asks. "That seemed crazy. There is no free-flowing exchange of data. We were just laypeople, but it seemed to us that these people have things in common. And it has proven to be true. When we get them in a room together, they drop the pretense and the ideas start flowing."

The cause drew allies rapidly. Donna Hanover, then wife of New York mayor Rudolph Giuliani, offered to hold a press conference at Gracie Mansion on Project ALS's behalf. The actor William Baldwin agreed to take part, to increase the media draw. During that event, while delivering her speech, Jenifer entered step five of her journey— empowerment.

She later wrote: "As I described the first twitch in my leg that Meredith had noticed, I saw reporters in the audience look down at their legs. When I talked about making ALS a topic of national concern, I saw them write in their notebooks."

Jenifer's influence was just beginning. She received a request to testify before the U.S. Senate Labor, Health, and Human Services Subcommittee, at the invitation of U.S. Senator Arlen Specter of Pennsylvania, a Democrat. Rolling down the aisle in her wheelchair, her black hair perfectly arrayed, Jenifer looked beautiful. But she spared no hard words for the committee.

"I am still here, and dreaming of an America that will protect the right to life, liberty and the pursuit of happiness for all. [Stem cells] one day may allow me to do the things I miss so much: brushing my hair, laughing out loud. Each day I speak from inside my body, which has now become a prison."

Christopher Reeve, the actor paralyzed in a horse riding accident, also spoke that day—about the need for stem cell research for people in his predicament. Government could not help but listen.

MEANWHILE THERE WERE the mice, four of them. In their tiny bodies lay all the challenges and all the potential.

The first kind is known as an SOD-1 mouse. Bred for laboratory use, the mouse has a genetic mutation that causes it to develop into ALS. "The amateurs," as Valerie called herself and her sisters, discovered there was essentially one company that bred these mice for research. And there was a shortage.

"The scientists couldn't get these particular mice for six months or a year," Valerie remembers. "There was a backlog."

Jenifer could not wait, and neither could Project ALS. So they bought the rights to the mouse, funded a colony to accelerate breeding, and now provide them to researchers for free. No detail was too small for Project ALS to improve.

The second significant mouse is called the wobbler mouse. These mice are bred intentionally with spinal defects. The sisters spotted an article in a scientific publication about a Harvard Medical School researcher who found a way to stop the mouse from wobbling. Evan Snyder, M.D., Ph.D., injected stem cells into wobbler mice, and they steadied.

"We read that paper," Valerie says. "We thought hey, if that trial works, if it fixes one kind of mouse with a neurological defect, maybe it will help humans."

So Project ALS funded a trial of stem cell injection in mice with ALS. It was an avenue of hope. In fact, the road remains open, as additional testing and protocol development now prepare the way for a human test.

The third rodent—actually a laboratory rat this time—was the focus of researchers at the Salk Institute in San Diego. Fred Gage, Ph.D., was experimenting with an idea called gene therapy. A quick background: Drugs work in most of the body because they can travel in the blood, and then penetrate the organ or tissue that is their destination. But the blood–brain barrier is far less penetrable.

Gene therapy uses smaller materials—pieces of a virus stripped of its negative attributes, for example—to cross the barrier. That method can either provide medicines or deliver genetic instructions to brain cells.

If that sounds like esoteric science, it is. But rodents Gage treated with gene therapy did something any layman can understand: They lived longer.

"These mice usually die like clockwork," Valerie says. "But in this research, ALS mice lived thirty-three percent longer."

In classic Project ALS style, the research involved collaboration with other scientists, in this case Jeffrey Rothstein, Ph.D., from Johns Hopkins University. Project ALS connected the Salk Institute with the Robert Packard Center for ALS Research at Johns Hopkins—a previously unheard-of partnership. Gage brought the basic science, Rothstein the clinical expertise to apply it. The potential was immense: By staying alive, these mice were demonstrating the most effective therapy since ALS had been discovered.

The fourth rodent, another rat, also had a deliberately induced illness, in this case a virus that destroyed nerve cells in the spinal cord. The common thinking is that a disease involving the spine would require many sites of intervention, vastly complicating any potential treatment.

Researchers at Johns Hopkins injected these sick rodents with human embryonic stem cells, which migrated to the spot where the nerves had died. There they implanted, grew as new nerve cells, and released proteins that spurred growth of new rodent nerve cells.

The implications were stunning, in two ways: First, they challenged the long-standing belief in the scientific community that neural cells cannot be repaired, nor new ones created. Second, they showed that stem cells actually sought and found the damaged areas.

"In a way, it was a perfect metaphor for what we've been doing," Valerie says years later. "Stem cells sort of know where they're needed. They tend to migrate to where there's need. That's us."

The politics of these discoveries was never far from sight. The stem cells Johns Hopkins used had come from five- to nine-week-old fetuses that had been electively aborted. Advocates of stem cell research therefore sought to play a video of the paralyzed mice walking again to senators and even President Bush. Some politicians did watch the film, including Health and Human Services Secretary Tommy Thompson. But government and the health care industry remained on the sidelines.

The stem cell controversy reached into new corners too. Missouri lawmakers killed funding for a $150 million research center in Columbia. A Kansas City institute likewise halted its $300 million research facility expansion. These losses made the sisters' work all the more important; funding for the Hopkins research came not from Washington but from Project ALS.

The hub of that effort was astonishingly modest: a bed, in a small apartment, in Greenwich Village. Family, friends, media interviewers, donors, above all Jenifer's cherished nieces and nephews, everyone came to that bed. The wheel around that hub grew too, as people with ALS or their families and friends heard about the project and made contact with Jenifer. And while the carpet absorbed countless spills, she lightened the burden of her illness for everyone with unrelenting dark humor.

In *Tales from the Bed*, a friend recounts these kinds of scenes: "Hi Jenifer. How are you?" "Fine except for this ALS stuff." "Jenifer, can I call you right back?" "Sure, but can you give me a few hours? I'm going to run a marathon."

Humor found room on the bed right beside hope. That word had special resonance for the sisters and their friends, but it also sparked caution.

"*Hope?* A lot of charities use it," Valerie says. "They don't do crap, but they still have a 'dinner for hope' or a 'walk for hope.'

"That's not hope. Hope is all about working your hardest, and dreaming as deeply as you can." She laughs archly. "I sound like Oprah, I swear to God, but if you work your butt off and you keep dreaming, the challenge doesn't matter. It just does not matter."

Dubious hope or not, the facts were undeniable. Suddenly where there had been no progress, it was happening in all directions. Scientific journals published study after study about progress with ALS issues. A popular arthritis drug extended the life of mice with ALS by 25 percent. Work began to prepare these ideas and others for human testing.

Should a researcher show doubt about the nonprofessionals in charge at Project ALS, he would be brought to Jenifer's bedside. There he would see both the organization's determination to accelerate science, and the urgent need of a person who could not raise a glass of water to her lips. Skepticism melted, and Project ALS won friend after friend.

The media was happy to help. Sisterhood, a medical mission, celebrity support, a beautiful woman dying—the combination was irresistible. *People* magazine did a profile, as did *The New York Times* and *Forbes*. The coverage wasn't fluff either. Said *Fortune*, "Project ALS serves as a model for how outsiders can force radical change in the scientific establishment."

In other words, the Estess sisters were exemplifying the determination, energy, and independence that characterize authentic patriots. Need a mouse? Or a million dollars? Or a spokesperson? Or an opportunity to be part of something larger? Or an answer to a medical question no one else has found? Here it is: three sisters, progress, urgency, and hope.

In contrast to the research successes, however, Jenifer's physical condition continued to decay. She had to be lifted in and out of bed. Her fingers stopped working, slowly curling in on themselves. Two years after moving into the apartment, she lost her trademark laugh. To her great chagrin, Jenifer's booming laugh had become a flat "Aaaaah. . . ."

The U.S. Senate invited Jenifer back to testify again. This time fellow speakers included Michael J. Fox, the actor who has been so open about his battle with Parkinson's disease. Once again Jenifer's appearance was striking, but not as much as the device beside her wheelchair. She explained to the senators, "I must rely on a ventilator because ALS is destroying the muscles I use to breathe."

And then, taxed merely by making that statement, she leaned to her right over a plastic tube, and sucked in her next breath.

* * *

MEANWHILE THE RODENT experiments were not developing as well as expected. The Harvard researcher who used stem cells to stop mice from wobbling did not have the same success with ALS mice. "What happened?" Valerie says. "Nothing."

Not quite. Snyder's work did lead to the idea that stem cells might offer a way to treat neuro-degenerative diseases. As so often happens in science, Valerie said, the failure of one idea "opened a whole new area of study. It put the ALS guys and the stem cell guys together."

As for the verdict on the other mice—the ones that lived longer—the jury remains in deliberation. Academic labs are not equipped to test enough animals to assure the FDA that a human trial of gene therapy would be safe. A San Diego biotech company is now performing that work. If those studies go well, then the application for a human trial will go to federal regulators.

"It has been frustrating," Valerie says. "The product had not been up to the standard of the academic batch. But we're making progress now. And meanwhile more people have realized that the findings could have meaning for other diseases. That company in San Diego is doing a test on Parkinson's now, for instance."

AT HOME IN New York, the challenge of breathing brought Jenifer into step six of her odyssey: dependence. The disease had reached her diaphragm. She had to begin using a bi-pap—essentially a triangular plastic mask that seals to the face and supports the patient's breathing.

Jenifer also began to realize that friends, and even her sisters, were having a hard time following her words. Between her weakening facial muscles and the bi-pap, they just couldn't tell what she was saying. She began repeating herself—in conversations, in interviews—not because she was confused, but because she was determined to be understood.

Ever the Naked Angel concerned with image, Jenifer did not like to be filmed wearing her mask. But she did it anyway. As she told interviewers from HBO in 2003, "I want people to see that this is where it goes to, ALS, if it's not stopped."

For the HBO taping, she dressed in black to hide the weight she'd gained. Medical caregivers sat her in a yoga pose, her hands now flattened and as motionless as paddles. Some of her emotions had stilled as well.

"I don't long the way I used to," she explained. "Like I used to long to have a cup of coffee in my hands. Your hands around a cup of coffee, it's like a simple moment. I used to want that. But I can't think about things like that.

"You know what sucks about illness? It so consumes you, you don't even have time for love. That's really hard for a girl like me. . . . Let me tell you something: If I get better, oh, they'd be jumped on. I'd be jumping all over them."

After interviews and strategy sessions, the sisters tried to buck Jenifer up. They insisted she was "going to get out of this." But then she leveled with them. Project ALS was giving them hope, yes. It was making progress, it was offering the promise of a cure for someone, someday. The work gave their lives focus; it meant that her illness was not a waste but an inspiration.

"You know," Jenifer told them, "even if we don't get out of this, we're still getting out of it."

THE FIRST THING a visitor notices at the Project ALS lab in Manhattan is large white tanks of liquid nitrogen. They're keeping stem cells securely frozen at −171 degrees Celsius. By contrast, the fertilization tables inside the lab are heated so that tissues there remain alive. Over the tables are glass hoods to prevent contamination. A doctoral student brings a tray of canisters holding stem cells to a microscope, then catches himself. It's a federally funded microscope, so only certain approved cell lines can be viewed on it. He fetches a different tray.

Under the microscope, stem cells are tiny gray blobs held together by darker gray tissue. Their deeper beauty may lie in the eye of the beholder.

"The motor neuron is one of the more elegant pieces of anatomy in the human body," says Christopher Henderson, hopping forward in his chair as he describes this minuscule piece of the nervous system. "That motor neurons exist at all is something of a miracle."

He spreads his hands wide: "It is incredibly long, up to three feet"—then he holds his fingers a fraction of an inch apart—"but very narrow. At the widest point you can't see one with a magnifying glass. Yet if half of this floor were the cell's nucleus, then the axon—the long fibers connecting to the muscle—would reach all the way to Boston."

The floor in his description is on 168th Street in New York City, a few blocks away from the Project ALS lab, at the Columbia University Center for Motor Neuron Biology and Disease. The center Henderson supervises involves forty labs, all working on topics related to motor neurons. Henderson, who has a Ph.D. in enzymology and biochemistry from Cambridge University in Great Britain, worked in several other nations before Columbia recruited him. While his research remains broad, he is fascinated by two particular motor neuron afflictions: spinal muscular atrophy (SMA), a leading genetic killer of infants, and ALS. He shows the most energy, though, when he is talking about neurons themselves.

"They're hard to see because they are virtually transparent. Yet they lend themselves to study brilliantly, because they light up all sorts of wonderful colors when we use genetic markers and antibodies." He gestures toward the walls, on which hang color posters of the cells. "It's sort of embarrassing that we don't really understand these amazing structures, and we're using them thousands of times a day."

That's where the Estess sisters come in, he says. "There's a perception that scientists aren't willing to collaborate. Project ALS has been unusually dynamic in fostering collaboration."

The sisters' passion spurs work at a different tempo. "The French have a great expression, 'The coachman's whip keeps the horse awake.' Sometimes I'm so busy running my own research center, I'm not able to pick up the phone to colleagues outside of this place. Valerie stays very current with our work, and she makes the call."

Project ALS money is essential too. "The brakes in the president's restrictions, and in National Institutes of Health funding, are real. This situation would have been disastrous without private and philanthropic support."

Leadership by Project ALS may eventually entice drug companies to address the disease more aggressively, because the hardest parts of the problem will have been solved for them. "Some people say the ALS market is too small for big pharma," Henderson says. "On this campus we clearly have more efforts for ALS and SMA research than the pharmaceutical industry. To kick-start the process, academics need to lead the way. A scientist with solid research results has a much stronger case to make with drug companies."

The common purpose fostered by Project ALS does not overwhelm scientists' predisposition to skepticism, Henderson says. "It's very important to have the freedom to criticize. It has been a very successful collaboration for us with people at Harvard's stem cell institute, for example, but when we meet, and analyze each other's work, there are still quite tough comments."

Henderson dodges any praise about the project's pace, however. "If you perform a postmortem analysis of a patient with ALS, where you should see tens of motor neurons in a section, you will see zero. There is just a massive loss. It generally takes about three years from diagnosis to death.

"We need to find drugs that will keep motor neurons alive, and will keep their axons from dying back. We cannot claim speed until we have a treatment for ALS. Until then, we are slow."

Jenifer developed pneumonia, a life-threatening complication for a person with ALS. She went to Saint Vincent's Hospital, across the street from her apartment, spending a week in critical care. She received antibiotics while her fever cooled and her breathing eased.

Hours after returning home from the hospital, a remaining plug of mucus clogged her airway and Jenifer lost consciousness immediately. The paramedics could not find a pulse. While they worked around Jenifer's head, Valerie knelt at her feet. "I love you, Jenifer," she said. "I love you."

The EMTs said they'd found a pulse.

"You can't leave anyway," Valerie said. "You're gonna be on Katie in an hour."

Katie Couric, in that era still a host on the *Today* show, was scheduled to sit at the Greenwich Village bedside later that day. Jenifer opened her eyes. "I'm here," she said.

*   *   *

A TINY GIRL dressed as a princess answers the door to Lewis Cole's apartment. "My name is Layla," she announces. Then she and a playmate in similar attire scamper down the hall to the living room, where two Columbia University writing students wait for a meeting with their professor.

Lewis is in the study, in an inclined, motorized chair. He uses a bi-pap, which makes each sentence start with a *kh-* sound before the words come out. He has to pause to breathe every five or six words.

"I couldn't button my pants," Cole explains. "I went to a doctor thinking I had a pinched nerve. That doctor told me I had six to nine months to live. He was an idiot. He let me walk out without even asking where I was going. I could have gone to Eighty-sixth Street and jumped."

Instead Cole kept working. That was three years ago. A screenwriting professor and department chair at Columbia, author of four books and thirteen screenplays, Cole was a powerful educational force. He helped build the university's film curriculum, recruited directors to serve as faculty, and lectured with legendary passion in the classroom known as 511 Dodge.

Now Cole sees students in small groups at his home. His study is walled with books. He's a tall man, bald, barefoot, and his brow furrows when he is thinking. The phone in his lap rings steadily with calls from friends and colleagues, which he answers by speaker.

"I've continued to teach," he explains. "I've continued to be a father to my child. She knows that I'm sick, that I'm handicapped. She is wonderful, helpful, considerate, loving." His face goes blank. "Today has not been a great day."

Over the years Cole has become an expert patient. He can recite from memory which services different medical equipment companies offer. But he insists he has not "become an ALS addict. In fact, one of the real problems with ALS is that, for such a catastrophic occurrence, there is very little central information about what you need to know."

Thus one of his earliest struggles was about how forthcoming to be. "I felt it was possible that the demands of the disease would necessarily lead me to so much hiding and shame that it would become an intolerable burden. This disease affects every dimension of your life—going to the bathroom, showering. If you don't want to become a complete invalid, you must make this part of your life or endure constant humiliation."

Then Cole met Valerie. "We liked each other a lot, right away. She's a source of enormous information about what's going on with research. I would call her from time to time. There are, as far as I can tell, quackeries in countries like Belize, where stem cell therapy costs hundreds of thousands of dollars. I called Valerie, she knew about it. She warned me off."

Project ALS invited Cole to a fund-raising event. "Now I knew about those things, because I'd been to one of another group and it was a pretty dismal affair. There was no education. The crowd never shut up. But Valerie said it would be good to have a dramatic presentation, to have people on the front lines of ALS talk about their day.

"I did it. I decided to be completely honest about it. I was in a wheelchair, much the same as now, and I did take the bi-pap. I gave them a totally straight characterization of what my day was like. Now this was incredible—a focused, superb group, and celebrities hosting it, combined information and entertainment. And when we people were talking, everyone was quiet."

Like many ALS patients, Cole is desperate to help find a cure. "There was a discovery that lithium might have a retardant effect. I said, 'Give it to me.' I've tried every kind of therapy there is. I've gone to faith healers, I don't care—partly because I have reason to believe that Western medicine has only a partial understanding of our beings, and partly because there's so much confusion on the part of the medical establishment about what ALS is.

"The reasons not to engage in trying to find some kind of cure are, to my mind, dismissible. I feel like there's very little to be lost. So when I heard about the stem cell stuff, I was eager to do it."

What researchers wanted to do, courtesy of Project ALS support, was determine if a person's adult skin cells could be turned back into stem cells—containing the patient's own DNA. That would enable scientists to try all manner of possible treatments, specific to that person, while avoiding the whole existing stem cell ethical obstacle course.

"To me it's a no-brainer," Cole said. "You do it because you're sick.

You also have an obligation to let people know what the sickness is, to use your body to promote understanding of the disease. I was also attracted to participating because I believe in the way they conduct business: communal work, complete transparency, quick results. These are all virtues."

With some fanfare, scientists sliced a quarter-inch square piece of skin from his forearm. Describing the procedure causes Cole to give a rare laugh. "They made it such a big deal. It's just a scrape."

But the work of Project ALS is not something he dismisses as readily. "I am a product of the sixties. I was a political radical. I believe in the value of radical social thought. And in a deep way I believe that the very good work that enterprising individuals do, like this organization, is a kind of surrogate for collective action. I believe that there is value in people coming together, that there is something extraordinary about revolutionary action, that people coming together can change history. Look at the Revolutionary War, the labor movement, the abolitionist movement. The Estess sisters, they are irreplaceable individuals."

Cole tilts his head back, his jaw working back and forth. "Look. All the things they're doing now? I don't believe any of that is going to result in a cure that will benefit me. I believe there's going to be a building of understanding of this disease, though, and a gradual erosion of its power."

His jaw frets a moment more. "This disease puts you in the privileged position of contemplating your end, and making it an end of your own choosing."

At that Lewis Cole clears his throat, then calls in his writing students. They enter without sheepishness, notebooks already open, and he digs right into their latest work.

In the front hall, Layla sits with her playmate. She bows while her friend waves both hands above her head, as if in blessing, and whispers, "I hope all of your wishes come true."

JENIFER ESTESS DIED on December 16, 2003, at about 5 A.M. It was a quiet event; her heart simply stopped. She was forty years old, five years past her initial diagnosis.

"I was working with her the day before," Meredith says. "She had a really bad day, choking a lot. We were on the phone that night. She said she was very tired, very tired, very tired. She never talked that way. I hung up thinking I might not see her again."

For the funeral Jenifer wore a black turtleneck and a favorite lipstick. Her trademark black hair was brushed to a shine. Friends stood by the casket in the Riverside Memorial Chapel viewing room, seeing her face without the bi-pap mask for the first time in ages. She looked pretty, as she had before the illness ever came her way.

"I learned about beauty from Jenifer," her friend Martha Mc-Cully said in the eulogy. "She could spot it, boy. In objects, places, and, of course, in people. She surrounded herself with beauty. She was always telling people how beautiful they were, inside and out, and not just gratuitously, she meant it. She wanted everyone to see what she saw.

"She bettered all of our lives, and the lives of millions of people who never met her, with her life. She will outlive all of us."

And thus, step seven in Jenifer's path was as an inspiration. With Meredith's help, Valerie finished the book she'd been co-writing with Jenifer. Then the surviving sisters went right back to work.

"I spent maybe a couple of days in bed," Meredith recalls, "but when you have three kids you can't do more than that. And then we just continued working. I don't remember taking time off. Any. Maybe I should have. But it was in honor of her too. And all the people we know now with ALS."

To this day the sisters speak of Jenifer in the present tense—"Jenifer likes that idea," for example, or "Jenifer thinks there's real potential in that direction." It's not craziness, though, or denial of the reality of her death. Rather it reveals a continued sense of common purpose. Three sisters experienced this disease, three sisters launched the effort to cure it, and three sisters persist in the mission today.

"In science, you see incredibly brilliant people holed up doing incredibly hard work," Valerie says. "I'm not sure they're lacking in dreams. But something is missing. That's our role.

"Now I admit, most of the feelings I've had have been very dark, feelings of anger. What drives me along is a love for my sister. That's stronger than anything. Jen went to Capitol Hill all those times, and now I say, 'You should help us, but even if you don't, let us do it. We'll keep on raising money, and putting it toward the most promising science.'"

So the fund-raising continues. At the most recent annual dinner, at the Waldorf-Astoria Hotel, Ben Stiller hosted for the eleventh year in a row, with support from the comedian Sara Silverman, and Jon Stewart of *The Daily Show.*

So the grants continue to support groundbreaking research. Project ALS so far has raised nearly $40 million to fund collaborative science. And it works. For example, a joint effort led by Kevin Eggan, Ph.D., at the Harvard Stem Cell Institute—and co-authored by members of Columbia's motor neuron lab—announced in mid-2008 that they had turned skin cells into stem cells, and stem cells into motor neurons. That means a patch of tissue like the one scraped off Lewis Cole's arm can be turned into motor neurons containing Cole's DNA. Researchers can watch these cells and observe precisely what causes them to die. By learning what that mechanism is, they hope to learn how to prevent it.

Moreover, because the stem cells come from the patient's skin rather than an embryo, Project ALS–supported research has rendered the ethical debate nearly moot. The Obama administration has reduced obstructions to stem cell studies and Congress is weighing a larger research appropriation.

That is what the authentic patriots do: They lead government toward solutions. When Project ALS–funded research one day results in a working treatment, and the drug companies turn that finding into a product, that will be authentic patriots again—leading the free market toward a better society.

Meanwhile Valerie and Meredith Estess maintain their creed that this always fatal disease can be cured. Until then, persisting is their patriotic duty.

"To stop now would be un-American," Valerie insists. "I love my country. And this is the only place on the planet where, if you're willing to work hard for what you want, you might be able to get it. And us? Well, we are getting closer. We are actually getting closer. That works for me. That's my sister living through me."

"It sounds so queer and corny," Meredith says, "but I always thought we were going to get out of it somehow. Save her? I always thought that we would. Now I realize. Science is a long process.

"We couldn't count on government. We couldn't count on the medical system. So you have to do something yourself. I know a woman who just died of ALS, three kids, just gorgeous, age thirty-eight when she was diagnosed, died in three years. How can that happen in America?

"We're patriotic, because we are fighting for a cause. Not a war, 'rah-rah,' but for people. We're trying to make a difference. My sister taught me that. Everyone told us, 'No, no, no, you can't do anything,' but here we are, standing up and making a difference. That's patriotic."

Above all, researchers maintain their determination that a treatment is possible. Articles about their findings appear in journals like *Science* and *Cell*. Project ALS recently doubled its laboratory space, improving conditions for the current scientists and recruiting more researchers to the cause. They reach a little further every day.

At a recent Project ALS tell-all meeting, for example, one researcher presented esoteric findings from a study on genetic markers. After severe interrogation by leaders of labs across the country, their skepticism rendered in language it would take a Ph.D. to understand, a senior cell scholar cleared his throat. As everyone in the room turned, expecting another scathing question, he rendered his opinion: "Perhaps I should give voice to what all of us are thinking inside, which is that this is astounding, spectacular work."

The room murmured its assent, but the researcher waved the praise aside. "It's a long way from a cure."

And everyone went right back to work.

At the meeting's conclusion, some scientists still had more to share. Christopher Henderson of Columbia crossed the room to sit beside Fred Gage from the Jonas Salk Institute. They both leaned over a piece of paper, making marks on it, their heads inches apart, speaking too quietly to be heard over other conversations in the room.

One person at the front turned to Valerie Estess. "What are they talking about?"

"Who cares?" she answered, smiling. "They're talking. It can only be good."

6

"The Noblest Question
in the World"

The youth of a nation are the trustees of posterity.

— Benjamin Disraeli

How far you go in life depends on your being tender
with the young, compassionate with the aged, sympathetic with the striving and tolerant of the weak and
strong—because someday in life you will have been all
of these.

— George Washington Carver

The children come pouring off the bus at the Benjamin
Franklin Institute of Technology in Boston. It's a Saturday afternoon, chilly and gray. The kids are noisy and boisterous, teenagers
and preteens who have been cooped up for the flight from Chicago and
then the ride in from Logan Airport. They are tall, short, skinny,
and fat. They are white, black, Asian, and Latino. They are laughing
and jumping around.

There to greet them stands another group of teens, similarly diverse, identically energized, who hail from Boston. The local boys
grab suitcases three at a time and bound inside, their strain masked
by enthusiasm. Girls squeal and hug, and a few wipe away tears. Inside the Franklin Institute's main hall, where stone floors and wrought-
iron railings reflect and amplify the sound, both groups of teens hail
and shout as though they were at a summer camp reunion.

But something much bigger than that is happening on this January afternoon in 2008. This meeting marks the start of a rite that in three days will touch hundreds of thousands of people: a yearly tribute to fundamental American principles, a dramatic annual reminder of a promise by the nation's Founders that thus far has gone unfulfilled. And this activist celebration will persuade not with marches or slogans or raised fists. It will happen because of the work of an authentic patriot, who did not seek social justice via government or the free market, but through individual courage and initiative. It will happen with song.

Chaperones call and wave their arms like cowboys herding steers, as the group hurries into the rehearsal hall. On a small stage up front, a few serious-looking grown-ups sit behind a table. Otherwise the cavernous room contains only rows of gray metal chairs facing the stage and, to one side, a piano. Kids bounce among one another like electrons, but over the next few minutes they usher themselves toward the chairs.

As if to reinforce the purpose of their gathering, some of Ben Franklin's aphorisms are painted on the walls:

"The doors of wisdom are never shut."

"I would rather have it said that he lived usefully than that he died rich."

"The noblest question in the world is what good I may do in it."

This room contains an answer. Just to see the children is to look on the embodiment of a melting pot. This is America made manifest, a demographic cross section gathered in folding chairs. But there are huge differences between the races in the United States and this crowd of teens. To begin with, here they are blended. Unlike kids of the same age in high school cafeterias across America, and unlike many urban and suburban neighborhoods, they have not divided themselves by race or socioeconomic status. Latinos stand beside African Americans beside whites beside East Asians beside West Asians.

More significantly, they are getting along. Unlike much of American society, there is no racial strife here—no name-calling, no hate crimes, no profiling, no discrimination. The only tensions in that rehearsal hall pertain to the musical task about to begin, and the performance that will result.

The difference between these kids and U.S. society as a whole becomes most apparent a moment later, after adults have droned their words of welcome and logistics. Then Anthony Trecek-King climbs to a riser in front of the stage. A slender black man with a brilliant smile, he is artistic director of the Boston Children's Chorus. He raises his arms wide.

"All right, all right, all right. Now: Where are my sopranos? Altos? Tenors? Basses?"

Hands fly up here and there, revealing that the children have segregated themselves after all—by vocal range. They arrayed themselves without prompting, basses behind altos to Anthony's right, sopranos in front of tenors on his left. They've even shuffled themselves like two decks of cards so that Boston and Chicago children alternate chair by chair through the rows.

That achievement, a deliberate mixing of race and background, might be impossible in some regions of the country. At the Franklin Institute that afternoon, it does not merit a mention. The adults onstage, as well as chaperones and staff lining the walls, do not interrupt their murmured conversations. Anthony raises his hands and the youngsters instantly fall silent. He nods in the direction of the piano, where the accompanist arpeggiates a chord. Anthony rises on his toes, says, "And—"

Instantly the children sing the notes, rising and falling through the chord: "Ba-da-da-*da*-da-da-daah." The piano rises a half step and the children follow. Then again. By the fourth arpeggio their voices have found themselves, and the singers nail the high note. The grownups, all of them, stop talking and look over.

The fifth annual joint appearance by the Chicago Children's Choir and the Boston Children's Chorus, with a televised performance forty-eight hours later on Martin Luther King Jr. Day, is under way.

FOR AS LONG as white people have lived on the North American continent, there have been struggles over race. It remains an astonishing hypocrisy, that the leaders of a revolutionary effort to establish liberty and equality in the New World should simultaneously have denied those gains to people who are not white.

This internal contradiction has directed government policy, shaped our economy, and bent even the best of people into self-contradiction. No less than Thomas Jefferson, who wrote that "the rights of human nature are deeply wounded by this infamous practice," nonetheless continued to own slaves.

Yet the widespread impression that American colonists were indifferent to slavery is not entirely accurate. Patrick Henry wrote that he much desired the great day "when an opportunity will be afforded to abolish this lamentable evil." In 1773 Benjamin Rush—a Philadelphia physician who had the ear of John Adams and others helping Jefferson write the Declaration of Independence—called on his fellow patriots to oppose "a vice which degrades human nature. The plant of liberty is of so tender a nature that it cannot thrive long in the neighborhood of slavery." John Allen, whose political pamphlets contained vehement exhortations in favor of human rights, excoriated slave owners and those who defended them:

> Blush, ye pretended votaries for freedom! Ye trifling patriots! Who are making a vain parade of being advocates for the liberties of mankind, who are thus making a mockery of your profession by trampling on the sacred natural rights and privileges of Africans; for while you are fasting, praying, non-importing, non-exporting, remonstrating, resolving and pleading for a restoration of your charter rights, you at the same time are continuing this lawless, cruel, inhuman, and abominable practice of enslaving your fellow creatures.

Religious leaders increasingly took up the cause of abolition, which commanded ever more public attention throughout the 1770s. Gradually some colonists awakened to their contradictory actions, and began efforts to extend liberty to all.

While many of the Thirteen Colonies lacked the courage to free the roughly half million existing slaves outright, several passed laws to inhibit the growth of slavery. Delaware outlawed the importing of slaves. Pennsylvania passed prohibitive taxes on the slave trade, and the world's first antislavery organization formed in Philadelphia in 1775. Connecticut and Rhode Island decided that any people imported to those states as slaves were automatically free.

Although these measures were clearly insufficient, as the eighty-six years between the Declaration of Independence and the Emancipation Proclamation would prove, they were significant steps nonetheless. Northern colonies relied nearly as heavily on slave labor as did those in the South. Slaves in Rhode Island comprised about one-eighth of the population. In New York slaves were nearly one-fourth of working-age males.

Meanwhile tens of thousands of white people also lived in compulsory servitude, for periods ranging from seven years to life. Some fifty thousand such indentured servants arrived from Britain and Ireland between 1718 and 1775. While some found apprenticeships and eventual freedom, others were bought and sold, abused and mistreated, perhaps as badly as their African fellows. In his heyday Congressman Matthew Lyon was a firebrand defender of free speech. But he arrived in the colonies at age fifteen under servitude, and at one time was sold in exchange for two bulls worth twelve pounds.

In response to slavery Massachusetts set the loftiest goal, and the one most in keeping with the virtues of liberty. In 1771 the colony's legislature voted to abolish slavery altogether. The governor vetoed the plan. The legislature acted identically in 1774, and again lost to a gubernatorial veto.

Not only did the issue of slavery not die, it remained central to American politics, and to the ongoing challenge to fulfill the promise of equality. When the colonies eventually gained independence, a region known as New Connecticut refused to join the new nation. Instead the people living between the Connecticut River and Lake Champlain declared themselves an independent republic, with their own currency and trade. They refused to assimilate unless their constitution was accepted wholesale, and that document specifically prohibited slavery. It took Congress until 1791 to consent, creating the fourteenth state, Vermont. Since that day, the nation has continually struggled to keep the unqualified promise of the Declaration: "We hold these truths to be self-evident: that all men are created equal."

IN THE LATE 1800s, as the nation's immigrant population swelled, the young United States imported an idea from Great Britain that sought to develop social justice at the most local level: the settlement house. These institutions, typically founded and run by women, provided an array of social services: day care, help finding jobs, medical care, assistance with learning English or with literacy, aid in finding housing. The first settlement house opened in New York City in 1886; three years later in Chicago the Hull House opened, and soon it became the most famous and progressive settlement house in the nation.

Hull House still exists, and still espouses its founders' values. Unlike the staff of most social welfare programs of the 1880s, for example, women working in settlement houses did not return to their comfortable homes at day's end, but instead lived among the people they served. The houses maintained that all people were equally deserving of dignity and respect, regardless of ethnicity or race. They also held that the crime, ignorance, and desperation of poor people did not reveal a moral failure on their part, but rather were results of the poverty under which they lived. If people received opportunities, they would rise.

The ideas took hold rapidly. By 1890 there were four hundred settlement houses across the country, primarily in Chicago, New York, and Boston. It was in the shadow of a Boston settlement house, in the 1930s, that Christopher Moore was raised. His mother, an active Unitarian Universalist, worked in a settlement house. Its effect on young Chris Moore is clear, because its values continually reappeared in his adult life.

Moore went to Harvard, where he majored in anthropology. But his principle occupation in college, his true devotion, was the Glee Club. A baritone, he was a fervent participant and by all accounts, he was good. He also sang off-campus with the Boston Symphony and the Boston Pops.

After graduation in 1950, Moore spent a summer traveling Europe and found himself in Austria. Ever the singer, he paid a visit to the renowned Vienna Boys' Choir. Established by an emperor's decree in 1498, the choir performs at state functions and religious events. The Vienna Boys' Choir worked with such composers as Mozart and Salieri; Schubert sang in the choir, as, briefly, did Haydn.

Five hundred–plus years later, the group consists of a hundred boys whose voices have not yet changed, hailing mostly but not exclusively from Austria. Although they range from ten to fourteen years old, the boys live in a palace converted to a boarding school, and perform in four touring groups before audiences that total half a million people annually.

Moore visited the choir and met the director, Ferdinand Grossman. He watched Grossman teach the boys to sing, to behave professionally, to expect high artistry of themselves despite their youth. After his travels Moore enrolled in Meadville Lombard Theological School in Chicago, then followed his mother's faith into an assistant ministry in Saint Louis. A recipe was brewing in Chris Moore's head and heart, all the ingredients for his future life's work, though he did not know it yet.

In the spring of 1951, a Chicago bus driver named Harvey Clark Jr. moved into an apartment building in the suburb of Cicero. An African American, he had come from the city's impoverished South Side. Cicero was almost entirely white. Some kids broke into the apartment building and trashed Harvey's possessions. Others damaged the building itself.

It was not the first such incident. Race riots broke out in some major American city every few years in the twentieth century. Until a backlash in the rebellious late 1960s, the rioters were predominantly white.

Chicago was no exception to this history. In 1919 a black teenager had crossed Twenty-ninth Street, apparently an inexcusably provocative foray into what was considered a white zone. The result was a seven-day battle between the races—fires, shootings, beatings. Fifteen whites died and 195 were injured. Twenty-three blacks died and 342 were injured.

It took the state militia to quell that incident, aided by a fortuitous downpour, but the issues were far from resolved. Arsons continued. From time to time a battle would erupt over African Americans using a certain park, or even a particular park bench.

In 1951, Harvey Clark Jr. revealed how many whites remained determined to prevent minorities from entering their neighborhoods. Competition for jobs, reduced property values, liberal political influence—reasonable or not, these were among the whites' fears.

Clark knew his rights. After the initial incident, he refused to move out. Instead he won a federal court order for police protection.

It mattered little. On July 12 a white mob rioted in Cicero. Police at the scene simply looked on. Estimates of the crowd's size reached five thousand.

Harvey Clark Jr. stayed put. He sued the town board, winning a $400,000 settlement. A grand jury indicted four town officials and three police officers on charges of violating his rights. His victory for African Americans extended beyond that summer's strife too; his daughter Michele was the first black woman to become a network television correspondent.

After Cicero the nation's attention on race focused elsewhere. The Supreme Court outlawed segregation in 1954. With the 1955 arrest of Rosa Parks, the subsequent Montgomery bus boycott, the lunch counter sit-in in North Carolina in the 1960s, the ascension of Martin Luther King Jr. as a leader of the nonviolent campaign for equal rights for African Americans, the march on Selma, King's jailing in Birmingham, his assassination as well as Malcolm X's, and much more, issues of race exploded from localized strife to national struggle.

Chicago took part, including a march for equal housing as late as 1966. Even today de facto segregation persists: Only 9 percent of the city's public school students are white.

While these conflicts persisted, some of the city's whites condemned inequality, segregation, and unwritten laws governing who could live where. Some white supporters took steps to show solidarity with the city's minority residents. A handful even sought to bring healing and peace.

* * *

BY THE MID-1950s Reverend Christopher Moore had attained a parish, the First Unitarian Universalist Church in Chicago's Hyde Park. The church is a classic neo-Gothic structure: ornate stone walls, a bell tower, a pipe organ, stained-glass windows, and a high-arched interior. That area, home to university faculty and some of Chicago's black middle class, was slightly less segregated than the rest of the city. As race issues burned through Chicago, Moore joined with the church's head of religious education to form a choir that would perform on United Nations Sunday in October 1956. Kids of varied backgrounds would sing the music of many different traditions.

Moore already had the artistic model of Vienna as his guide. But his aims would be the opposite of palace elitism. Right from the start his goal was to create as diverse a choir as possible, in race, gender, and socioeconomic status. One of the first members was the child of a Japanese American couple who had met in the World War II internment camps.

Moore's strategy was simple but idealistic. The place to start building a Chicago that respected all people without regard to race was among kids. The way to do it was by giving all races a common purpose. The means to do it was music.

United Nations Sunday was a success, and with that launching Moore could not let the choir fade away. Rather, he began drawing singers from neighboring parts of the city. With no basis for inclusion other than talent and potential, not only was the choir of mixed races, it also bridged divides of class. Rich kids and poor kids sang beside one another. Thus the two major influences on Moore's life—the settlement house and the Vienna Boys' Choir—were merged in a new idea.

Some parents objected to Moore's high artistic standards. Singing in the chorus was too stressful, they said; he pushed the boys and girls too hard for their age. His answer came when the Vienna Boys' Choir toured the United States. Moore threw them a party at the church—and asked them to serenade his kids.

"The message was plain," remembers Chris's wife, Judy. " 'These are kids like you, your age, and they're doing it this well.' They had to buy into this vision of producing music at this level."

Increasingly, the choir dominated Moore's life. When he met Judy

Manwell in 1960, their first date was *Carmen* at Chicago's prestigious Lyric Opera. Moore's choir members were performing as street urchins. "He took me, yes. And then he deposited me so he could take care of the kids. It was a really big deal, a huge auditorium, a real audience and not just your parents loving you, real critics. And afterward, he had to take the kids home."

Still, it was love. They courted while she finished graduate school in social work and fulfilled a fellowship requirement in California. In 1964 they married and she moved to Chicago. Meanwhile Moore had become close friends with the principal of a school adjacent to a huge housing project on Chicago's South Side. When federal funding became available in the mid-1960s for inner-city artistic programs, Moore joined with his friend to win a grant. Now the choir would grow beyond the confines of one church; its reach would extend into areas that were decidedly not middle-class.

By this time Moore was becoming a classic authentic patriot. Government was struggling even to discuss matters of race; the Civil Rights Act was years away, its fulfillment decades in the future. The free market generally showed little interest in race relations. If the nation were ever to fulfill its promise of equality, the effort would take individual initiatives converging toward a common purpose.

That was Moore's mission. As the choir became a consuming interest, it required concomitant familial sacrifices.

"I knew at the start that the choir was the organizing influence of his life," Judy Moore recalls. "I could like it or lump it.

"Sometimes I had to lump it. He wasn't making much of any money. He did less work at the church. The choir's budget was always dicey—he would sit and figure out their bills while I was the income earner. For five years I worked at a children's hospital with very, very sick kids. There is only so much you can do, and the work is very stressful. But I'd get home and Chris would say, 'I have some kids who need to be taken home.' We each had VW Beetles; we'd pack in the kids and away we'd go."

Chris was reluctant, but Judy persuaded him to start a family. Their son Jonathan was born in 1969. If the child grew fast, the choir grew faster.

The Chicago Children's Choir of the twenty-first century is a multiracial, multicultural, professionally run, choral music education organization. The project teaches singing and music theory in fifty Chicago schools. When cities struggle to pay for basics like science instruction or safe buildings, arts education is always among the first things cut. The choir offers an alternative for children who might otherwise grow up without learning anything of the performing arts. There are seven neighborhood choral groups, one in nearly every section of the city. The best singers comprise the professional-level Concert Choir. This world-class group has performed in more than a dozen countries, on television, in collaboration with Chicago's Lookingglass Theatre Company, the Chicago Symphony Orchestra, and the Lyric Opera. Chicago children have sung in the White House, as well as at inaugurations for mayors of Chicago and governors of Illinois.

These high-profile events belie the routine work of developing young voices, and providing music education in schools and neighborhoods. If Moore had merely replicated Vienna in Illinois, then his achievement would be artistic only. But the measure of his larger purpose, and its unmitigated success, may be found in a census: The choir's current membership is 44 percent African American, 40 percent Latino, 10 percent white, and 5 percent Asian. In a typical year, the overall number of children singing in its programs hovers near 3,200.

Each level of the organization has common attributes. Kids from beginners to experts are expected to behave like adult musicians: to arrive on time, bring their sheet music, and pay strict attention to the conductor. A day's instruction might focus on tasks as complex as preparing an operatic piece for the Concert Choir, or as fundamental as learning how to sustain a note on pitch for the beginners, but artistic excellence is always the common denominator. The kids are challenged, and their efforts to meet the challenge are taken seriously.

Each of the member choirs also performs. Of course, the immediate intent is to display the children's progress. The beginner choirs sing for their parents, and for other schools. Dressed in identical uniforms—red sweater or jacket, blue pants, white shirt for a striking and patriotic look—the children learn that they represent not only themselves, but also the citywide choral enterprise. To reinforce the point, every May the entire choir joins in a single Paint the Town Red concert. Imagine thirty-two hundred trained children's voices, lifted in common purpose.

That leads to the second reason for performing: to foster in the audience the same bridges among races and across classes that connect the choir. The shows create community, one of the unique gifts of the performing arts, as parents and friends gather to hear the children sing. Because the choir involves kids of all races and socioeconomic status, audiences are much more mixed than at other arts events in the city.

Imagine the children touring the South, singing songs of racial harmony in towns where the struggle for civil rights faced condemnation or violence. Imagine them as pitch-perfect emissaries to Korea. Imagine them performing in a rebuilt Hiroshima, appearing jointly with a Japanese choir.

Ironically, by making race and economic status irrelevant to musical ability and shared purpose, singing may be one of the least important things the choir teaches. The standard of seeking artistic excellence is contagious, affecting not just how the kids sing but how they behave at rehearsals, and by extension how they behave in school and at home.

As children become friends through the choir, they share play dates, sleepovers, and of course the choir's tours, and thus they learn how others live. With a foundation of practicing and performing together, with the shared goal of high musicianship, they have a preexisting basis for accepting the differences among them.

The aim is not tolerance. That word suggests some superior person deigning to put up with some inferior person. Instead the goal is appreciation. Every voice is needed to achieve full harmony.

Thus the ultimate lesson, for this choir and for American society, is the value of having a common purpose with other people. What matters at each choir practice is whether the singers are on pitch, if they remember the conductor's directions, if they pay attention to details like when to breathe or how to shape their mouths so a word sounds right when sung by dozens of voices at once. When the most important thing is working together in common purpose, a singer's skin color or economic status matters not at all.

For this nation, with its ugly history of racial strife, the lesson bears repeating: When the most important thing is working together in common purpose, a person's skin color or economic status matters not at all.

"I love it," says Tamaiya Clayton, a sixteen-year-old African American Chicago girl, between Boston rehearsals. "I love seeing the audience. I love making people happy. I want to be a professional when I grow up."

Tamaiya has not had an easy road. Difficulties at birth meant that her life began with a long hospitalization. Her father, "a really big man who always was happy," died of a heart attack when she was ten. Tamaiya's mother lives in Indianapolis, "because she wanted a better life, but in Chicago she gets into a lot of trouble. She was selling drugs."

Tamaiya tried living with her mother, but wound up in foster care. "I cried every day for my grandmother. I would cry so hard at night that I had to go to the hospital."

Tamaiya lives with her grandmother now, in the Evergreen Park section of Chicago's South Side. "There's a gang community, yes, a lot of boys seventeen, eighteen, twenty years old. All they want is trouble. They hang out by the fire hydrant looking for someone who gets out of pocket. And drugs, weed, you can get it from anybody."

Her school, Morgan Park High, is a tough place too. "There are slow kids, and they're angry. They like to hurt people's feelings. They seem to be in charge. Plus there are, I don't know, two thousand kids there now. So the school is very, very packed."

One element of stability in Tamaiya's life is religion. "I am a Baptist, and in hard times I just keep praying and keep the faith." The church's values come through in her appearance: straight hair, modest clothes, black-framed glasses. She has a soft-spoken manner, and rarely looks grown-ups in the eye. Only the studs in her ears hint at an artistic sensibility. As she has grown up, Tamaiya has learned race relations the hard way.

"At school I would never date African Americans, and the boys didn't like it. They would talk about, is it racist? People are always looking at you, there's a lot of competition. If your hair's not a certain length or a certain texture, it's not looked at well. I used to be talked about, because of the way I dress. People said that I talked white too, but it's really just proper talk. And I need it to be clear for the times when I speak in the front of church."

Church is also where Tamaiya started to sing. In one choir or another since she was little, she has always been a standout. "We do a praise dance. We have a ministry of music."

In sixth grade she tried out for the Chicago Children's Choir, aiming for the top. "I auditioned for the Concert Choir, but they ended up making me go to the Beverly Choir, a neighborhood choir. I was very upset. I was always in the top group. Why did I have to go in a neighborhood group?"

Tamaiya was so embarrassed, she did not even tell friends when she had performances. But gradually she gained self-awareness. "It turns out I needed to work on my sight reading. And in Beverly I was an older kid, so I learned being responsible and I gained confidence."

Tamaiya's knowledge of music theory deepened, as did her appreciation for artistic precision. "I didn't know that every note meant something. It does. It is the purest purity. In Chicago life is so complicated, so much is happening and not much connects. In the choir, we connect with each other, we connect with people."

Tamaiya did attain the Concert Choir, before her sixteenth birthday. The Boston trip is her first tour at that level. While the boys practice a song, she sits to one side and whispers. "I felt scared. But Boston is really similar to Chicago. I'm staying with a family where no one is black. The girl is Chinese, the parents are white. At first I felt left out, do my own thing, you know? But I knew that's not the way to go. So that's a thing to work on.

"I've connected a lot more with the Boston singers. Sometimes we get laughing. Yes, we're all different, but you also see a sense of connection."

* * *

THE CONNECTIONS ARE not limited to singing. Just ask Cece Hill. A thirty-three-year-old African American woman with an easy laugh, she grew up on the South Side too. "It was very bad, poor, a lot of the buildings being condemned. Gangs, drugs, you name it. It was kind of the peak of crack. I lost a lot of friends along the way."

Her household was stable, though, and strict. Children could venture only so far from the front door; bedtimes were set in cement. Cece sang each Sunday in the church choir. She also performed the national anthem at Carter Elementary School functions, singing "The Star-Spangled Banner" so often, the school recorded it to play after the Pledge of Allegiance every morning. "The principal at our school was a kicker on knowing that song."

Teachers had spotted Cece's inner ham, and encouraged it. "They had these school assemblies, where we'd do things we weren't used to doing. One time they had a square dance. Mrs. Smith wanted me to do it." Cece laughs at the memory. "Well, I wasn't about to get up there. But she said, 'You be the caller.' The caller? I could see my friends cracking all these stale jokes. But I did it. And I liked it."

Soon after, Mrs. Smith told Cece about the Children's Choir.

"I was interested right off. Convincing my parents was the thing. They all worked. My dad was geeked: 'How can we get her back and forth?' We didn't have a car. But he took me to the audition after all. Probably he'd decided I wouldn't make it in."

Cece was nervous too. The audition involved matching notes on the piano, testing her tonal memory. Then came the moment of truth, when she was asked to sing a solo without accompaniment. The requested song? "The Star-Spangled Banner."

Cece was in. But that day's nervousness was just beginning.

"I knew no one. It was very mixed racially, that was a first for me. I truly applaud my parents for their open-mindedness. Staff members encouraged older kids to mingle with us. I'm rubbing up against all kinds of people, a variety of ages from eight to eighteen. And if you could sing, they took you in. I was excited, because I was doing something more than my next-door neighbor. The traveling, the people I met, the exposure to different points of view, learning songs in another language, it was more, just more."

Cece's musical education was intensive, and included theory, movement, performance skills, discipline, professional etiquette. At home she sang so much, she irritated her family. Still, her parents rode the bus with her to rehearsals several times a week, waited outside, then rode home with her. With each concert, meanwhile, with each new song in her repertoire, Cece's confidence grew. "You have achieved something: the feeling of standing there delivering something so strong, you bring these people to tears of joy. Here is something and I know how to knock 'em dead with it."

When Cece attained the Concert Choir, real travel began: Japan, England, Mexico, Austria. One of her most memorable shows, though, was a bus ride away in Sparta, Illinois.

"Sparta was not ready for us. We went to an elementary school to perform one evening. Well, the people come walking in, and the blacks sit on one side, the whites on the other side. That blew us away.

"We had a talk: Are we upset? Is there friction? But there was none. We're here together, we're a family. Then our conductor was making jokes, and saying, 'Let's give them what we are. Let's give them what the Chicago Children's Choir represents.'"

Cece's favorite song from that time was a Yugoslavian piece. Recalling the melody, she bursts spontaneously into song. Her voice soars through the cubicles around hers, in the Chicago Cultural Center where the choir's administrative offices are located. Singing out, in that workplace, does not even bring a comment from surrounding cubicles. This is an office with a piano in the entry. Reams of sheet music lie stacked along the walls, on which hang photos of the choir singing to Nobel Peace Prize winners such as the Dalai Lama and South African Archbishop Desmond Tutu.

"If I had stayed in that neighborhood, without the choir, I don't think I would have gone to college," Cece says.

That is true in many ways. There was the influence of the choir, its discipline and standards. There also was personal support to create opportunities for Cece.

"One of the vocal counselors was talking to the kids, you know? 'You're juniors, you need to start thinking about where you want to go.'" Neither of Cece's parents had finished college. "And they could not pay for me either. Mainly I didn't have the sources to know how to find help."

The choir director connected her with music professors and financial aid advisors at Roosevelt College. Cece received a full scholarship. She landed a part-time job with the choir as well.

Cece now has a degree in music education. She sings in churches and anywhere there's demand for a sight-reading soprano. As the choir's program manager she attends to the children's nonmusical needs—sheet music, performance uniforms, permission slips, medical forms. "I'm the mom away from home."

The longer Cece works on the choir's two missions—music education and respect for diversity—the more opened-minded she has become. "This has broadened my horizons. I'm not afraid to walk up to somebody because they don't look like me. I love everybody.

"Hey, if people want to know what's coming up, in the future, we've got it right here. We represent the world that is ahead, the mix of people. It's already happening, with a lot of struggle, but with the choir we're showing how it could be. If you start with that idea at a very young age, we're breaking down walls. Here we teach that music has no color."

IF ALL THE choir did was lift voices and raise the sights of disadvantaged kids, those would be notable achievements. But appreciating diversity is a two-way street; it is also important for children of privilege to learn how everyone can contribute to the greater mutual good.

"We don't really talk about backgrounds much," says Isaac Sherman, a white, just-shy-of-seventeen-year-old from Chicago's Wrigleyville neighborhood. "It doesn't matter to us. It all really depends on what you do here, in the moment. It's all about how you sing."

The son of an award-winning playwright whose work has appeared on Broadway, Isaac attends Northside College Prep High School. "It's a very nice school. The faculty is very good, I love all my teachers. There are about a thousand students, and the music department is very good—a full orchestra, band, and chorus." His neighborhood is "very nice, quiet, safe."

Isaac is consistently polite, with a firm handshake and a clear expression. "I'm an average student, but it's a very rigorous program. I'd like to go to a college with a good theater program, Columbia College in Chicago, or Carnegie Mellon if I really wanted to shoot for something."

When he was twelve, Isaac joined a subset of the Chicago choir designed for boys whose voices were changing. "I realized how my passion is voice, that's what really stuck to me."

As he progressed, finally making the Concert Choir as a bass, Isaac also learned lessons about race, and how relations across classes could be. "There's no friction at all. We're a very accepting group. It doesn't matter what your history is, you'll still be accepted into the circle of trust."

That circle has grown to contain more than one city. "There was a great moment when we arrived this time," Judy Hanson, Chicago's director of choral programs, says during a Boston rehearsal break.

"One boy, couldn't be nerdier, reconnected with another boy who is all hip-hop and urban fashion," she says. "They'd become friends last year, and they just ran off together. Couldn't be more different, and they're friends through performing together. That's the whole point here, isn't it?"

"As a society, I have to say, we are a little ill," says Josephine Lee, artistic director of the choir. A daughter of Korean immigrants, she was classically trained in voice and conducting, and drawn to the choir by its social mission.

"Music has that ability to unify everyone's voice," she says. "It transcends race, gender, sexuality." Still, the choir cannot succeed on good intentions alone. "Unless there is musical excellence, no one will recognize the mission and spread the word."

Thus she and Hanson take turns at the podium in rehearsal, providing continually fresh energy to spur the children on. Hanson concentrates on choreography, which she teaches in a style somewhere between cheerleader and drill instructor. She bounces around the stage, arranging the children's locations by inches so every face will be visible. Honing in on individual gestures, and individual singers, she is relentless.

"If you pull your hands toward your heart, and really mean it, then when you sing 'there is a feeling' right there, it won't come out phony. Sing with your whole body and it will be sincere. . . . And can we have more precision on the *t* in *might*? Let's hear your diction there."

Lee's style is more professorial, perhaps because on the Boston trip she's seven months pregnant. If Hanson leads with her whole body, Lee conducts with three parts: her mouth, which exaggerates every word of the lyrics to keep the singers synchronized, and her hands, which are as expressive as a dancer's. Her hands implore, cajole, focus, and encourage.

Choir members, for their part, maintain professional standards throughout—jumping from cue to cue with their conductors, barely speaking during interruptions, paying such close attention that not one instruction is repeated all weekend. If these kids are tiring, they refuse to show it.

Seeing the Chicago Children's Choir at work is a moving experience because the singers' conviction is so visible. Working together, gathering diverse audiences, singing songs that celebrate differences and similarities among cultures, the children believe it works. They do so because they are among adults who also believe. And the grownups in turn depend on the audiences, who if they do not explicitly believe at least have an ardent desire to believe. The racial troubles of this nation have fostered an appetite for reconciliation, for progress, for signs that change is possible. To watch these kids of every color onstage, working hard together, pouring their hearts into their voices—this is a story that America wants to be true.

Those believers include Hubie Jones. He is the right person to have faith in an idea if you want to see it succeed. Jones has founded or helped found literally dozens of civic programs in Boston. His City Year project served as inspiration for the AmeriCorps program established by President Bill Clinton. If there is an authentic patriot in this host city, a person not waiting for government or business to solve problems, Jones fits the description.

A former protégé contacted him seeking fund-raising ideas for a film about the Chicago Children's Choir. Jones had never heard of the choir, but he saw them perform a few years later.

"I was blown away. And I just filed it away, thinking: We could bring this to Boston. We have the Museum of Fine Arts, the symphony, and they are excellent. But I'd already been thinking, how do we make the arts a high civic priority in Boston?"

Jones had built a partnership with higher educators, businesses, and city officials, creating a program that brings Boston's leaders to cities around the world to observe various organizations' best practices. When that group visited Chicago, the agenda included a performance by the choir. The idea of a Boston version won some well-placed friends.

In 2003 Boston finished construction of a new landmark bridge, which would be named for a deceased director of the Anti-Defamation League. Jones suggested joining various kids' choirs from around the city to sing at the dedication.

"Maybe this is the time to do the Chicago thing, build a new arts organization, provide excellent musical education and instruction for kids, but also use singing for social change, social healing, and youth development."

The idea took hold, with seed funding from the state turnpike authority and local businesses. More than two hundred children performed at the bridge's dedication, their singing broadcast on local TV. The response was enormous and immediate. "I've done a lot of projects here in fifty years. I've never before had money arrive unsolicited."

The Boston Children's Chorus was born. The following Martin Luther King Jr. holiday, Jones invited the Chicago choir to a joint performance. As when the Vienna Boys' Choir came to Chicago, it was a one-sided affair.

"I wanted them to come show Boston where we could go, what we're going to give the world. We'd had our first rehearsals that October, we had about twenty kids I'd guess. They sang a few songs, and the rest of the show was Chicago. They blew Boston away, just blew us away. But people got it.

"And now, this concert? People look forward to it. It's the biggest dose of inspiration they get every year."

The inspiration is spreading too. Boston's WCVB-TV broadcasts the show, which also airs in cities across the country. Jones puts icing on the sales pitch: "This is probably the most joyous thing I have ever done."

There's a little secret among both choirs that neither readily admits: They are cheap. That is, what they accomplish—arts education, shrinking racial barriers, bridging the chasms of class, healing the public, and providing high-quality entertainment—is astonishingly inexpensive. The whole Boston chorus' budget is about $1.4 million annually; Chicago's is about $1 million more, including all the travel, neighborhood groups, school programs, and scholarships for kids who need help affording choir participation. Ticket and CD sales reduce the need for fund-raising by about half.

Given the massive cost to the nation of racism and classicism—in diminished opportunity, in bitterness fostered by inequality, in condescension resulting from an erroneous sense of superiority, in violence and protest and discontent, in jail terms and housing denied and jobs lost—these choirs are practically free.

But nobody is talking about these concerns, as the rehearsals change locations on Sunday, arriving at the site where the choirs will perform for a paying audience and the TV cameras: Jordan Hall at The New England Conservatory of Music.

The building itself has historical significance. Jordan Hall is where Martin Luther King Jr. spoke when he came to Boston. At one of his talks in that hall, a college student was so inspired, he decided to devote his life to civic activism: Hubie Jones. Jordan Hall figured in King's personal life as well; on the steps outside he met Coretta Scott, who eventually became his wife and the mother of their four children.

The hall is visually stunning, its deep stage backed by high rows of organ pipes. The ceiling rises easily forty feet overhead, with ornate gilt woodwork on the walls. The rows drop steeply so every seat has a clear view, and the balcony is curved so the back of the seating is highest and the sides closer to the stage are lower—as though huge arms are embracing the crowd. The acoustics are lively, like in an old church.

Every year the Martin Luther King Day show sells out quickly, so dress rehearsal is open to the public as well. Some eight hundred people fill the seats, while TV crews test production plans and camera angles, the sound team fine-tunes the band's sound mix, and the children gain familiarity with the stage. More importantly, they practice backstage procedures—where there is room for about ten people, a far cry from the hundred and twenty or so who will need to file on and off in a matter of seconds, in an order that changes depending on which song is next. During entrances, program managers and conductors stand just offstage whispering, "Hurry. Smile. Hurry. Smile." When the children come off, the same adults chant: "Hurry. Costume change. Hurry. Costume change."

Onstage, Tamaiya maintains the same serious expression she wore during rehearsals. Her place is with the altos, stage right, on the second step up on the risers. It's a choice position, on the end of the row, but she keeps her eyes on the conductors. "I've been practicing all my moves. The Boston singers, I think they look up to Chicago Children's Choir a lot. There's maybe kind of a competition, who's going to sing best."

After dress rehearsal, the two choirs gather in a recital hall. Gathered in groups on the floor, they do homework, flirt, debate which Harry Potter book is best. They seem like ordinary teenagers, all acne and energy, one showoff at the piano ignoring the chaperones' repeated commands to shush.

When no one else is around, Tamaiya confesses a complaint.

"I'm not being seen. As I look at the audience, I don't see eyes on me. My engagement comes from the audience, and their faces. I like to be significant and unique, not seen just in the group. I love to be seen."

She takes off her glasses, frowns at them, puts them back on. "It's not happening. I'm not being seen."

NOT BEING SEEN is hardly a new experience for a black person in North America. The condition of minorities is, by many measures, dire.

- **Education.** Black children receive early education in large numbers, learning words and reading at home in rates comparable to whites. They do well in elementary school too. But their achievement collapses in high school; black teens' dropout rate is 25 percent higher than whites'. Possible reasons? More than one-fifth of teachers in majority black school districts have less than three years' experience. Also, per pupil spending runs nearly 20 percent less than in white majority districts. Education gaps grow with time too: By age twenty-five, 81 percent of blacks hold high school diplomas, compared to 86 percent of whites; 18 percent have college degrees, compared to 28 percent of whites.

- **Economic factors.** Education dictates earnings, so schooling problems affect later job prospects. Some 9.5 percent of black men were unemployed in 2006, compared with 4 percent of whites. The median income for a black man that year was $34,443, while the median white man's income was $46,802—a span of $12,359, or 26 percent. Nearly 25 percent of African Americans live below the poverty line, triple the rate of whites. Among children, 33.5 percent of young blacks live below the poverty line, while the rate is 10 percent for white children.

- **Justice.** A higher percentage of blacks are convicted of criminal charges, and they receive longer sentences than whites. Five times as many blacks are in prison as whites, and Hispanics go to jail at double the rates of whites. The disparity is greatest in Iowa, where only 2 percent of the population is black, but African Americans comprise 24 percent of the prison census. Nationally, the prison population reached a record 2.38 million in 2007, with 905,600 black inmates—also an all-time high. One study found more African Americans in prison than in college. Another found that the present rate of incarceration in America (4,789 out of every 100,000 black males) is more than five times the rate in South Africa during apartheid (851 black males per 100,000 in 1993).

- **Equality.** Not all injustice occurs in courts. Homeownership among blacks is 47.9 percent, compared with 75.8 percent among whites. One reason is that blacks receive higher-priced mortgage loans at double the rate of whites, even when they earn high incomes. Later in life, blacks also receive unequal nursing home care. They are 10 percent more likely than whites to live in a nursing home that is understaffed, 40 percent more likely to reside in a facility cited for a deficiency causing a resident harm or jeopardy, and 70 percent more likely to live in a home terminated from Medicare and Medicaid because of low-quality care.

There's much more. The median income for white families in 2001 was $45,200, for Hispanics $25,700, and for African Americans $25,500. Voter identification laws, passed to solve a voting fraud problem that does not exist, deter nearly 6 percent of African Americans from voting—mainly because they don't have driver's licenses.

Even setting aside statistics, the nation routinely suffers paroxysms over cases of obvious prejudice. All the world saw the 1991 videotape of Los Angeles police beating Rodney King, long after he had stopped resisting, long after he was flat on the ground. And all the nation suffered when those officers were found innocent. What did those riots express but anguished disappointment that a nation founded on principles of equality could somehow harbor such injustice?

The story was not so different fifteen years later. *The Jena Times* in Louisiana named high school football star Mychal Bell player of the week three times in the fall of 2006. But when the sixteen-year-old beat up a white student that same autumn, he was charged as an adult with attempted second-degree murder. When a black student asked if he could sit under a certain tree at Bell's school, white youths hung nooses from the tree. The public's readiness to be inflamed now had its requisite spark.

Bell's legal tangles included ten months in jail for lack of ninety-thousand-dollar bail, conviction as an adult of a lesser crime, a judge overruling that verdict and saying he should be tried as a child, and eighteen months in a juvenile home. Somehow, though, Bell's hopes remain intact; he says in interviews that he still hopes to win a football scholarship so he can go to college.

But what of the nation's hopes? Perhaps they are expressed in the

September 2007 protest that brought twenty thousand people to Bell's town of three thousand. There is that disappointment again.

One reason these incidents are so difficult to fathom is that they contradict the fundamental principle on which this nation was founded: that each person is inherently as noble and worthy as every other. Every human being is endowed with inalienable rights purely by virtue of having been born.

Noble as that principle is, this country has not yet fulfilled its promise. One document after another has proclaimed the goal: the Declaration of Independence, the Preamble to the United States Constitution, the Emancipation Proclamation, the Civil Rights Act, the Voting Rights Act, the countless court cases affirming equal opportunity. Yet in each instance there has also been an opposing view, a resistance to change, a Congress that sees a black man as three-fifths of a human, or a court that reverses affirmative action. The notion of equality often has been more dream than reality.

When the sin of oppression spans generations, there is no atonement, there can be no reparations to the dead. There remains, however, a centuries-long imperative to provide an antidote, a commitment to learn from history and build a better day.

Leaving millions of Americans in the mire of inequality exacts a spectacular price: nothing less than the squandering of humanity. But America can no longer afford the luxury of wasting lives. To overcome the serious challenges that face a nation adrift, the energy and effort and intelligence of every American is needed. There is not one person to spare.

FOR REVEREND CHRISTOPHER Moore of Chicago's Hyde Park, the choir was a way to include everyone. Its explosive artistic and social successes, however, brought plenty of growing pains.

"Chris could get really stressed out before performances," Judy Moore recalls. He would smoke cigarettes incessantly. "Also it was important for him to maintain good relations with the [Unitarian Universalist] people. Sometimes I had to do the 'minister's wife' thing. I believed in the faith path, so it wasn't a huge thing. But there was a lot of committee work. I felt beleaguered.

"Meanwhile the choir grew and grew and grew. More schools involved, the fund-raising more sophisticated and complex. Now today, the folks there are really in thick with the establishment of Chicago. But that took a long time. The choir needed to get more professional, not just in music but in administration. It was rough and getting rougher."

Rapid growth required Chris Moore to surrender some control of the beautiful thing he had created. That was difficult, partly because he had a big ego, and partly because it takes a high personal investment to make such a new idea succeed. Judy explains: "You have to maintain a strong sense of denial about why it won't work."

But with every new child's voice added to the choir, there also came the opinions of new parents. Sometimes those parents had more to offer than opinions.

"They brought lots of competencies," Judy says. "They would try to persuade Chris of one thing or another. He would try to listen, but often he'd shrug and keep going."

In those days Chris would try to quit smoking too. But he would become impossible, irritable and short-tempered, and when he started smoking again people would actually feel relief.

By then the choir had a board, which endured a hard power struggle with Chris. Eventually the board hired an administrative director. Chris remained in charge of the music.

"They were really good people," Judy says, "well meaning, and doing what they knew how to do. Things could be pretty tense between Chris and them. He ended up feeling discouraged. Like maybe the choir was getting bigger than he was."

By 1987 Chris Moore was thinking about what lay ahead, what other activist roads he might travel. He decided to attend the Unitarian Universalists' General Assembly in Little Rock that June. As it happened, he and Judy had a spat, and there wasn't time to make up before he left.

Their son was seventeen by then, and he spent much of the next afternoon rounding up friends to go to a Grateful Dead concert. When the phone finally was free, it rang right away. Chris had been trying to get through for hours. He told Judy he'd had a long and wonderful talk with a minister from Washington, D.C., who wanted to start a choir.

"We had a nice, a really nice conversation," Judy remembers. "Later I thought, 'Thank God for that.' You always want to leave things on a peaceful note, because you never know."

Chris Moore died in his sleep that night, of a brain aneurysm. "It's a good way to go," Judy says.

By then the choir was in professional hands; there was no question of its continuing, and thriving. Chris Moore had two memorial events. The first was a normal service, for family and friends; the second a special gathering for the choir. "A bunch of alums sang Brahms' Requiem and it broke everyone up." The choral masterpiece features a second movement renowned for its use of tenors and basses. "All these male voices that had trained under him were singing, only now their voices have all changed."

Once the singing ended, Judy's life took a new path. "I loved that guy very much, I was never meant to be married to another man. But there were also a lot of things I'd wanted to do in my life." That meant studies in ecology, working in environmental education, and returning to the Connecticut River valley of Massachusetts of her family's origin. Her home sits among a former artists' colony, with writers and painters living nearby. "I am not an artist," Judy says, "just a fellow traveler."

Her connection with the choir waned though the years. "When they had the fiftieth anniversary, they wanted me to come out. And I did. By that time it was so much more. They had a great big fund-raiser in a ballroom on Chicago's Gold Coast. And they sure flashed Chris' picture huge on the wall. He was supposed to be an icon, I guess."

Judy says she knows what caused Chris's success, and the choir's: "Strong but loving expectation. Damn it, you can achieve, you can do this stuff, and society needs for you to do this stuff. He expected kids to know how to learn and perform, so they can sing Brahms like Brahms is meant to be sung. This is just as important as that on UN Sunday kids get some idea of the vastness of human experience, the many forms that humans take, and the need to coexist.

"Choir kids get to know folks they would otherwise have no idea about. And so the choir did present a way kids could become aware of their shared humanness, and could pass that on to lots of folks the world over."

Judy says she likes contemplating Chris's last evening, his excitement at the prospect of starting a new choir. As with all authentic patriots, the idea of all that work did not daunt him; it filled him with hope.

It is not difficult to imagine his dream: choirs in more than one city, engaged in common purpose. Clearly his dream has come true.

THE FIFTH ANNUAL joint Chicago–Boston concert on Martin Luther King Jr. Day begins with male singers from both choirs onstage. They smile at the silent audience and wait for the TV producer's signal to begin. Two boys' hands hover over African drums. Another boy in front hums the opening note over his shoulder, so the other singers know the starting pitch.

Ten rows out sits the mayor of Boston. To his right, the governor of Massachusetts is seated. There is not an empty spot in the house.

The producer counts down with his fingers, then points at the boys onstage. Instantly their voices are raised to deliver "Tshotsholoza," a South African folk tune, with gusto. The drums drive a thrumming beat, the mood light, the song short, and when it ends the audience roars. Next out hurry the girls of both choirs, who form a quick semicircle around Josephine Lee. She raises her hands, and in quiet voices they deliver a richly harmonious rendition of "Strange Fruit," which Lewis Allan wrote and Billie Holiday made famous. Their voices remain quiet, and any time the volume creeps higher Lee presses downward with her hands, and the level drops again. The harmonies lean in angular ways, like those of Eastern European music, so listeners must concentrate to follow the melody. As the message of the words becomes apparent, the audience turns to stone:

> Southern trees bear a strange fruit,
> Blood on the leaves and blood at the root,
> Black bodies swinging in the southern breeze,
> Strange fruit hanging from the poplar trees.

Pastoral scene of the gallant south,
The bulging eyes and the twisted mouth,
Smell of magnolia, sweet and fresh,
Then the sudden smell of burning flesh.

Here is the fruit for the crows to pluck,
For the rain to gather, for the wind to suck,
For the sun to rot, for the tree to drop,
Here is a strange and a bitter crop.

The silence at the song's end lasts several breaths. Then the roar of applause endures a full minute. Now boys and girls of both choirs join for a rowdy gospel tune, hands clap, spirits rise, and the performers have the audience exactly where they want it.

IN HIS *NARRATIVE of the Life of Frederick Douglass, an American Slave*, published in 1885, Frederick Douglass describes his journey from plantation slave to free man in the North, and the lessons he learned along the way. Perhaps his greatest insight comes when he is given to his master's relative Hugh Auld in Baltimore. Mrs. Auld has compassion for Douglass, provides him with proper clothes and decent food for the first time in his life, and even begins to teach him the alphabet. When her husband discovers that this instruction is going on, he demands that his wife stop at once. Teaching Douglass to read will make him forever unfit to be a slave, Auld argues, because it will make him discontent with his life.

Mrs. Auld withdraws her help; Douglass determines to learn to read however he can. But then something worse happens: The woman becomes cruel. "She lacked at first the depravity indispensable to shutting me up in mental darkness," Douglass writes. "It was at least necessary for her to have some training in the exercise of irresponsible power, to make her equal to the task of treating me as though I were a brute."

Mrs. Auld finds Douglass with a newspaper, and flies at him in a fury. She grows vigilant that he never be left in the presence of a book. She becomes, he wrote, "more violent in her opposition than her husband himself.

My mistress was, as I have said, a kind and tender-hearted woman. . . .
There was no sorrow or suffering for which she had not a tear. She
had bread for the hungry, clothes for the naked, and comfort for
every mourner that came within her reach. Slavery soon proved its
ability to divest her of these heavenly qualities. Under its influence,
the tender heart became stone, and the lamblike disposition gave
way to one of tiger-like fierceness. . . .

Slavery proved as injurious to her as it did to me.

Douglass was correct, of course. Slavery demeans the slave; it also
demeans the slave owner. One suffers forced subservience, the other
moral decay. "As I would not be a slave," Abraham Lincoln said in
1858, "so would I not be a master."

The same logic holds true for situations less extreme than slavery.
When minorities are denied jobs, housing, education, and opportunity, it harms more than them alone. It damages the whole nation.

The choir shows what happens when people share a common
purpose. Despite their differences, they learn to see one another as
individuals rather than stereotypes of skin color or economic status.
As they strive together, they develop affinity, understanding, respect.

The ways in which Americans could apply this thinking are
endless—in schools, in churches, in workplaces, in communities. For
this nation's painful race relations, neither government nor the free
market will be coming to the rescue any time soon. It will take the action, selfless and sustained, of every American.

Granted, America has seen minority men and women rise to the
pinnacles of government, business, the arts, faith communities, and
more. But the achievements of these remarkable people also signify
how much potential is lost when millions of other Americans routinely experience limited opportunity due to their race.

The election of Barack Obama to the presidency represents a spectacular milestone for the nation, even among those who voted for
John McCain. There is cause for national pride when a black man becomes the nation's commander in chief. There is an unmistakable influence as well, a political gravitational pull: Immediately following
the election, the Republican National Committee named its first Afri-

can American director, former Maryland Lieutenant Governor Michael Steele.

And yet, Obama's success also delivers two kinds of rebuke. First, it took this nation 232 years to see beyond skin and elect a member of a minority to the top office—though younger democracies have been led by blacks and women years sooner. Second, the ascent of Obama ends all argument about the potential of his race—and thus reveals what a treasure of human possibility America has squandered through the generations, by failing to see all people as equal.

When the Chicago choir performed in Memphis, the crowd numbered only a few dozen. Families that had agreed to host the visiting kids backed out at the last minute. And national choral organizations, which are predominantly white, frown on the Chicago choir because its repertoire is insufficiently classical. That the arbiters of choral status would undervalue the choir's message sounds distinctly out of tune.

Whether it is slavery 140 years ago, or segregation fifty years ago, or poverty today, whatever form that squandering of human potential takes, if somehow it did *not* occur, imagine the resource this nation would discover. Imagine the human power America would reap. Imagine the harmony.

AT LAST THE television broadcast ends, the audience gives a long standing ovation, and it's time for the choirs to perform their off-camera encores. Boston goes first, girls streaming into the aisles to sing a Scandinavian hymn so pure, no translation is needed to feel the sacred hush. Afterward the crowd claps a long time. Then Chicago delivers its closing number, "A Praying Spirit" by Twinkie Clark: "Lord, when I pray, give me what to say. Lord, when I pray, give me what to say."

The kids start smiling, nodding their heads as the chorus comes around: "Yes. Yes. Yes, Lord."

It's slow like a march, dignified, and the children savor every note. This song is not about religion, but it is about the spirit. This moment is not preaching, but making a declaration through proud affirmation. Form and content have merged: What the children sing is what they represent is what they have to teach. "Yes. Yes. Yes, Lord."

Their voices are strong, nearly enough to raise the roof, more than enough to lift the heart. With the TV performance behind them, having stretched themselves socially and musically, no longer responsible for providing healing to an audience, a nation, and one another, relieved of all of this weight, the children seem vastly lighter—still precise, but looser. Mouths wide, heads tilted back, they are all but laughing as they sing.

"Yes. Yes. Yes, Lord."

Josephine Lee stands before them, honing in on each word, every syllable, its volume and depth and color.

During the final chorus, while everyone on stage proclaims in full voice, a serious-looking girl in black glasses, standing on the end of the second row of altos, turns away from the conductor to scan the crowd. Suddenly a smile spreads across her face, bright as any stage light, and it remains as she mouths the song's final words, incandescent. It endures even as she bends with the others to take a bow, then straightens to her full and dignified height.

Yes, Tamaiya, we see you. We see you.

7

A Culture of Caring

It is in our lives, and not from our words, that our religion must be read.

— THOMAS JEFFERSON

I see millions of families trying to live on incomes so meager that the pall of family disaster hangs over them day by day. I see millions whose daily lives in city and on farm continue under conditions labeled indecent by a so-called polite society half a century ago. I see millions denied education, recreation and the opportunity to better their lot and that of their children. . . . I see one-third of a nation ill-housed, ill-clad, ill-nourished.

It is not in despair that I paint you that picture. I paint it for you in hope. We are determined to make every American citizen the subject of his country's interest and concern. . . .

In every land there are always at work forces that drive men apart and forces that draw men together. In our personal ambitions we are individualists. But in our seeking for economic and political progress as a nation, we all go up, or else we all go down, as one people.

— FRANKLIN DELANO ROOSEVELT

A LL THAT MORNING A crowd stood waiting to see what would happen. Philanthropists had donated hundreds of thousands of dollars. State legislators had changed laws to make the idea possible. The local newspaper, despite some stiff local opposition, had repeatedly endorsed the proposal. The mayor had agreed to lease a site on public land for a dollar a year. Everything was present but certainty.

Yet there had been so much optimism, only three months earlier. On a cool March day, eleven community leaders stood with hard hats and shovels at the groundbreaking ceremony. Then dozens of companies provided their work—architecture, construction, landscaping, project management, painting—at reduced cost or even for free. Donated equipment was installed, tested, and readied. All of this labor, all aimed at opening a free clinic for medically underserved people in Hilton Head, South Carolina, took years to bear fruit.

Finally opening day arrived, June 3, 1993—but no patients appeared. That morning, doctors, nurses, dentists, and pharmacists stood at the ready. Volunteers had decorated the entry, and they planned to greet the clinic's first patients. A photographer and reporter from *The Island Packet* had their front row seat to history, as well as a local television reporter. The doors were open, the lights were on.

Still no patients came. The hours dragged by; people fidgeted. A TV reporter turned to one of the clinic's founders and asked, "You sure you built this in the right spot?"

He did not answer. He only knew he had seen a problem that had stymied the past ten presidents of the United States, and which had grown worse regardless of whether the economy was good or bad. And he had decided to do something about it. He was an authentic patriot, not waiting for government or the free market to solve a problem he believed could be remedied by individual initiative.

And yet the hours passed and no patients arrived. Had it all been a mistake? Were the poor people of Beaufort County so accustomed to receiving minimal medical care—or none at all—that they would not take advantage of a free facility built, equipped, and staffed entirely for their benefit? Had this leader wasted everyone's time, money, energy, and faith?

* * *

THE ANSWERS TO those questions lie in the past, more than seven decades back, and hundreds of miles away. That is where the trail begins that arrives at this morning in Hilton Head.

The year is 1936, in the fall. The place is a small house with its shades pulled down, in the Appalachian coal town of Big Stone Gap, Tennessee. Reverend Enoch Luther McConnell, the local Methodist minister, is known among his flock for two types of leadership. During revivals, he shouts and storms: All men are sinners and there will be hell to pay. The rest of the year he offers a gentler message of redemption: We are all God's children.

Reverend McConnell is an itinerant preacher, traveling from town to town praying and teaching, baptizing and singing, performing weddings and funerals. His wife and seven children are part of the touring package, and provide vocal ballast for the local choirs. Son Jack, age eight, sits at the piano to play "What a Friend We Have in Jesus."

Like most work of the cloth, the rewards tend more to the spiritual than to the material world. In his best days McConnell earns no more than fifty dollars a month. But he is instrumental in the people's faith. With the nation struggling through the Depression, sanctity and community are more important than ever. And so, on that 1936 Thursday, friends advise McConnell not to come to his door that night. He must pull the blinds down as well. A "pounding" is taking place.

Pounding: Over the course of the night, people sneak onto the porch to leave parcels—a bushel of beans, half a ham—to see the preacher's family through the winter. Giving what they have, in humility because of their limited means, but with their generosity all the more meaningful because it does not come from homes of plenty, this is how the poor support the poor. Until spring, the only groceries the McConnells need to buy are bread and milk. Everything else is supplied by the community.

Pounding is one of Jack McConnell's earliest memories. The autumn ritual provided more than one kind of sustenance, he says. When you receive food from your neighbors, most of them as poor as you are, some of it feeds the body and some the spirit. And certain debts of kindness can never be repaid—or at least, they convey the message that giving is a necessary way of life.

Now eighty-two, Jack McConnell has fond memories of traveling with his father from parish to parish, across Tennessee into Georgia and West Virginia. "You'd get to meet people. And anytime you went into a community you were welcomed."

Jack McConnell is slender, with dwindling white hair and eyes bright behind metal glasses. His voice is soft, his country upbringing evident in certain elongated vowels. Mostly, however, his speech is shaped by enthusiasm, from the near constant smile on his face to the accolades he continually showers on others. A colleague is "the smartest man I ever met." A benefactor is "the most generous person on earth." His wife, Mary Ellen, naturally, "is the sweetest woman I could ever imagine, and I am the luckiest guy." With three children, five grandchildren, and forty-nine years of marriage, his raves seem justified. But the path has not always been easy.

"When I was six or seven my mother took ill. I would do for her things that the doctor had left instructions for. I told her, 'I'm going to grow up and be a doctor and take care of you the rest of your life.'"

On the road to that future, though, Jack was shaped by another force: the family dinner table. Each night, his mother and six siblings gathered with the good reverend at the head. "After the blessing, Daddy would talk with us about how our neighbors were doing," he recalls. "What had we noticed? What did we know? He taught us always to think about others. Then Daddy'd assign something specific: Mow their yard, chop their wood. We were always givers, without any expectation of anything in return."

As Jack speaks, some of the minister's genes peek through. "That business of isolating ourselves that we do so much of now, we will pay a price for that downstream. If you start from thinking of others first, once you do that you have a much richer life."

But not one without challenges. His mother would later suffer years of dementia. Jack himself would fulfill his childhood promise by attending medical school at the University of Tennessee—paying his way in part by performing stand-up comedy—only to learn that along the way he had contracted tuberculosis.

"They discovered I had a hole in the upper lobe in my right lung. Turns out there were seven of us contracted TB in the same year, during our residency training. One of our professors died with it. So did one guy I trained with. I was twenty-three years old. Back then the treatment was isolation, and one drug. Just one. If it didn't work, so long."

Expecting a long hospitalization at best, Jack broke an engagement. "I didn't have a job, no money. She married well though, had herself eight or nine young 'uns."

He also had to surrender his hope of being a pediatrician, because of the risk that he might one day infect a young patient.

Doctors put Jack in a hospital bed. After the long hours and intense challenges of residency, within days he was bored to distraction. He asked for medical journals, to keep his mind active. It proved to be his salvation.

"My feet never touched the floor for a year. I got as weak as a kitten. Oh, I ate well, and gained weight, but it was all blubber. Toward the end even to sit up was a bit of a chore. But I read voraciously. All the stuff in training I hadn't had time to read about."

When friends learned that he was broke, Jack experienced a reprise of the pounding. They chipped in fifteen dollars a month to keep him afloat. Still, he had to borrow money when he finally left the hospital, until he found work as on-board physician for a cargo and passenger ship cruising between New Orleans and Trinidad. That job led to a post at a New Orleans hospital.

In the mid-1950s, the pharmaceutical industry was beginning the rapid growth that continues to this day. Drug salesmen—Jack calls them "detail men"—routinely pitched their wares to hospital doctors. After all of his convalescent reading, Jack was a hard sell.

"I was asking questions. No one else was asking. Someone must have noticed, because one company's director of research came to see me. He said, 'I understand you have doubts about pharmaceuticals, is that right?' We spent half the night talking about it, and then he offered me a job.

"Well, that's what I was looking for, a place to land and know about this. I was fascinated by it. So I went to work for Lederle Laboratories, in Pearl River, New York. They had five thousand people there. I went to work for them, and I was on my way."

Jack's first major achievement had personal relevance: a new TB test. Previously the only way to determine if someone had tuberculosis was a blood test, which was both expensive and slow. Jack led the team that delivered the TB-tine test, a cluster of pinpricks that redden on the skin to provide a clear diagnosis. It was a massive success as a product for Lederle, but more importantly as a tool for battling TB across the globe. A similar test is still in use today. "It sounds bigger than it was," Jack says. "Someone else invented it, but they didn't know how to finish it."

At the time, Jack says, he was "living in a basement apartment." Two women rented the upstairs, and one day he invited the brunette to join him in New York City to see *The Music Man*. Three weeks later he asked her to marry him. "She's an expert at listening, Mary Ellen," he laughs. "I wish I'd learned it from her."

A job opportunity arose at McNeil Labs (now McNeil Pediatrics) outside Philadelphia, where a new drug was promising explosive growth. The McConnells moved there, but the drug began to reveal serious side effects. The head of the company told Jack to find a new product right away or the business would be ruined.

"I went rummaging around the lab. The fella up there was the nicest guy I ever met in my life. I said, what have you got up here? Well, what he had was Tylenol, only just for kids. I thought, this could be used the same as aspirin. But he said the chemistry was not the issue. It was that the taste was so horrible. I put one in my mouth. I could barely get it out fast enough. And it left a taste for six or seven hours."

Jack led a team that worked on the flavor, until it was "pretty darn good." Double-blind tests found people received reliable pain relief without side effects, which was also promising. But a bigger challenge remained—overcoming the popularity of aspirin. In a meeting with management, Jack suggested an approach based on pounding.

"We're going to give it away. Tylenol is not known at all. Everyone knows and loves aspirin. We're going to give it to surgeons and pharmacists for a year. The boss came out of his chair. 'A damn year? You'll break me.' I said, 'No, I'll make you.'"

The experiment with generosity could not have gone better. "We had a fantastic result. People grew into it gradually. Now it is a billion-dollar product. And next thing I know, I went up to corporate head-quarters, Johnson & Johnson in Basking Ridge, New Jersey. We were there twenty-some years, raised our children there. It was one of the most peaceful places I've lived in my life. The church atmosphere was good, the schools were better than good."

In 1980, a peak in those years of prosperity, Jack and Mary Ellen McConnell took a vacation in Hilton Head. Though his job was still going strong, that trip set the stage for an encore career, in volunteer work, with achievements equal to all that Jack had done in his years with a salary.

HILTON HEAD IS the nation's second-largest barrier island, its roughly sixty square miles dwarfed only by New York's Long Island. European settlers established themselves there in 1698.

The region's history is colorful, to say the least. Beaufort County held the first secession planning meeting in the nation. On December 20, 1860, South Carolina was the first state to secede from the Union. As a result Hilton Head was chosen as an early target by the army and navy of the North, becoming the Union's base of operations in the region.

After the Civil War, relations between the races were marked more by tolerance than cordiality. The population, 80 percent white, also included descendants of the former slave communities of Gullah and Ogeechee. Gradually, more Hispanics gathered in Beaufort County than anywhere else in the state.

But the miles of white sand beaches, the two-thirds of the island preserved as salt marshes and tidal pools, the wildlife that ranged from sea turtles and alligators to all manner of aquatic birds—these resources eventually contributed to making Hilton Head a different kind of place. After construction in 1956 of one of the nation's first planned communities, and with municipal government setting strict limitations on development's potentially negative impacts, such as roadside signs, tree-cutting, and excessively bright outdoor lighting, Hilton Head took shape as a tourist destination. Today the area boasts more than thirty golf courses, hundreds of tennis courts, and more than 250 restaurants. The population hovers at thirty-eight thousand in the off-season but surges to a hundred and fifty thousand at the peak. Some 2.5 million people visit annually.

The economic and demographic impacts of these annual waves of visitors have been profound, especially as more of them have chosen to stay. In the last ten years, the population has grown by 45 percent. Median household income reached $72,750—almost 45 percent above the state median of $50,334, and a solid 50 percent above the national median of $48,451. The median home price hit $320,000—59 percent higher than the national median of $200,700. Prime beachfront lots now trade in the range of $1 million.

But such statistics can be misleading, because for every restaurant there must be waiters and bus staff, for every golf course there must be groundskeepers to mow all that lawn, for every garden there must be a gardener.

The travails of such people in Hilton Head were not immediately visible to Jack McConnell during his first vacation, nor when he and Mary Ellen visited in subsequent years. Only later did his eyes open in that regard. Meanwhile his career flourished. He achieved positions of increasing seniority, working with colleagues in medical product development around the world. He led the team that built the first MRI machine in the United States. He participated in the Human Genome Project, which mapped the coding for the minutest building blocks of life. Jack helped Mary Ellen raise three children, and became a formidable golfer and a nationally competitive paddle tennis player.

It was, in other words, a successful life—well insulated from concerns like choosing between paying the rent or buying medicine, between going to the emergency room or going to work, between suffering with pain or seeking care to alleviate it. And yet those were precisely the issues that would occupy Jack's thoughts and energy soon enough.

WHEN RETIREMENT FINALLY beckoned, Hilton Head was the chosen land. But the idle life did not turn out as expected. To Jack, retirement felt eerily similar to the days when, as a young resident, he had been confined to bed for a year.

"I thought I would come here, play golf, eat in good restaurants with my wife, and travel," Jack recalls. Then he laughs. "I never got so bored in my life. The last time I played Augusta National, I birdied every par three in the course. I even got bored with golf."

Years later in a privately published memoir, Jack cited Robert Frost's observation that every poem begins with a lump in the throat. The same goes for good deeds. One morning after a hard rain Jack was driving on a dirt road when he saw a black man walking in the drizzle. As the son of a preacher who had hitchhiked all over the South, Jack offered the man a ride. After hesitating, the man accepted. Ever friendly, Jack struck up a conversation. The man's name was James, and he was a native islander. He'd been laid off from a construction job, he was looking for work. And no, he did not have access to health care. Neither did his wife, nor his two children.

Jack brought the man to another construction site, they shook hands, and the doctor drove off with a head full of notions. And that is how the Volunteers in Medicine clinic in Hilton Head began: "With a serendipitous meeting on a rainy day that transformed a rather routine retirement into one of the most exciting and rewarding experiences in my life."

WHEN JACK MOVED to Hilton Head he had given an MRI machine to the local hospital, which responded by promptly putting him on its board. After meeting James, Jack made a tour of the facility on his own.

"I didn't see any African Americans here," he said. "I asked around, and people said, 'No, they don't come here, they go somewhere else.' I said, 'That's the oddest thing I ever heard.'"

Jack surveyed local businesses and performed telephone polling. "We discovered that about one out of three of our fellow citizens, eight to ten thousand, had little or no access to health care, and that over ninety-eight percent of them would welcome a clinic where they could obtain treatment for themselves and their families."

He picked up more hitchhikers. "None of 'em had been immunized, no TB shot, nothing. I kept thinking, we ought to do something about that."

In the early 1990s Jack announced his dream of building a clinic, independent of any medical institution, whose sole focus would be to serve people without access to health care. The staff would be volunteers drawn from the many medical professionals—doctors, dentists, nurses, pharmacists—who had chosen to retire in Hilton Head. Patients would be treated for free.

He was surprised at the response. "I went through some troublesome times. The hospital literally threw me off the board. Some of them I thought were my friends. I bought my house from one of them."

Likewise, his speech to a local physicians' group raised objections. One doctor feared his practice would suffer if the clinic opened.

"I am surprised you feel the Volunteers in Medicine clinic will take patients away from you," Jack answered. "Just tell me how many of our nonpaying patients you want, and I will see to it that you get every one of them."

The crowd laughed, but Jack said the problem of people lacking decent health care was no joking matter. "Look here: I think we now have probably the worst health system in our history. A significant segment of the population is left outside to fend for itself. The number of Americans without health insurance is 47 million at a minimum."

Jack's number may be an underestimate. Because a portion of the uninsured population has sporadic episodes of coverage, the actual total of people without insurance in a given year is likely millions higher.

Government helps deal with part of the problem: Medicare provides health coverage to seniors, as does Medicaid for people who are poor. The free market contributes too, with more than half of employers offering health insurance benefits to full-time employees.

But these efforts are wholly inadequate. The United States today has more people lacking access to proper health care than the rest of the world's developed nations *combined*.

That matters for several reasons. Foremost, low-income people do not receive proper screenings and preventive medicine. Thus they develop severe illnesses that could have been avoided. Instead of taking a blood pressure medicine, for example, these people arrive at the emergency room after heart attacks, with long hospitalizations and extensive procedures necessary to keep them alive. The human costs are huge; many studies have quantified beyond dispute the correlation between poverty and shortened lifespan.

That leads to the second reason that limited access to health care is damaging: economic consequences. A heart attack patient's emergency room trip, cardiac catheterization, hospitalization, and rehabilitation all cost vastly more than the preventive blood pressure medicine would have.

Moreover, Medicare and Medicaid pay only part of the bills for their beneficiaries' treatments. The unpaid portion is added directly to the bills of people who have health insurance. Patients who lack that protection, and do not qualify for state or federal health programs, must pay out of their own funds. Again, the unpaid portion becomes part of the bills of people who have insurance. In other words, when government does not meet its medical care obligations, it increases the cost to businesses of providing health benefits. That burden forces some employers to cut coverage, leaving more people without insurance—and thus eligible for government programs. The cycle is not saving any money, nor making anyone healthier.

Further, it is fair to ask if the current approach undermines the nation's economic competitiveness. If an American company must compete with a foreign manufacturer, the cost of U.S. care is a distinct disadvantage. About $1,400 of the cost of a General Motors car, for example, goes to employee health benefits. That is more than GM spends per car on steel. And if GM moved its factories from Michigan north to Canada, where the government provides health care, that $1,400 expense would vanish. (Granted, some portion would certainly appear in GM's taxes, but that does not negate the fact that Toyota, for example, has vastly lower employee health costs.)

The United States spends the most on health care of any nation in the world: $6,600 per person annually. The results, however, are far from the best. This country ranks third among the developed nations in the rate of deaths that could have been prevented with timely care. Infant mortality is 7 deaths per thousand live births, compared with 2.7 per thousand births in the world's top three countries. Medical bills are the leading cause of bankruptcy for Americans, even for people who have insurance. And this country spends three times as much of its health care dollar on administrative costs as the world's most efficient nations.

You would think that the strongest economy in the world would work to prevent such a problem, that the initiative of American capitalism would find ways to afford and even profit by caring for people who need treatment. You might also think government would have an answer to this problem, if not for the human cost then for the sake of the economy.

Instead, both private enterprise and government have sat by while the number of people without health insurance continues to climb—steadily, year after year. It doesn't matter which parties control Congress and the White House. Reform proposals languish in partisan battles or wither from inattention.

At the time of this writing, the Obama administration's health care financing reform proposal is the primary issue occupying Congress. Opponents have lined up with questions and objections that range from the legitimate (How can we afford it?) to the fictional (Death panels will decide whether elderly people receive care or not). The plan's affordability depends on cost cutting, though the source of those savings remains uncertain at best. Perhaps a bill will pass, however, because the human and economic consequences of failing to act may have finally grown too large. If so, that achievement would provide a rare exception to the usual fecklessness of Washington on this issue. Perhaps America will actually shed its highest-cost, most-uninsured status.

Until then, administratively, there is paralysis. For instance, it is fascinating to contrast the income tax system (in which a median-wage earner completes roughly the same documents as a billionaire, and both remain confident that the information will remain confidential) with the health care system (in which a patient may write his name multiple times on multiple forms within the same medical office, with justified uncertainty about whether the information is confidential).

Private enterprise has not improved the situation. It doesn't matter if the economy is weak or strong; the number of people without health insurance continues to rise. Meanwhile spending devoted to elective surgery and advertising for pharmaceuticals grows much faster than access to basic care.

It does not have to be this way. Many other nations, with economies far weaker than that of the United States, have found the means to provide every citizen with access to decent health care. These systems are not without flaws—what human enterprise is?—but their existence reveals a national commitment to treating every citizen's health and illness as a societal issue.

It is a matter of common purpose. When you are sick, whether you are my parent or sibling or child or co-worker, your illness affects me too. For authentic patriots, our common woes cannot wait for government or the free market to provide answers; individual initiative will have to do. For Jack McConnell, the answer is attainable by those willing to work for it.

"If we had resources in place, we could provide much if not most of the service to the forty-seven million that they need," Jack says. "I wouldn't be surprised if we could provide three-quarters of it."

By *resources*, Jack McConnell means people. While the nation reckons with a shortage of perhaps 350,000 nurses, and while the cost of educating and training new doctors has reached an all-time high, in Hilton Head he tapped a different source.

"We have two hundred and fifty thousand retired physicians in this country. We have more than twice that many retired nurses. They are trained, they are seasoned. Every day that goes by, we're wasting their expertise."

JACK McCONNELL DID not invent the idea of the encore career. The ranks of the Peace Corps are thick with retirees. Visit any Habitat for Humanity construction site and the home-building crew invariably includes retired tradesmen. In some states, retired engineers have formed a service corps that consults for free with young entrepreneurs and inventors.

The potential for an encore career is greater than ever today. When Social Security was created in 1935, the average American's life expectancy was sixty-one. Now the average is seventy-eight, a jump of 28 percent. Millions of people are not exhausted at sixty-five, nor do they need decades of essentially free time to recover from their work lives. In fact, in retirement many lifelong workers experience restlessness, even boredom.

The encore career is a perfect antidote. These people are skilled, experienced, and available. For those who have built financial stability in their working years, an encore career can be less about monetary rewards and more about personal satisfaction and contributing to society.

The idea of an encore career can be applied beyond retirees too. The average American woman who quits her job to raise a family is absent from the workforce for eleven years. Returning to work that benefits others could be an ideal reentry strategy. Certainly the need for these women exists, at all levels of professional experience and skills.

ESTABLISHING A VOLUNTEER medical clinic actually proved to be harder than Jack expected. The problem wasn't finding willing souls; sixteen doctors signed up before the clinic had a name or a location. The three largest obstacles—ironically enough—came from the very institutions that should have been finding solutions: government and private enterprise.

The first challenge was licensing. Each state has regulations to assure that people who practice medicine are sufficiently expert. A state board reviews applicants' credentials, verifies their training, and in general polices the profession. In several states, M.D.s. cannot be licensed to practice until they have met with this board or its representatives. The board also serves as an enforcement agency, sanctioning doctors who provide substandard care or violate ethical standards. The process of certifying that a doctor will provide competent care can take months and cost several thousand dollars.

In Jack's view it did not make sense to require retired doctors to undergo this scrutiny and incur this expense just to practice on a part-time, volunteer basis. The licensing gauntlet would prove an insurmountable deterrent to retired doctors, who after all had decades of experience in their home states before retiring. Yet licensing review was the law in South Carolina, no exceptions.

The second challenge was insurance. Since even excellent doctors face the possibility of being sued for the care they provide, they must maintain malpractice insurance policies as a safeguard. For the primary care clinic Jack envisioned, insurance could cost more than $50,000 per physician. With so many doctors potentially involved, the expense could run into the millions. Again the obstacle appeared to be insurmountable.

In other words, although the needs of people without access to health care are acute and often urgent, government and the capitalist system not only failed to solve this problem, they also created impediments to solving it.

The third challenge, of course, was money. Building a clinic was one thing. Equipping it was another. Maintaining staff and supplies could be financially prohibitive. Jack's clinic would be a test of Hilton Head's character, a measure of the capacity of its financially successful people to care for others far less fortunate.

To tackle the licensing issue, Jack first tried with dentists. The South Carolina dental oversight board required license applicants to complete a supervised test on a dummy, conducted in Charleston, a hundred miles from Hilton Head. The board also mandated that the clinic have a licensed dentist on-site at all times. Jack wrangled a compromise on that requirement, and the board consented to have practicing South Carolina dentists review the charts of the volunteers' patients to monitor the quality of care.

The ease of winning that arrangement sent Jack into the doctors' licensing project with optimism. But there the glass was half empty.

"I went from joy and exhilaration to frustration and disappointment," he says. He drove to Columbia, the state capital, to introduce himself to the state board that regulates doctors. His plan was to ask for a waiver of the test and fee for physicians willing to work without pay in a clinic for needy South Carolinians.

While in the waiting room, Jack saw a young doctor coming out of a meeting with the twelve board members. A native of the Philippines, the man was a well-trained cardiologist who'd been offered a job in South Carolina. Jack recalls what the man said: "I have just gone through the worst experience of my life. I have been grilled and treated as if I have come to the United States to steal something from the members of the board. All I want to do is just practice my profession and be a good citizen of the United States. What can I do?"

When Jack's turn came, he entered the meeting room and swiftly formed his own impression. The board "seemed to be a rather unhappy and joyless group, and unfortunately, not at all open to new or creative ideas, particularly when the idea was offered by someone who had just moved to the South from the North."

A board member explained that the physician rules were needed to ensure that all residents of South Carolina received high-quality care. Jack responded by noting that the state ranked among the bottom three in the country by many medical measures. The leader of the board jumped to his feet, and in a rage told Jack the meeting was over. "If you want anything done in this state you gotta go through the legislature," Jack remembers him saying. "You might as well get your hat and coat."

Instead he picked up the phone, called a friend who was familiar with the capitol, and asked him if there were any doctors serving in the legislature. In fact, there was one: Representative Billy Houck, M.D. Houck had served on the medical board, but resigned because of the other members' stubbornness. The legislature was only weeks away from adjourning, though. That left no room for educating representatives and senators about Jack's clinic or its merits.

Houck and other sympathetic lawmakers resorted to a maneuver known as a "Christmas tree," in which an amendment is quietly hung on a noncontroversial proposal like some kind of legislative ornament. In this case, a bill to create a computer database of South Carolina's veterans received a one-sentence amendment—including a deadline—instructing the medical board to write rules for a special license for volunteer doctors.

Jack received an invitation to the bill's signing. Then he called the medical board to volunteer to help write the new rules. The board staff member denied that any such amendment existed until Jack faxed it to him. Still the board delayed until three days before the deadline. At the single public hearing on the issue, Jack arranged to have a crowd present: state officials, physicians and hospital leaders, and most persuasively of all, a native islander who was both the grandson of slaves and an expert in the terrible health conditions of poor people in the region.

The board approved new rules, the waivers were in place, state government was no longer an obstacle to this citizen initiative. Now it was time to solve the second problem and find affordable malpractice insurance.

As he had come to expect, Jack found that most people responded to his idea for the clinic by finding fault with it. One insurer after another turned him aside. Then he met Cal Stewart of the Joint Underwriting Association, who "turned out to be one of the wisest, most concerned, compassionate, and solid businessmen I have ever met." JUA investigated the clinic concept in detail. The fact that the volunteers would be providing primary care, rather than surgery or specialized treatment, and that previously underserved patients would more likely be grateful for care than litigiously critical of it, led to a remarkable deal. The company decided to offer coverage for $5,000— not per physician, but for the entire clinic.

Again the marketplace had been an obstacle to progress, but the forces of individual initiative had proved stronger.

The final obstacle, raising money, turned out to be the least difficult. Charity golf tournaments and dinners, generous donations by local retirees, sustained editorial support in the region's newspaper, a deal with the mayor for an essentially free parcel of land, plus all kinds of reduced-cost or free construction work, and the Hilton Head community had contributed more than enough to build the Volunteers in Medicine clinic.

JUMP BACK NOW to that opening day in June 1993. The clinic is a trim one-story building, tucked among trees a few hundred yards from the island's main road (and thus, conveniently for the people Jack hoped to serve, the bus line). Nearly three dozen companies have contributed to the construction, as well as several local philanthropists. Jack and others have haggled with medical equipment companies, persuading them to donate and install machines, examining tables, and more. By opening day the clinic has four paid administrators, managing fifty-five doctors, sixty-eight nurses, seven dentists, two chiropractors, two social workers, two dental assistants, two medical technicians, and a hundred lay volunteers. A crowd is gathered. Volunteer greeters stand at the ready. The doctors have been working already at a free immunization clinic at the local hospital, to ease them back into practice. The medical records room is ready too, though the filing cabinets are empty for now.

And no one comes. The morning passes and a kind of anxious dread sets in. It's not that people don't know about the opening; *The Island Packet* has covered Jack's work each step of the way. With fund-raising golf tournaments, the groundbreaking, the legislation, and so on, the public is well aware. Is mistrust of the health system so acute? Do the people who most need this clinic not have confidence in the care they will receive? What about those survey results, early in the process, which had nearly every respondant saying they would come to this clinic?

Finally, at about 1:45 P.M., a mother comes up the walk carrying one child and holding another's hand. Jack McConnell bends to embrace Malikah Housey, but she wants to walk in herself. So Jack steps back, holds the door for her, and a three-year-old girl inaugurates the clinic.

DEMAND GREW SLOWLY in subsequent weeks, then exploded. In a few months Volunteers in Medicine had opened a satellite facility, a mile across the sound on Daufuskie Island. Relations with the local hospital improved too: The emergency room began sending patients who had arrived with nonurgent needs to the clinic for more appropriate and less expensive care. Likewise, when patients at the clinic needed more advanced treatment, they received referrals directly to the hospital.

That's systemic change—no small feat. But the progress is best seen in human terms: a thousand children immunized in the clinic's first six months, twenty-seven hundred patients in the same period, and countless individual success stories.

"Let me tell you about a woman who came in last night with a toothache," says Stan Stolarcyk, volunteer director at the Volunteers in Medicine clinic. "Now that is not a big deal to you and me, we know we can get treated. But she has no dentist, and she is in pain. And by the time she got here, it was late and there was no dentist on to see her. So we gave her some medicine for the pain, and she came back in first thing today. The tooth was extracted because of an abscess. She left not an hour later. The pain was under control, she'd received good care, and she learned about how to prevent the problem from getting ahead of her the next time."

Stan's office sits in a prefab building behind the clinic, tucked away from where the medical action is. But his face is bright with enthusiasm.

"It's just a great feeling. I can't explain it, except to say that you feel happy. You're helping folks who truly need your help, and you get to see immediate outcomes."

When a patient arrives at the clinic there is a greeter at the door to welcome them, to say they're sorry the person is not feeling well, and to escort the patient to the registration desk. Not only is this a stark contrast to the cold, fill-out-this-paperwork experience at most doctors' offices, but the greeter is also typically multilingual—a valuable asset given the large Hispanic community in Hilton Head. The greeting process is also important for prioritizing patients' care, because the clinic does not work by the same scheduling rules as a regular doctor's office.

"We saw a hundred and four patients this morning," Stan explains. "About forty were walk-ins."

The waiting room is unusual too, lacking the typical outdated magazines and stale music. Instead, public-health videos play on a screen at the front of the room—about nutrition and exercise, for example. Bilingual signs on the doors and halls remind people about healthy habits. No one complains about waiting.

When low-income people receive decent and immediate care, Stan says, it contributes something even more significant to their lives. A person has many needs and concerns beyond the medical; good care limits the effect an illness might have on other dimensions of life. The woman with the toothache, for example, "did not have to miss a day of work due to pain. If she had, I'm sure she was an hourly employee, so there'd be the lost income. Maybe she'd lose her job. Maybe she'd miss a rent payment and lose her home. Maybe her kids would suffer in some way. All kinds of things could go wrong in her life, just because of an untreated toothache. Instead she's gone back to work. And she'll be able to sleep tonight."

Stan leans back in his chair, hands behind his head, and laughs. "Of course, I know if I called my dentist, it would take a couple of days to get in to see him."

THE VOLUNTEERS IN Medicine clinic in Hilton Head had fifty-four hundred patient visits in its first year. The number nearly doubled the next year, to ten thousand.

Fund-raising was an ongoing task, of course. But ironically for physicians, the clinic's freedom from normal financial concerns had a liberating effect. No one worried whether a procedure was covered by one patient's insurance, or what portion Medicaid would pay of another person's bill. The only paperwork was medical record keeping. There were no financial forms. Unlike virtually anywhere else in American medicine, money was not an issue in patient care.

Word spread. Soon the clinic had practicing physicians volunteering to work a shift or two a week, to supplement the retirees, because providing care without worrying about who would pay for it was so liberating. The clinic tended to concentrate those volunteers on Tuesdays, because that was when the older folks played golf.

Not everything went smoothly. Some doctors wanted to practice medicine even when their age meant that the care might not be of top quality. That meant hiring a paid executive director to oversee a credentialing process, and to deliver the bad news if a volunteer's time of service had to end. Screening of nonmedical volunteers had to be likewise rigorous, because occasionally they arrived with issues of their own that they sought to alleviate through the clinic.

"Of the many good people who want to participate here," Jack explains, "there are definitely some who need to do their own healing."

* * *

IN ITS THIRD year of operation, the clinic treated thirteen thousand patients. The next year, the tally was fifteen thousand. Six years after the idea was born, Volunteers in Medicine was already treating more people than it had identified in the initial surveys. By the clinic's fifteenth year, four hundred medical volunteers and two hundred lay volunteers were handling thirty thousand patient visits annually. The problem of people lacking health care in Hilton Head had been solved. And yet this success was just the beginning.

PICTURE NOW A little girl named Shelley DeLaurentis, meandering the neighborhoods of Union, New Jersey, collecting coins for the March of Dimes. Kids like this are a fixture in some suburbs, marching around on Halloween with the orange box for UNICEF. Then they finish grade school, pour their energies into the taxing tasks of adolescence, and good deeds become a thing of the past.

For Shelley, however, the gratification of those neighborhood walks left a distinct feeling. It lingered through high school, Mount Holyoke College, and the Wharton School of Business, where she earned an MBA. Shelley married and took a job with a division of Johnson & Johnson—the massive health and beauty company whose products span a wide range: Neutrogena to Mylanta, Band-Aid to K-Y Jelly, Splenda to St. Joseph Aspirin. One of the most successful products is Tylenol.

Over the years Shelley rose to become director of the company's consumer care center, a telephone and Internet system that handles more than a million customer questions and requests a year. Shelley's work placed her squarely at the intersection of selling health-related goods and communicating with the people who buy them.

Although her career soared, Shelley faced serious trials in her personal life. Her second child has cystic fibrosis, a genetic disease that affects the pancreas, glands, and above all lungs. Although the disease is always fatal, the family has rallied through years of hospitalizations, physical therapy, and medications, and that daughter is now twenty-two years old.

"It's gratifying," Shelley says, "but it's also tough."

Ever that girl raising money in her neighborhood, Shelley and her husband joined the local cystic fibrosis foundation. She received a leave from her job to serve as a loaned executive to the effort. Here is another authentic patriot, exercising individual initiative toward a larger purpose.

Meanwhile Shelley's next daughter, at only two years old, developed brain cancer. They battled to their utmost, but Susanna died at age ten.

"We suffered with her for eight years," Shelley says. But in time she and her husband turned their grief toward the positive. They created Susanna's Foundation, which awards college scholarships to children who have overcome adversity.

"We're both really proud of that," Shelley says. "These kids have illnesses that could limit their abilities, but against all odds they are doing well. It's so heartwarming to see. I mean, if you think about just what it takes for them just to get to school, much less do well? But one scholarship winner this year had multiple kinds of cancer in middle school, yet she graduated having never gotten anything but an A."

Shelley says the sadness in her life has been healed somewhat by making a difference on others' behalf, and by realizing just how precious a healthy life can be. "People just don't even get how lucky they are to have normal everyday lives."

In 1999 Shelley learned that the mother of a close friend had died. The mother had a vacation home in Hilton Head; her obituary asked that in lieu of flowers contributions be made to a charity: Volunteers in Medicine.

Shelley had heard of the organization, but vaguely. Because of her job, she received copies of any news coverage that involved products within her purview. Since the list included Tylenol, coverage of Jack McConnell's project in Hilton Head crossed her desk from time to time. But she had treated the information like any story about a retired McNeil executive. When she saw that obituary, though, a light went on.

"To me it was like a message, something way beyond coincidence," she says. At the woman's funeral, Shelley met Jack McConnell.

He invited her to visit. By then he could do so with confidence; the clinic was seven years old, seasoned and established.

Although it was outside her role, and crossing lanes of responsibility in a multibillion-dollar company can resemble crossing a highway at rush hour, Shelley approached the directors of the Tylenol brand. Someone ought to go to Hilton Head, she said, to investigate a possible corporate sponsorship. That someone, the company decided, should be her.

The trip, from Shelley's perspective, could not have gone better. "It's such a dichotomous population in Hilton Head," she says, "the very rich, and the very poor who serve them. And nationally, it's daunting. The need is so great. . . .

"That clinic, though, with the respect for people's dignity in everything they do—it should be the model for health care. I know I sure wish *my* doctor's office was like this.

"And it's impossible not to be taken by Jack." Shelley laughs at the memory. "He's so charismatic. And his story is so amazing, his father at the dinner table saying, 'Who did you help today?' What can I say? We fell in love."

Jack retells a more grueling version of events. "Three females and a male arrived here and said they might want to be involved. We had a lengthy discussion, a tour, spent the whole day, had dinner, agreed to meet the next morning. After that I couldn't hold it in any longer: 'We've been here together a day and a half, and you haven't once mentioned McNeil.' 'Oh,' they said, 'what did you do there?' 'I helped invent Tylenol.' Well, one of them stood up so fast he knocked the chair over."

Jack laughs. "Turns out they've been the best supporters we've got. Fact is, we couldn't survive without them."

McNeil not only embraced the clinic, it brought to the project the larger vision that a multibillion-dollar company is accustomed to relying on every day: What about building Volunteers in Medicine clinics all over the country? The company agreed to finance an institute to pursue exactly that goal. Later, McNeil employees—including senior management—served as volunteers when the institute helped launch a clinic in Pennsylvania.

To Shelley DeLaurentis, there is a feeling of destiny to the whole experience. "I think of it as a little like when you have your first kid. You give it a name, and declare it to the world. And this amazing thing happens. People call the kid by that name, and on it goes. The same thing happens with making a difference. You name it, declare it, and on it goes."

ON IT GOES indeed. At the institute's headquarters, a U.S. map bristles with pins for each location of a Volunteer in Medicine clinic: Ohio, New York, Georgia, Tennessee, Alabama, Oregon, Florida, California, Massachusetts, Louisiana.

The map hangs in the office of Amy Hamlin, executive director of the institute since Jack began his second retirement. Hamlin had been a nursing manager for a large hospital, but during a 1997 reorganization she was offered a generous buyout. Simultaneously, a friend mentioned wanting to start a free clinic in Alaska, and Hamlin offered to do some research. She wanted to help because she had experienced the health system's problems firsthand: preventable suffering, illnesses that could have been minimized if treated sooner, economic ruin. "All the time I would see people coming in who were uninsured, and whose lives were destroyed because of it."

Hamlin's homework led her to Volunteers in Medicine. She called Jack, who said he had too much work on his hands. Forget aiding others, he needed help himself.

"This is providential," Hamlin said. "The hospital had just offered me a year of full pay with health insurance. Ten days later I flew to Hilton Head."

Her friends worried: She was a single parent, she had a child in college. "It felt just right," Hamlin said. "This was an opportunity to have an impact, to right the injustice of access to care."

Jack and his wife checked her out fully, she said. Then they put her to work in the executive offices—above Jack's garage. "I'd get there every morning, go on up, start working while he and Mary Ellen were having breakfast. All of a sudden there'd be Dixieland jazz on, and he'd come up the stairs singing, 'Hi, baby,' and then we were off working."

Her imitation of Jack's voice is uncanny. Her attitude echoes his too. "It wasn't hard work. It was soulful work. It was joyful work."

Hamlin became executive director in 1999. Now she says the potential growth seems nearly limitless. "In the pipeline we have another thirty to forty sites, and that's with no marketing, just word of mouth."

Some governmental obstacles have begun to fall away. Malpractice protection for medical volunteers in free clinics—a proposal ignored in Washington for years—received support from Johnson & Johnson's lobbyists. As a result, federal law has helped the cause since 2005: A Department of Health and Human Services program provides medical malpractice protection to health care providers who volunteer their time at free clinics. If more states can resolve how to license retired doctors and nurses, the number of Volunteers in Medicine sites could explode.

The potential human effect is equally promising, Hamlin says. "When a marginal breadwinner loses their health, it starts a spiral. They never recover. So this may keep families together, or preserve a life."

The institute helps assess a potential clinic's capacity, quantify the need, and teach local residents how to build a facility that will succeed. The resulting clinics operate entirely due to local volunteers and philanthropy.

"Every time we open a clinic, it means that people who are poor—maybe working, but poor, on the edge, life's so difficult—but they know if they get sick they can come to this wonderful, nurturing place and someone will listen to them, treat them with respect, and give them what they need. There's no judgment based on people's ability to pay. There are no lawsuits. It's a culture of caring, and you feel it when you're in the clinic."

Hamlin, sounding every bit as much an authentic patriot as Jack, adds that today the role of service organizations is more important than ever. "I really think nonprofits are around to pick up the failures of the marketplace. We represent capitalism's failures. And the political process? I always thought we would have national health care. I'm cynical now."

Thus society needs authentic patriots—whether the few rare visionaries who launch ideas like free clinics, or the countless donors and volunteers who enable them to succeed. Oddly enough, though, Hamlin says, the volunteers say their involvement is not a gift. They insist it is a reward. "They say it has improved the quality of their life. And they tell you over and over again, they don't just want to play golf."

All told, Volunteers in Medicine clinics are providing health care for some three hundred thousand patients every year. It's not all 47 million people who don't have access to care today, but it is a substantial start. And it's free.

JACK MCCONNELL RISES from his seat in the administrative building, and wanders into the clinic. There's a retired urologist he's playing golf with next week. There's an administrator whose arm Jack gives a squeeze. He holds a door open for a woman in a hurry, calling after her, "Have a great day, sweetheart." He ducks into an examining room to boast about how he browbeat a manufacturer into donating the equipment for free. In a hallway he hails a ninety-three-year-old pharmacist: "How are you today, young man?"

A volunteer in the waiting room greets him, and says what a pleasure it is to spend the afternoon at the clinic. Grinning, Jack McConnell stands his straightest and takes her hand. "Isn't it the most beautiful day?"

8

Until Proven Innocent

Truth is great and will prevail if left to herself. . . . She
is the proper and sufficient antagonist to error.

— THOMAS JEFFERSON

THE POLICE CAME FOR Alan Newton at eleven o'clock in the
morning on June 28, 1984. It was a Thursday.

A customer service representative for New York Telephone, Alan
worked in the towers of the World Trade Center. He lived with his
mother and four of his eight siblings in the Bronx, where he'd grown
up. Alan had graduated from DeWitt Clinton High School in the top
third of his class. His character had been shaped largely by four older
sisters who were vigilant, determined that their baby brother would
grow up properly despite the tough neighborhood.

Alan was a small man, five foot eight and 140 pounds, with a
handsome face and a quiet manner. He had not been entirely a saint;
a high school fistfight years before had led to a misdemeanor assault
conviction. But by 1984 life was definitely on the climb: He was engaged; his work was going well. Normally Alan would have been at
work, but as a new hire completing the job's probationary period, on
rare days he might be home in the daytime.

"When the police came, it was just a coincidence that I happened
to be there," he remembers. "There were four of them, three males and
one female. They were in plain clothes. They came and took me down
to the precinct."

Alan did not resist, nor did he see any reason to. He was anxious because of his past experience with police, but he had no idea why he was being held. No one interrogated him, no one accused him. "I had nothing in my head, you know? Just thinking, 'You all made a mistake.'"

The police had Alan stand in a lineup; he stood second in a row of six black men. He waited a while in another room, and then walked in another lineup, again in the second position. This time the police asked him to approach the one-way window and show his teeth. He has ordinary teeth. The police asked each man in the lineup to speak, then told Alan his voice had not been loud enough.

"They told me to go to a crack in the door and shout: 'I'm gonna cut you so you can't identify me, bitch.'"

Alan did as he was told. "I just tried to maintain my composure," he says. "Then the female officer told me I had not been picked out. She said, 'We're just going to put you in the holding pen while we void the arrest.'"

It was a trick. Once Alan was behind bars, the police told him he had been identified by the victim and a witness as the perpetrator of a violent sexual crime.

"I started acting up then, sure. I was screaming, cursing, kicking the bench. That was why they trick you into the bullpen I guess, so you won't act up."

After Alan calmed down, the police took him to central booking, where he was photographed and fingerprinted. He spent the night in jail. At his arraignment the next day, he was charged with robbery, assault, and rape. "Now that I knew the charges, I realized I was facing some serious stuff."

The judge set his bail at two hundred thousand dollars. "We call that a ransom," Alan says. "They give you a bail you can't make. When you're earning like twenty thousand dollars a year, and facing charges like that, now you understand: You are not coming home. You turn around and see your family and you realize: Shit, I am not coming home."

Instead he went to the Bronx House of Detention. He was twenty-two years old. Alan Newton would not see the free light of day again for twenty-two more years.

IN COURT DOCUMENTS she is known as "VJ," a twenty-five-year-old woman who stopped at a convenience store at the corner of Third Avenue and 180th Street. It was 4 A.M. on June 23, 1984. Although she'd had eleven beers already that night, as well as Dilantin, an epilepsy medicine that is not supposed to be mixed with alcohol, VJ went into the store to buy a beer. A man entered at about the same time, purchased cigarettes, then exited. As VJ later recounted to police, when she left the store the man grabbed her, held a razor to her throat, and forced her into a car.

He drove about six blocks to Crotona Park, where he raped her. Once he'd left, she went to find a cab. But the man returned, forcing VJ into an abandoned building. They struggled, but he took her to the third floor. There he raped her again. She felt his semen on her leg. Then he told her he was going to "fix it" so she couldn't identify him. He took the razor and slashed her left eye. She passed out; he took her money and fled.

When VJ regained consciousness she called the police. She was taken to Jacobi Hospital, twenty blocks away, where she received emergency care.

Emergency staff also performed a rape-kit study on her. These kits collect physical evidence from the victim's body: any ejaculate, hair, blood, skin under the fingernails. A kit is about the size of a box lunch, white with identifying markings on the side and top; it contains swabs and plastic bags, and upon completion is sealed with tape. Strict guidelines govern these procedures—including who possesses the completed kit and at what secure location it is kept—so the evidence may be used in any later trial.

At the hospital VJ said her attacker was "physically large" and his name was Willie. Her eye received extensive treatment but could not be saved; she remained permanently blind in her left eye.

Over the next two days, in her hospital bed, VJ reviewed more than two hundred police photos to see if she could find her attacker.

Alan Newton's mug shot, on file from the schoolboy fight five years earlier, lay in the stack. She chose his picture. Four days after the crime, the store clerk also reviewed police books of photos. She too selected Alan.

The next day the clerk reviewed a police lineup of suspects, and identified Alan. In her lineup, VJ was unsure if her assailant was among the six men. She asked for each one to show his teeth, then speak, and then for Alan to speak up. He shouted at the door, as instructed. VJ said it was him. And later, when he began screaming in the holding cell, VJ overheard and said, "That's him. That's the voice. That is the way he yelled at me."

There was one problem. Alan was innocent. He had never seen VJ before. He didn't smoke. He didn't drive. What's more, he had an alibi. On the night of the crime he had gone to Brooklyn to see *Ghostbusters* with his fiancée, her son and daughter, her sister, and her niece. Afterward he went to his fiancée's house in Queens, where he stayed till morning.

"I kept that movie stub a long, long time," he says.

It took until the following spring for the case to go to trial. Alan experienced Christmas in jail, Easter, his twenty-third birthday. "By that time, being locked up for eleven months, it was an adjustment every day."

Shortly before the trial began, some legal problems arose. VJ called the prosecutor and said she was "not sure" if Alan was her attacker. At a hearing a week before trial, with Alan in the room, the store clerk was asked if she could spot the rapist among the people present. She said no—but that she would be able to do it if she ever saw him again.

Once the trial began, however, VJ identified Alan as the assailant. The store clerk did too, saying in her twelve-hour shift that night he had been the only person coming into the store that she did not know personally. She contradicted the victim, though, testifying that the cigarette-buying man had tooted his horn and VJ had gotten into the car voluntarily.

Alan's defense raised additional questions: Why after the first attack did VJ go for a cab instead of the police? What about the differ-ence in size between him and Willie? What about his alibi?

"They figure your family is going to lie for you," Alan says of the prosecutors and jury. "They think, 'We're going to get somebody to pay the price for this crime.' The public is happy, they see someone arrested. But in the rush to judgment, we wind up denying justice."

In this case the jury split the difference.

"They must have decided that we knew each other and something went wrong," Alan says. "Now the only difference between the park and the building was that she was cut. But . . . everything in the park I was acquitted of. Everything in the building I was found guilty of."

On May 31, 1985, Alan Newton was sentenced to eight and one-third to twenty-five years in prison for the rape and robbery convic-tions. He received an additional five to fifteen years for the assault. The sentences would be served consecutively—meaning one would not begin until the other had been completed—for a total of thirteen and one-third to forty years behind bars.

"I was numb," he remembers. "I didn't speak at sentencing. I looked at it as futile."

Alan went first to Downstate Correctional Facility, a six-year-old maximum-security prison in Fishkill, New York. Over the decades he lived in a dozen New York jails: Dannemora, Sing Sing, Great Meadow, Wyoming, Elmira, Attica. Some cells measured six feet wide by nine feet long; others were seven by eight, adding two more square feet of living space. The best cells were at the end of a block, because there was less traffic. His inmate number was 85A3854.

Alan went before the parole board three times, and might have won release had he shown remorse. "But how can you have remorse for a crime when you're innocent?"

Alan also could have been eligible for early release, once he had served his minimum sentence—if he completed sex offender counseling. That process had one fatal prerequisite, though: an admission of guilt.

"I refused," he says. "I refused to do any kind of sex offender pro-gram for a crime I didn't commit. In my mind, I was prepared to do the whole forty years."

In other words, Alan Newton may as well have told the state to throw away the key.

BARRY SCHECK WAS born in 1949 on the Lower East Side of Manhattan. His father, one of eight children, escaped an impoverished childhood by dancing. A black janitor taught him tap, which he learned well enough to join the USO in World War II, to share the stage with Buddy Ebsen, to perform at Harlem's legendary Apollo Theater. As he aged and his feet grew heavier, he turned to managing entertainers to make his living—singers, musicians, songwriters of Tin Pan Alley. His star client was Bobby Darin, who stood among the rare few to make the transition successfully from big band stylist to pop sensation. His shows had packed the Copacabana nightclub, with lines stretching around the block. But after his hit "Splish Splash" sold a million copies, Darin became one of rock's first teen idols.

Darin also was among the first rock stars to use his celebrity to draw attention to public needs. He was no stranger to want. Darin had never known his father. Only in adulthood did he learn that the woman seventeen years his senior, whom he'd always called his sister, was actually his mother. Darin said he had grown up in such poverty, his crib was a cardboard box. Darin also had lifelong health problems resulting from childhood rheumatic fever that had left him with a damaged heart. In all, he was aware of public health needs and often worked to help. In later years, for example, Darin became an ambassador for the American Heart Association.

On top of all that, he was a pal to his manager's son. "I remember going to his show at the Copacabana," Barry Scheck recalls. "I was a little kid staying up late. And Bobby used to take me to Yankees games."

Between innings, man and boy must have conversed. In addition to reverence for Willie Mays, some measure of Darin's impulse toward generosity must have rubbed off.

"I was just a kid from Queens," Barry says. "But I grew up right at the time of the civil rights movement. In junior high it was, that I recognized these were the great forces of our time—the antiwar activities. I met Robert Kennedy. I worked in New Hampshire for Eugene McCarthy."

Barry was the first person in his family to go to college. He was admitted to Yale, where he immediately became politically active. "My freshman year I was elected president of the Yale Democrats, because we kicked out the Humphrey people." He chuckles. "Also, we let in girls."

The activist spirit of the time, plus unabashed liberalism, were fundamental to the young man's development. He wrote his undergraduate thesis on the social novel in America, from John Dos Passos to Norman Mailer.

"Political change was a major part of our identity," Barry recalls. "And what we learned from the civil rights movement was that *law* could be an instrument for social change."

Thus Barry applied to law school. He was accepted at the University of California at Berkeley and it was a perfect fit. "The people in my class were very progressive, while our faculty was very conservative. It was a liberated place. And law school cost me only four hundred dollars a semester."

During those three years, some of Barry's illusions about law took a beating. "We were learning how Richard Nixon's Justice Department had allowed illegal wiretaps without warrants. I wanted to get involved, to go to Washington. But then my father was quite ill. I needed to come back to New York. So I came, and decided to be a public defender. I arrived right when [President Gerald] Ford had said to the city, 'Drop dead.'"

The tough job and poor timing were both auspicious for a man starting his career. "They sent me to the Bronx, where they sent all the 'people's lawyers,'" Barry says. Resources to defend clients were rarely sufficient.

As a result there were unwritten rules, mostly about keeping cases moving swiftly, which Barry was reluctant to obey. On his first day as a defense attorney, he went to deal with a series of arraignments. "The judge was filing really huge bails. Well, we can challenge that, right? So I walk to the court reporter and ask for the notes. The judge screams, 'What are you doing? What are you doing?' I said to the reporter, 'Let the record reflect that the judge is standing, shouting, and red in the face.'"

The judge cited Barry for contempt of court. "My first hour on the job, and I was put in jail." Barry shakes his head at the memory. But then his face brightens at what happened next.

"Of course, word spreads. All the lawyers walk out of court in protest. Someone called *The New York Times* and the *New York Post*, which was a liberal paper back then. At two P.M. the judge holds a hearing on me, lets in all the legal aid lawyers and all the district attorneys, a hundred and fifty people in all. He looks at me and says, 'Do you apologize?' I don't say anything. Not a word. He bangs the gavel. 'Apology accepted. Case dismissed.'"

If the courts were tough, the neighborhood was tougher. "It was a wild time. That movie *Fort Apache: The Bronx*? That's the place. Pam Grier shot the two cops right where our legal office was. You had to step over derelicts to get in the door. We had one phone for six lawyers. We actually at one point went on strike, with demands like a phone for every lawyer, and x feet of space per person."

For three years Barry worked in that environment, learning firsthand how hurried and incomplete criminal justice could be. Then life took an unexpected turn. Yeshiva University in Manhattan wanted to start a clinical program at its Benjamin N. Cardozo Law School. Law students would receive field experience to enrich their book and lecture learning. When the university's chosen candidate turned them down at the last minute, the law school asked Barry if he would take the job.

He jumped. The clinic defended protestors at a nuclear power plant, worked on a case involving gunrunners in the Irish Republican Army, even freed a Brooklyn man convicted of a murder he hadn't committed.

Barry loved it—the students, the energy, and the bigger understanding he was gaining about law. "It created a larger view, not just this one-case-at-a-time life I had been leading, but looking across many cases. I guess I was developing what you might call perspective. It wasn't entirely clear how I was going to use this. And then we learned about Marion Coakley."

In the world of criminal justice, Coakley was like a precursor to the Alan Newtons of the world. His case was the first instance of a problem that afflicted many men in the years to come—and still does irreparable damage today.

Marion Coakley moved from South Carolina to New York and found jobs in unskilled labor, unloading trucks and working in a stonecutter's shop. He read at the second-grade level and his IQ was in the seventies. On October 13, 1985, he spent the evening as he often did: with a Bible study group in the basement of a building on Beekman Avenue where his sister lived. A minister and six other people were present.

While they were studying the Bible, across town a man broke into the room of a couple staying at the Bronx Park Hotel. Waving a gun, he took their money, ordered the man into the bathroom, then raped the woman. He demanded more money, which the woman said she had at home. He ordered her to tie up the man, get dressed, and drive them to her apartment. They rode together in the car, they were in the elevator together, they reached her place on the nineteenth floor, she opened the door, and when her brother-in-law stepped into view the attacker fled—with her car. She immediately called 911, thus fixing the crime at a particular time of day.

About a year previously, a woman with a record as a prostitute had demanded payment from a man she'd met at a bar and spent the night with. When he refused, she called the police to say she'd been raped. So unconcerned was the man, he waited in the apartment for the police to arrive. The woman did not make any formal appearances, even to swear out a complaint, but the man's arrest photo nonetheless remained in a file of possible sex offenders. That man was Marion Coakley. When the Bronx Park Hotel victim identified him from the mug shot, he was behind bars within hours.

The limits of criminal defense bore heavily on his trial. One lawyer handled the case early on, gathering evidence, but then she changed jobs. The attorney who took over had just finished another case and barely had time to prepare. Two more legal teams would become involved in Coakley's case before it was finished.

At trial—once the victim, her male companion, and her brother-in-law had all identified Coakley as the rapist—he was cooked. The alibi, including the minister's testimony, had no impact. The jury deliberated only briefly. At the sentencing hearing, the prosecutor noted the defendant's lack of remorse and asked for a sentence of up to twenty-five years.

Coakley exercised his opportunity to speak, and while he rambled, the ring of innocent truth was unmistakable: "I never seen these people before in my life," he began. "I wasn't there when this crime happened. . . . And the Bronx Hotel, I don't even know where the Bronx Hotel is. . . . I never carried a gun in my whole life. . . . They probably got someone confused and said they can't find the right person, so they said Marion Coakley. But God knows I didn't do this. It's wrong for you to send an innocent man to jail. I know I didn't do this. I'm not the one. . . . I never drove a car in New York City. I can't drive a car. I can't drive a car. That's all, judge, that I have to say."

His sentence was fifteen years. They led him from the room screaming. Later that day Marion Coakley received his first of many involuntary doses of antipsychotic drugs.

By then Barry had teamed up with Peter Neufeld, another former Legal Aid attorney. Neufeld came from a different background; instead of Barry's entertainment world, Peter was practically weaned on political engagement. His parents were activists, and his brother held a national position with the campus antiwar group Students for a Democratic Society. While still a young man, Peter worked with community organizers in Appalachia, collected books for segregated school districts in the South, and was suspended from high school for leading antiwar protests.

Peter and Barry both also fashioned themselves screenwriters, and in later years managed to pen several films and a book on their legal work. But they first joined forces with Barry's asset of the clinic students and Peter's growing expertise with using science to examine forensic evidence.

In the fall of 1986, the team took up the case of Marion Coakley. Cardozo students, investigating with Barry, found many problems. Prosecutors had not told the defense that the victim had sued the hotel, for example. That information mattered because juries need to know if the accuser stands to benefit financially from their verdict. The issue was especially pertinent in this case, because the hotel was arguing that the attack had never taken place. Moreover, before the trial the victim had told a prosecutor that since the crime, she felt anxious at the sight of all black men's faces—weakening the force of her identification of Coakley. Also, her companion at the hotel said prosecutors had told them Coakley committed another rape and got away with it, which was both prejudicial and untrue.

As for the science, the rape-kit evidence had not been properly preserved. Nonetheless police scientists had identified, before the semen was destroyed, the blood type of the rapist as either type B or O. With legal help from Barry and Peter, Marion Coakley was tested; he proved to have type A blood.

On July 7, 1987, a forensic chemist wrote an affidavit that the semen had not come from Coakley. Barry and Peter promptly filed court papers for his release. In late September, after nearly two years in jail, Marion Coakley won his freedom. His sister picked him up at the state prison in Greenhaven and took him home. He went back to work at the stonecutter's shop.

But Coakley's exoneration could hardly put an end to concerns about the criminal justice system. On the contrary, it left many important questions unanswered: Was eyewitness identification sometimes unreliable? Were the haste and presumptions of criminal cases leading to convictions of innocent people? Could science play a larger role in fostering actual justice? And if so, who was going to do this work?

From such difficult questions is a nationwide movement born. From the unrelenting desire to find answers are authentic patriots made.

ALAN NEWTON, BEHIND bars, had to find a whole new way of living. "You have no say-so, about almost anything, so you adapt. I came from a normal environment, and had to get used to abnormal."

He learned to avoid men wearing the colors that communicated membership in gangs. He learned to avoid most of the foods. He started exercising. He rejected the prison pecking order that placed sex offenders lowest. "Here's a guy, he killed four people for forty dollars, but he feels better than you because you raped someone? I'm not going to let you hurt me."

Alan also decided, lonely as prison life was, to keep to himself. "Let's say you're walking around the yard with a new guy, and he was stealing in another facility and you don't know it. Or you get conned, and you take it personally. Well, I learned to let it go and move on. I learned you have to do your own time. Don't be doing anybody else's time. Just do your own time.

"I saw people, when they got angry, they might stab someone over a cigarette. You think, Are you serious?"

In 1991 VJ died of natural causes. The news did not reach Alan for years.

WHAT IS IT that identifies an individual human being, that sets him or her apart from all others on earth? The metaphysical answer to this question may be unsolvable, but for many years the physical answer has been the fingerprint. Each person's whorls and ridges are as unique to them among humanity as each snowflake is in a blizzard. In court cases, however, fingerprints can prove unreliable. They smudge. They can easily be wiped away. The justice system has perpetually sought more reliable indicators.

In 1953 James Watson and Francis Crick identified the double-helix structure of deoxyribonucleic acid (DNA), which governs the development and functioning of all known living organisms. It is DNA that determines how deep a tree's roots grow, how wide a flower opens, and whether a person will be tall or short, black or white, likely to contract cancer or prone to deliver babies easily. Their discovery won the scientists the Nobel Prize in 1962; Watson remained a controversial and abrasive figure for the rest of his days (his autobiography was called *Avoid Boring People*).

In the early years following its discovery, DNA remained within the realm of science, in genetics, biochemistry, and medicine. It took decades for the criminal justice system to become aware of the power of this molecular fingerprint. In 1985 a British scientist determined that certain repeating patterns in DNA were unique to each person. Thus organic evidence at a crime scene could provide evidence to profile the criminal that was vastly—perhaps definitively—more useful than fingerprints.

The first appearance of DNA evidence in a criminal case occurred in England, when a seventeen-year-old boy confessed to two murder-rapes. DNA profiling not only proved his innocence, it also led to the arrest of the actual perpetrator.

DNA evidence first saw use in this country in 1987, in a Florida case. The defendant's blood matched the DNA profile of semen on his victim, leading to his conviction. Today DNA evidence is used so commonly, it appears in TV shows and crime novels. Courts recognize the science behind DNA profiling, and it can prove invaluable in criminal cases.

But not always. By the time Alan Newman went to jail for VJ's rape, only six states permitted reopening cases based on new evidence. Many prosecutors believe reinvestigating solid convictions is a waste of resources that could be better used to solve new crimes.

Remembering the reasoning of one South Carolina prosecutor, Barry allows himself a bitter laugh. "He actually said this, 'I can't consent to this or there will be a flood of innocent people trying to get out of jail.'"

The effect of such laws and attitudes is no laughing matter, though. For crimes committed before DNA forensics gained acceptance, people wrongfully sent to jail were condemned to stay there.

Alan Newton had seen the inside of many prisons by the time DNA evidence reached common usage. "You just transfer to a facility that has a program you want—culinary programs, industrial programs, college. All that time I just learned to adapt."

Alan filed appeals of his verdict; they were all denied. Sometimes he would be overwhelmed with feelings of anger, but what could he do? "You learn to swallow it. You learn to redirect it. I put it into my legal work, and my studies. I got an associate's college degree. But then I would have a motion denied, and the anger and depression would be back.

"Now there were other guys, if they were innocent, still by this time they'd be into gambling, drugs, fighting. They would have become another number. Too many blows to the head, they just give it up.

"I know I might not have made it home. I was on the edge sometimes. But something, something always pulled me back. Strangely enough, not doing the sex offender program, holding out that I was still innocent, that helped. It gave me a sense of peace. And as long as I was able to do my work and read and think, and keep contact with my family on the outside, that helped me swallow it."

When Alan learned about DNA evidence, he felt a whole new hope. By then he had been in jail for ten years, trying procedural maneuvers exhaustively. But now there was something substantial and powerful on his side: science. On August 16, 1994, he filed a motion for DNA testing of the rape kit. Surely that would prove his innocence.

While awaiting the ruling, another interest arose in his life. He called his brother's house one night while a party was going on. People passed the phone around until it reached one woman, who stayed on with Alan the longest. "I got her address, I got her number. Six months later we were married."

New York is among the more lenient states when it comes to such matters. If both parties write to the superintendent, the prison will make a chaplain available for the ceremony. At that time Alan was jailed in Elmira, which also was equipped for conjugal visits.

"You get forty-four hours every three months or so," he explained. The facility constructed trailers inside the walls but away from the regular prison yard. "You can go in, it's usually a weekday, like Tuesday at one in the afternoon, and stay till Thursday at eight or nine in the morning."

On November 17, 1994, Alan learned that the DNA was not available from VJ. The rape kit, which was supposed to be stored at the city's evidence repository in Queens known as Pearson Place, could not be located. Somehow it had been lost.

The setback, though a huge disappointment, did not stop him. Alan continued filing motions, year upon year, saying the lack of evidence at this point ought to raise reasonable doubt of his guilt. He argued that VJ's eye wound had gangrene, indicating that it was caused well before the night of the rape. He learned that VJ's boyfriend had previously abused her, and argued that another of those incidents was being blamed on him.

As regularly as Alan filed those motions, the courts turned them aside. Then, in 1998, Alan remembered that VJ had said she felt semen on her leg. Perhaps there would be DNA evidence on her pants. He filed a motion for the pants to be tested, which in time the courts granted.

During that period, meanwhile, corrections officials took away Alan's conjugal visit privileges. "I knew the termination was going to come one day. They said because I refused to take any program connected to the nature of my offense, I was no longer eligible."

The marriage waned, then ended. Family became increasingly essential for keeping his perspective, Alan says. "I was always able to call somebody. I have twenty-two nieces and nephews now. At first they didn't always want to tell me what was going on outside. But I told them they had to. I needed the distraction. It was the only thing keeping me sane. Focusing on my case twenty-four hours a day? No. If I lost that connection, I might stop caring for myself. My family, they did the time with me."

Eventually a state lab scanned VJ's pants, and found no biological evidence. The legal procedures for that dead end had consumed another two years. Imagine an innocent man, living in prison, and waiting day after day to hear if the courts will open an avenue to freedom—the frustration it would cause, the patience it would require.

Alan's mind kept turning over a simple question: How could the best evidence be missing? He filed a motion requesting a search of Pearson Place for the rape kit. A police sergeant's reply dashed those hopes.

"Currently there is no original voucher in the active file, therefore it must have been destroyed," the officer wrote. "Unfortunately there was a fire in our facility during the summer of 1995 which destroyed those files."

There seemed to be no further options. By then Alan had spent nearly half his life in jail. He might plausibly remain behind bars for twenty more years.

One day in 2004, though, one of Alan's brothers was online, trolling through criminal justice Web sites, when he found the Innocence Project.

* * *

YES, MARION COAKLEY'S case had created something. Within
three years Barry and Peter had founded the Innocence Project, a
nonprofit legal group that would take cases in which DNA evidence
could determine definitively the guilt or innocence of a person behind
bars.

It was a classic authentic patriot project: Government was indifferent to legitimate complaints about unfair trials, from misidentification by witnesses to racially biased sentencing. The free market
could not care less who goes to jail, provided crime is kept to a minimum and thus does not interfere with commerce. Solving the problem of wrongful convictions would therefore take individual initiative,
and a commitment to fundamental American values of justice.

The Innocence Project began with the two lawyers, an assistant,
and the Cardozo clinic students. Right from the start, they won exonerations.

Gary Dotson of Illinois was convicted in 1979 of rape and kid-
napping. The victim later recanted, saying she fabricated the incident,
but it took four more years—and DNA evidence—to win his 1989 release. Mentally handicapped David Vasquez pled guilty to a 1985
murder, but DNA brought his freedom four years later. Another suspect in a rape and murder implicated Bruce Nelson, but in 1990 DNA
evidence proved Nelson's innocence.

Instead of feeling that they were finding rare exceptions in a fair
justice system, Barry and Peter gained a stronger sense that these
cases were not exceptional at all. They rented an office, they began
hiring staff. "From the beginning, we were a policy group. But then
we got on Phil Donahue's show, and that brought us a huge pile of letters. Then in the middle of this, we did the Simpson case."

Former football star O. J. Simpson was charged with murdering
his ex-wife and a friend—and acquitted. A civil suit later found him
liable for the deaths, and he was ordered to pay $35 million. Barry
helped the criminal defense as a technical consultant, for which he
makes no apologies. "Some people are still angry at us about that.
What we point out, though—and we were right—was that the way they
collected evidence was totally improper.

"I can see almost nothing good that came out of the O. J. trial. It was terrible for race relations. And now we have an industry of people bloviating on television about the law, and we have legal shows that have distorted courts and trials. But through that case there was a sea change that we can support. All of a sudden people realized that we had twenty-first-century evidence technology, and we were still using a nineteenth-century collection method."

So the business of using contemporary methods for gathering and processing evidence boomed, but not without growing pains. "We knew nothing about how to run a nonprofit. Nothing, zero. We had problems with the law school, and gaining independence. If we had known, we would have raised so much more money. And we'd have two times as many people out of prison by now. That's on us. But we didn't know."

Thus Scheck and Neufeld began assembling professionals to run the operations.

"I was really impressed with their deep commitment to justice," says Madeline deLone, the project's executive director. "They were freeing people, of course, through extraordinary acts, many of them miraculous. But also they believed the work could be used to improve a system."

With degrees in public health and in law, plus long experience in corrections operations and policy, deLone embodies the nonprofit professionalism—communications materials, fund-raising operations, the Web site, the social workers who help exonerees reenter society—that now characterizes what was once a three-person endeavor. "My job is to make sure we're using the amazing power of these exonerations to advocate for systemic change."

Today the project occupies several stories of a building in lower Manhattan. The staff of fifty is complemented by dozens of law students each year, plus scores of volunteers. Most of the office is nondescript: cubicles, copiers, and so on. But there are signs that this is not an ordinary workplace. The art on the walls is either large portraits of exonerated men, or posters of superheroes. The exception is Barry's office, which has a large painting—perhaps echoing Bobby Darin's influence—of Willie Mays.

One hint of DNA's importance hangs on a restroom door, below the sign saying MEN: an enlarged photo of male chromosomes. Inside, meanwhile, there is evidence of the strain of this exasperating work: an enormous bottle of headache medicine.

With greater public exposure, demand for the Innocence Project's services became a flood. Inmates from all over the country wrote, insisting that they had been wrongly convicted. Of course not all of them were, but the torrent meant there needed to be a system for vetting the claims, determining which cases seemed promising and whether there was any opportunity to use DNA. The compelling need—and the Innocence Project's growing list of successes—exerted an almost gravitational pull.

"The plan was to get my MFA in poetry and then make my living as a poet," says Huy Dao, who joined the Innocence Project at twenty-three. Born in Laos, raised in Pennsylvania, and educated at Cornell University, he grew too concerned about social justice for the path he'd planned. "I had a lot of political fire in me."

Dao has held eight different jobs with the project, but for most of the time he has handled the intake process. Imagine opening the mail from thousands of prisoners who see you as their only hope for freedom. The letters reveal all of the emotional turmoil of a person behind bars, and can go on for dozens of pages. Dao's job is to cull, to prioritize, to perform a kind of justice triage. "It's not for me to know if a person is innocent or guilty, but to determine if science can prove it."

The process begins with a form containing ten pages of questions as chilling as they are essential: Where were you convicted and of what crime? How did you plead? When were you sentenced and for how long? Who were the victims and did you know them? How did you become a suspect? Was there physical evidence? And then the show-stopper: What items of evidence, if subjected to DNA testing, would prove your innocence?

The work requires a cold focus, Dao says, because potential clients present so much background noise. "We work with so many unknowns: literacy level, mental illness, the shock of being incarcerated." He shrugs. "I've trained myself to overrule them in order to focus on the mandate. You need to strike a balance, such as do you make the questionnaire longer—literacy levels are appallingly low in prisons— with the need to get specific answers. The hope level is so high. We humans are all so skilled at deception and self-deception. In actuality you need eight thousand things to go your way to even get a glimpse of the exonerating power of your evidence."

Even so, there are three hundred new potential clients every month. Hallways throughout the office are lined with chest-high white filing cabinets, each packed with papers pertaining to cases in progress. More filing cabinets stand in rows in storerooms. The contents of one long row of steel cabinets are revealed by a single word affixed to the top drawer: MAYBE.

The work exacts a toll, Dao says. "You don't want to deal with what it says about you if you process these cases without emotion. But you also don't want to delve too deeply into someone's life, not if you want to get to the others waiting their turn. My old anger carried me through a lot: Here's a pile. If I can get through them, something good has been done."

The difficulty of the job meant clashes with Barry. "In the first two years, every situation was a screaming match. He'd pound his desk. I'd bang my table. It was never personal, though. At some point I found my voice."

He helped his co-workers find their voices too. Huy's contribution to the office culture was an unlikely expression of the need to release: karaoke.

"There was a fair amount of resistance from Barry to the idea of people making spectacles of themselves. At first it was just a fun after-work thing. Then the old-schoolers began to do it. Gradually it became the default option."

When a missing rape kit is found, when a court agrees to admit DNA evidence, especially when an innocent person is freed from jail, the staff goes around the corner to a tiny bar—and sings. "It becomes cathartic. We are free to be as cheesy or earnest or whatever as we like. It is some kind of weird, unifying force."

One time, after a particularly trying exoneration, Barry joined the festivities. "But he couldn't take off his director's hat," recalls policy advocate Rebecca Brown. After she'd sung Janis Joplin's version of "Me and Bobby McGee," she remembers, "he came over and told me how to do it better. To do it grittier."

The evening remains emblematic in the staff's minds.

"It is a basement place," Dao explains, "no natural light. He came in, and he didn't even take off his sunglasses. He just took part in the celebration by singing with us."

What song did the founder choose? "Papa Was a Rolling Stone."

ONE THING WAS definitely worth singing about: The pace of the exonerations was accelerating. As they accumulated, the cases also revealed patterns in how wrongful convictions occur, and how profound the resulting injustice can be.

In 1993 Kirk Bloodsworth became the first person rescued from death row. He was arrested in Maryland for raping and killing a nine-year-old girl, after police received an anonymous call. DNA evidence cleared him eight years later. He now works in criminal justice reform for the Justice Project in Washington.

Based on eyewitness misidentification, Ronald Cotton spent ten years in jail for raping a college student before DNA freed him. Today he and the survivor speak publicly together about wrongful convictions.

Kevin Green was convicted of attempting to murder his wife and thereby killing their unborn child. His wife, who experienced brain damage in the attack, testified against him. DNA evidence cleared him after more than fifteen years in prison. It also led police to a suspect who confessed to that crime and five murders.

Timothy Durham, found guilty of the brutal rape of an eleven-year-old girl based on hair evidence—despite having an alibi with eleven witnesses—received a sentence of thirty-two hundred years. DNA evidence proved his innocence three years later, implicating a convicted rapist.

Ron Williamson came within five days of execution for murder in Oklahoma, before DNA evidence cleared him—and implicated a man who had testified against him in his trial.

Kenneth Waters was convicted of a Massachusetts murder and

robbery, after ex-girlfriends testified he had confessed while drunk. His sister put herself through law school to clear his name. DNA testing proved his innocence after he had served more than seventeen years. He died six months after getting out of jail.

Ray Krone went to jail for an Arizona murder based on a comparison of his tooth marks on a Styrofoam cup to bite marks on the victim. He was sentenced to death, plus twenty-one years. He served ten years before DNA evidence cleared him.

Michael Mercer was convicted of raping a seventeen-year-old girl based on her misidentification. After ten years DNA testing not only cleared him, but also matched with a convicted rapist. The perpetrator could not be charged, however; the statute of limitations had expired.

Frank Lee Smith spent fourteen years on death row for rape and murder. DNA testing proved his innocence and implicated another man, but by then Smith had died of cancer.

"Regardless of how you feel about the morality of putting someone to death for committing the most heinous of crimes," Barry says, "the system itself is an obscenity: unfair, inefficient, inaccurate, and far too often, mistaken."

When Larry Mayes left an Indiana prison in 2001, after serving more than eighteen years for a rape he did not commit, he marked a proud milestone for the Innocence Project and a troubling one for America's criminal justice system. He was the group's one hundredth exoneration.

MARCH 5, 1770, was a cold night in Boston, the cobblestone streets spotted with ice. At about 9 P.M., a British sentry stood guard at the Custom House while a group of men and boys insulted and mocked him. Someone rang a nearby church bell in alarm, and people hurried into the streets thinking there must be a fire. Hundreds of Bostonians gathered at the Custom House, where the lone soldier had been joined by eight more. The men had muskets, bayonets attached. The crowd shouted at the soldiers, then began throwing things: garbage, chunks of ice, rocks. Suddenly the soldiers fired. Five men died.

Boston's sharpest propagandists leapt on the incident as evidence of the crown's oppression of innocent colonists. Paul Revere created a print depicting the event in the worst possible light. Sam Adams, who quickly distributed Revere's interpretation, declared the incident a "bloody butchery." Thus the legend of the Boston Massacre was born. In some schools, the event is taught as a slaughter of unarmed innocents to this day.

When the soldiers and their captain were charged with criminal conduct, a thirty-four-year-old local lawyer was asked to defend them. It was not an easy choice. He would receive only eighteen guineas for his labor. He said himself that working on behalf of the Redcoats would mean "incurring a clamor and popular suspicions and prejudices."

There were other reasons to decline. His wife was pregnant. He and his family could be placed in physical danger. He was already touchy about public opinion, possibly because he harbored political ambitions.

Writing in a diary about his deliberations, this young man copied a quotation from an Italian scholar on crime and punishment:

> If, by supporting the rights of mankind, and of invincible truth, I shall contribute to save from the agonies of death one unfortunate victim of tyranny, or of ignorance equally fatal, his blessings and years of transport will be sufficient consolation to me for the contempt of all mankind.

The lawyer took the case. In order to allow calm to return to Boston, the proceedings were delayed for months. The captain's trial began in October, and was based on whether he had given the order to fire. His guilt was never proven, the young man's defense argument was considered "a virtuoso performance," and the captain was acquitted.

At the soldiers' trial in December, the young lawyer described the crowd that March night as a mob, "a motley rabble of saucy boys" and "outlandish jacktars." Meanwhile he called the sentries "wretched conservators of the peace."

The mob had caused the incident, he argued. These people, far from being innocents, had thrown ice and rocks, had cried, "Kill them! Kill them!" One soldier had been hit with a club, and had struggled to his feet only to be clubbed again. Ultimately the British fired in self-defense.

"Facts are stubborn things," the lawyer argued, "and whatever may be our wishes, our inclinations, or the dictums of our passions, they cannot alter the state of facts and evidence."

Six of the eight soldiers were found innocent. Two, guilty of manslaughter, were branded on their thumbs.

Many years later, when the young lawyer had grown to be an old man, he would reflect that the Boston Massacre defense marked "one of the most gallant, generous, manly and disinterested actions of my whole life, and one of the best pieces of service I ever rendered my country."

This man was John Adams, signer of the Declaration of Independence, ambassador to Great Britain and France during the nation's infancy, two-term vice president under George Washington, and one-term president of the United States.

Adams' sensibility reflects many of the fundamental concepts undergirding the American justice system. When the nation's Founders created this model of a judiciary, it was an entirely new idea. Until then, the king appointed judges and the king's word was law. Even the courtrooms themselves were the property of the crown.

In the fledgling United States, the judiciary was established as an independent arm of government, separate from and equal to the legislative and executive branches. Courts have standing to strike down laws as unconstitutional. They have the power to sit in judgment of elected officials. And their work is symbolized by Themis, the Greek Titan who represents justice: a woman, blindfolded, holding a scale on which both sides are in perfect balance.

Isn't that what we believe too? Yes, rich people get better lawyers, black people get tougher sentences, many cases take too long to resolve. Even so, don't we at some level believe that the general quality of justice in this country is good? Maybe even excellent? Don't we want to believe that these founding principles remain vital today? And don't the Innocence Project's stories of injustice give us a claustrophobic feeling, or at a minimum, chafe against our idea of how America works?

That is why Barry Scheck is so important. He was just a simple defense attorney in a tough district. He wasn't famous, or rich, or powerful. He just cared. And once he started caring, he didn't seem able to stop. We need him to be out there, serving his idealistic purposes, or our belief in American justice might collapse. We need him beating the bad guys—even if they turn out to be someone other than we'd thought—because such a battle for justice is integral to the intrepid spirit that is so much a part of the American character. Every time he succeeds, it delivers a terrible verdict on the criminal justice system. But Scheck's work also reinvigorates our faith in truth ultimately prevailing. In this nation adrift from its founding principles, his victories redefine what is possible.

By the time Alan Newton contacted the Innocence Project, the group had exonerated 180 men. Missing evidence made his case an unlikely one; Huy took it on, though, and handed it to Vanessa Potkin, one of the longest-serving lawyers at the project.

"My brother called her God," Alan says. "She's small in stature, but big in heart. You know that line 'Speak softly and carry a big stick'? She gets the job done."

"Tony Newton," she says, smiling, remembering Alan's persistent brother. "I used to get calls from him all the time."

Potkin's office and desk are cluttered with legal briefs. They are stacked several feet deep on her office's spare chair. The walls are adorned with enlargements of newspaper pages about men getting out of jail.

"Today I have fifty cases ongoing," she says. "The latest news is a Mississippi death row case, and the prosecutor agreed pretty quickly to DNA testing. Oh, and one in Illinois, in Chicago, where they've had exculpatory test results for years. Right now I'm working on one in New Jersey, where we have favorable DNA results, but the judge denied a new trial so we're appealing. You know, the run of the mill."

It says something about criminal defense work in America that Potkin considers such situations commonplace. Her strategy in Alan's case was similarly workmanlike. "The first thing we did, because they couldn't find the rape kit, was reconsider biological evidence in the pants. There was an expectation that there would be biology in there, based on the stated facts of the case. But the labs did a mapping, all over the garment. There was nothing there. We were going to close out the case."

In fact, the Innocence Project closes one-third of its cases because of lost or missing evidence. Half of the Project's New York City cases conclude for that reason. This time Potkin had an intuition, though. "I had a nagging feeling inside of me: I can't close this case without personally trying to find the rape kit."

In her experience, even though a life behind bars is at stake, it's not uncommon for evidence requests to go simply ignored. "You know, a student asks a court clerk, and the answer is, 'Oh no, it's too old.' So we file a motion. And then someone has to get up and look."

In Alan's case that supposedly had already happened, twice. "The egregious thing was that NYPD had made representations in writing that officers looked in the actual bin where the evidence is stored. It wasn't there. And it was thus presumed destroyed. New York, by the way, has one of the worst evidence storage systems I've found in this country. It's better in the back roads of Mississippi."

New York's evidence all goes to Pearson Place in Queens, where it is placed in bins—more like barrels, really—with a date on the outside. There is no bar coding of data, no computerized catalog of locations. As a result, not only are exculpatory materials misplaced, so is evidence that might lead to convictions—such as a bloody shirt from a crime committed before DNA evidence. "It is this city's ugly secret," Potkin says. "It is a debacle."

When the hearing on her motion for Alan finally took place, Potkin recalls, "I said to the judge, let *me* go in. Issue an order and I'll go in and look myself."

Instead the judge ordered Elisa Koenderman, a prosecutor, to conduct the search. She went willingly, Potkin said, but not instantly.

"That ruling was before the summer, I remember," she says. "I was hesitant to check in with her; I felt sheepish. Towards the end of summer, though, I was just so curious. So I sent an email: 'Just checking in, how's it going?' And she responded, it was November seventh: 'They have the rape kit.'"

In fact, VJ's evidence was located exactly where it was supposed to be, in barrel 22, as the storage voucher had always said. The authorities found it eleven years after Alan had first asked them to search.

"I screamed," Potkin recalls, beaming at the memory. "I told everyone here. They screamed. We announced it on the intercom. You have legal things still to accomplish. But that, that was the victory moment."

It has happened, in rare cases, that a person represented by the Innocence Project reaches that moment of truth, the prospect of irrefutable scientific evidence, and admits guilt. Sometimes too the evidence has been degraded by time.

"When I was telling Alan, I was cautious," Potkin says. "I tried to represent all the possibilities. It didn't matter. Regardless of what I said, he knew he was coming home."

"I started crying on the phone," Alan remembers. "When they found that evidence, I was at Wyoming prison, right next to Attica. I told my brother Tom, if this evidence has not been tampered with, I am coming home."

Sequencing a DNA sample can take up to a year, and cost up to twenty thousand dollars. In this case, in addition to testing by the state lab, the Innocence Project sent evidence to a premier private lab as well. One more time, Alan Newton's job was to wait.

AS THE INNOCENCE Project continued to win more cases, patterns emerged. Sixty percent of the wrongfully convicted people were black, 10 percent Latinos. The average length of time served was twelve years. About 8 percent were either sentenced to death or served time on death row.

More striking were the reasons these innocent people went to jail. The list was surprisingly short. It also revealed a systemic rush to judgment.

- **Mistaken identification.** Seventy-seven percent of the Project's exonerated clients have been proven innocent despite an eyewitness report that the suspect had committed the crime. The reliability of such evidence, though instinct tells us it would be nearly infallible, has proven weak too many times. Many cases reveal sloppy protocols for showing suspects to witnesses, in ways that imply that the suspected person has already been spotlighted by other evidence.

- **Junk science.** Sixty-five percent of wrongful convictions involve misuse of forensic evidence (despite the spectacular success of these techniques on TV shows). In many cases there are signs that police or forensic scientists exaggerated findings, presenting evidence as conclusive when it decidedly was not.

- **False confessions.** Twenty-five percent of wrongful convictions result from statements by defendants. One-third of these cases involved a suspect who was either under eighteen or developmentally disabled. Others were simply coerced. John Kogut of New York withstood eighteen hours of interrogation before confessing to raping and murdering a sixteen-year-old girl. DNA proved him innocent, but only after he'd spent seventeen years behind bars.

- **Snitches.** Fifteen percent of wrongful convictions are due to false jailhouse testimony. An inmate, promised a reduced sentence in exchange for testifying, insists that the suspect has confessed to the crime. Some snitches have contributed to multiple convictions.

By the time enough exonerations revealed such patterns, the Innocence Project's work had completely transcended its founders' liberal politics. Their effort had become about justice itself, in the broadest meaning, and about upholding the lofty principles of fairness and human worth that were born in the nation's founding. These should always be bipartisan goals.

"As long as the wrong person is in jail," Barry says, "the real person is out there, usually committing more crimes. So if you can get to the causes of wrongful convictions, everyone wins. That's a powerful mainstream message."

It's also not just rhetoric. More than a third of the Innocence Project's exonerations have led authorities to the actual perpetrator.

Moreover, DNA testing has also cleared thousands of people who were prime suspects in crimes. A National Institute of Justice study of more than ten thousand cases found that DNA disqualified a stunning 25 percent of suspects. Science has become an essential tool in a crowded and hasty justice system.

"People have this idea of a person who is charged with murder getting a long, Perry Mason–type trial," Potkin says. "That's just not reality. Sometimes it's one day long, the whole thing."

Indeed, the quality of legal representation for people facing long sentences or even death is notoriously poor.

The 1984 murder conviction of Calvin Burdine became a famous example. A court clerk later testified that Burdine's lawyer "fell asleep for long periods of time during the questioning of witnesses." The state court of appeals in Texas, where Burdine was tried, denied his appeal. Burdine has been scheduled for execution six times. The U.S. Supreme Court eventually granted Burdine a retrial, which at the time of this writing had not begun.

Consider too the less well-known case of Jesus Romero, charged in a 1989 rape and murder. Here, from court transcripts, is the entire argument his lawyer presented at the sentencing hearing:

> DEFENSE COUNSEL: Ladies and gentlemen, I appreciate the time you took deliberating and the thought you put into this. I'm going to be extremely brief. I have a reputation for not being brief. [To the defendant:] Jesse, stand up. Jesse?
> THE DEFENDANT: Sir?
> DEFENSE COUNSEL: Stand up. [To the jury:] You are an extremely intelligent jury. You've got that man's life in your hands. You can take it or not. That's all I have to say.

The jury took it. Romero's argument to the Fifth Circuit Court of Appeals, that he had received ineffective counsel, was denied. His last words, spoken on May 20, 1992: "Tell Mom I love her." Then he was executed.

A rare few mistaken cases would be one kind of problem; a litany of them represents a far more serious situation. That was the finding in a 2000 study on error rates in capital cases. A group of scholar-attorneys investigated all 5,760 death sentences issued in thirty-four states between 1973 and 1995. The work took them nine years. They discovered that appeals courts found serious, reversible, prejudicial errors in *68 percent* of the death sentences. Forty-seven percent of the sentences were thrown out wholesale, and there were major flaws in 40 percent of the remainder. Eighty-two percent of the cases that went to retrial resulted in lesser sentences. Seven percent of the time, the person who had been sentenced to death was subsequently found innocent.

In all, the authors said, their findings "reveal a death penalty system collapsing under the weight of its own mistakes. They reveal a system in which lives and public order are at stake, yet for decades has made more mistakes than we would tolerate in far less important activities. They reveal a system that is wasteful and broken and needs to be addressed."

The governor of Illinois declared a moratorium on executions in that state. The legislature in Nebraska followed suit, only to have the governor veto that bill. Nebraska lawmakers responded with funding for a study of that state's capital punishment system. Florida and Mississippi have acted to improve the quality of defense lawyering. Legislators in Indiana, Maryland, New Hampshire, and Oregon are either studying the fairness of their state's capital punishment convictions or facing protests in favor of eliminating the death penalty altogether.

U.S. Supreme Court Justice David Souter, dissenting in a 2006 decision that upheld the death penalty in a murder case, noted "an unusually high incidence of false conviction, probably owing to the combined difficulty of investigating without help from the victim, intense pressure to get convictions in homicide cases and the corresponding incentive for the guilty to frame the innocent."

That concern apparently did not trouble Justice Antonin Scalia, who wrote in the same case, "One cannot have a system of criminal punishment without accepting the possibility that someone will be punished mistakenly." As for the many exonerations, Scalia continued, "Reversal of an erroneous conviction demonstrates not the failure of the system but its success."

It might be hard to persuade the Innocence Project's clients, whose total incarceration surpasses twenty-six hundred years, that their experience marks a success. Judges who are more accepting of the uncomfortable realities of capital punishment admit that exoner-ations make them question the system over which they preside.

"On six separate occasions it was my duty to be in our office at six-thirty in the morning for an execution that was scheduled for seven o'clock," recalls Gerald Kogan, former chief justice of the Florida Supreme Court. The procedure involved a conference call with gover-nor's counsel and the warden at the state prison, to confirm that there were no last-minute stays or delays. By then the prisoner was already strapped into the electric chair. After the conversation, the judge would stay on the line while the sentence was carried out immedi-ately. Then the warden would come back on the line to pronounce the time of death.

Kogan remembers what he would do during those phone confer-ences: "Pray to God that this person is truly guilty.... The responsi-bility just sits on your shoulders.

"As human beings in a civilized society, we must do everything within our power to make sure the innocent in this country are not put to death. I have learned the imperfections in our system. Is it worth executing one innocent person just to get the other scoun-drels? . . . I know for a fact that we have, on occasions in the past, ex-ecuted people who are in fact innocent."

As that thinking spread, so did Barry's influence. Although he still argued cases and filed motions, his work enlarged: educating other lawyers, helping jurisdictions that wanted to improve, testify-ing before legislatures, and eventually instructing members of Con-gress.

"One of his gifts is that he anticipates what people are going to be cynical about," explains Rebecca Brown, who works in the Innocence Project's policy division. "Whatever their skepticism, he puts the ques-tion right out there at the start. It defuses people. Let's move past whatever emotions we feel and look at the science. He is very conver-sational, and very effective."

The other essential attribute Barry brings to those presentations is familiarity with decades of wrongful imprisonments. "Always at his fingertips he has ten or twenty case examples of why a policy change is important. He talks about these individuals who were mistreated, and it humanizes it for lawmakers."

Barry rose in legal circles, eventually becoming president of the National Association of Criminal Defense Attorneys—a group with nearly fifty thousand direct and affiliate members. His face appeared in newspapers. His life became increasingly consumed by the project's work.

"You get emails at four o'clock in the morning, literally," Brown says. "When does this person sleep?"

Barry did make time for two things: family—his wife, son, and daughter—and Yankees games. "But then he goes right to defense conferences, to being in a courtroom, advocacy, litigation," Brown says.

Barry and Peter's work began to gain traction outside of courtrooms. As awareness of faulty criminal defense work spread, some hawks on crime began to realize that perpetuating injustice makes no one safer.

U.S. Senator Patrick Leahy, a former prosecutor and now Judiciary Committee chairman, held a news conference in 2000 in which Innocence Project exonerees told Congress and the Beltway media about what had been done to their lives. By then Barry and Peter were national leaders in criminal justice reform, and they flanked Leahy at the event.

"The American people are entitled to something better than 'Whoops,'" Leahy said. The criminal justice system is making so many errors, he added, that it appears "medieval."

"I've prosecuted murders," Leahy said. "It is one thing to be tough on crime. It's another thing to do what the American people want us to do—make sure the criminal justice system works."

A recent Virginia case again proves that the system often does not work. Four sailors, charged in a 1997 rape and murder, were told that they had to confess or they would face execution. They later recanted and another man confessed to the crime. His DNA matched evidence at the scene.

Under Virginia law a retrial is not possible, nor can a judge commute a sentence. It takes a gubernatorial pardon. Thirty retired

FBI agents called on Governor Tim Kaine in 2008 to pardon the sailors. Former attorneys general and members of the original jury also called for these men to be freed. In August 2009 Kaine gave the sailors conditional pardons; they still must register as sex offenders. As for the timeliness of this half-response, the pardons came after these men had served more than eleven years. One of them was already free, having served his complete sentence.

Justice should not be so arbitrary or so political, Barry Scheck argues.

"We've always noted the spiritual power and moral force of these exonerations," he says. "It reveals a total system failure. What we need is Innocence Commissions, like they have in Britain and Canada, that investigate what went wrong and how it can be prevented from happening again. Like the National Transportation Safety Board does in the U.S., right? If a plane goes down, they do a complete investigation. We need that in criminal justice, after every exoneration. Otherwise the integrity, legitimacy, and confidence in the system collapses."

Shy of that step, the Innocence Project's exonerations have influenced state and local policies. Hundreds of jurisdictions, for example, have begun videotaping interrogations. That investment should have a profound effect on reducing false confessions. Some jurisdictions have likewise embraced new standards for naming suspects and conducting lineups, to minimize the risk of misidentification. A few states even enacted laws permitting courts to consider new evidence that arises after a conviction.

In Maryland, for example, Bernard Webster was charged with rape when he was eighteen. The victim and other witnesses identified him. After that state passed a post-conviction evidence law, DNA proved he had not committed the crime. Granted, by then he was forty years old. He had missed a huge and irreplaceable portion of his life. But at least he was free.

EACH TIME THE Innocence Project wins another prisoner's release, the implicit question about the quality of American criminal justice looms larger. The United States incarcerates more of its population than any other nation on earth. There are now 2.3 million people in jail in this country. The United States has 5 percent of the world's population, but nearly 25 percent of the world's prisoners. We jail people at five times the rate of England, nine times the rate of Germany, twelve times the rate of Japan.

Quite apart from the issue of whether mass incarceration has made Americans safer—our violent crime rate still vastly exceeds the rest of the world—what about cases in which there is no DNA evidence? There's no skin left behind at a bank robbery, no semen at a carjacking. But countless convictions in those crimes have depended on precisely the kinds of evidence the Innocence Project has revealed to be unreliable: snitches, forced confessions, and misidentifications.

Are we Americans able to have an honest conversation about how many people, out of those 2.3 million, should not be in jail?

IN APRIL 2006, the state lab came back with the report from VJ's rape kit. The scientists had obtained only a partial result, an incomplete profile. The private lab managed a full profile, however, and its results did not contradict the state lab's findings. Meanwhile the state drew fresh blood from Alan, for comparison with the rape-kit DNA. The subsequent court filing put it succinctly: "The DNA testing by both laboratories conclusively excludes Mr. Newton as the source of the sperm recovered from VJ immediately after the rape."

That filing, which asked the court to vacate his sentence, was signed not only by Potkin but by District Attorney Koenderman as well.

"She was the epitome of a prosecutor working to get the truth in a case," Potkin says. "Too often we encounter prosecutors who try to find some new way of seeing the case. You could tell she really felt the magnitude of the situation—not the callous attitude that this is just the cost of doing business, but the devastation, you could tell she knew it."

"She was subsequently appointed to a criminal court judgeship," adds Alan, who has followed Koenderman's career. "People like her need to be put in a position where they can do more good."

Waiting for the results, and for the joint filing to receive court action, made doing time suddenly harder for Alan. "I was on pins and needles all those months. Come on, people, hurry up and get me out of here."

All the pent-up emotion eventually led to a fistfight. "Because of all the frustration, it happened. Over a stupid thing too, a fan. It was hot as hell in there that month."

Alan was placed in solitary confinement, which he actually welcomed. "I didn't fight it. I knew I was going home. I figured, I'll just lay back and not have to worry about going back into the population. 'Cause I was going home."

Finally word came for Alan's transfer to New York City for a hearing. "Well, there's a holding facility, different buses, they always have to do everything a certain way. I had seven days of making my way to court."

No one told him to pack his things. They all assumed he would be coming right back. Alan knew differently. "I gave away most of my stuff. When I come home, there's nothing here that I'll need. It was like you're cleaning yourself."

He arrived at Rikers Island on a Wednesday afternoon, the fifth of July. A close friend brought a new tan suit for Alan to wear in court. "I didn't want to be wearing some jailhouse jumper suit, no sir. Especially if I'm going to be walking out the door."

On the sixth, he remembers, "They said, 'You're going to court this morning.' So I was washing up in the bullpen. I didn't know that the Innocence Project had put the story out, and it was in the newspaper. But I'm on the bus on my way to court and I hear my name on the radio. I'm baffled. A little later one of the corrections officers comes over with a paper and says, 'Hey man, this is about you.' And there's me, in my high school graduation picture. They were already treating me differently."

WINNING A MAN his freedom is only the first step in restoring a life with decades taken away. For many Innocence Project clients the task of rebuilding, of reentering the functioning world, can be its own prison. These men exist in the justice system's limbo—not qualifying even for the modest supports that convicts receive. Thus no government aid exists to help them find work, housing, health insurance, stability. Some states treat these catastrophic errors so cavalierly, it is breathtaking.

Charles Chatman was serving ninety-nine years in Texas for rape when the Innocence Project won him DNA testing that proved his wrongful conviction. His exoneration was, by the way, the fifteenth in Dallas County since 2001. When Chatman came to court for his hearing in January 2008, the judge offered to buy him a steak dinner.

Still, that surpasses what Michael Anthony Williams received. He was only sixteen when, because of misidentification by the victim, he was sentenced to life for aggravated rape. After he'd served more than twenty-three years, DNA testing proved his innocence. Because he was not a parolee, though, nor a prisoner who had served his full sentence, Williams was ineligible for the state's reentry programs. Instead the Louisiana Department of Corrections gave him a check for ten dollars.

"You can never make people whole," Barry says. "But when they have lost years and years of their lives, wrongfully? It doesn't matter whose fault it is. If you're in a democracy and the system makes a mistake, you have to compensate the victims."

THE COURT HEARING Alan's release motion opened at nine, but his case was not scheduled till ten-thirty. "I always had patience," he says, "but by then I was feeling joy. Just joy."

Alan was still in handcuffs when he came before Judge John C. Byrnes. The courtroom was windowless, utilitarian. The usual crowd of people awaiting arraignment for minor offenses was squeezed into the seating area. So was Alan's extended family, dressed in Sunday best.

The judge reviewed the filing. Potkin, with Barry Scheck at her side, offered the motion for Alan's sentence to be vacated. Koenderman stood and agreed. There was more paperwork to be resolved. Alan was moved to a holding cell just behind the courtroom.

He laughs at the memory. "I waited twenty-two years, I guess I could wait another hour."

"We were making a million cell phone calls," Potkin says. "Getting information to Rikers Island that he's being released, that sort of thing."

Then, at 10:47, the judge ordered Alan Newton released.

His family cheered. There were countless hugs and tears of joy. Alan's brothers teased him about his out-of-date haircut. The people awaiting arraignment pumped their fists in the air for him. Potkin warned him there would be a crush of people outside.

"I took a public speaking class during my time," Alan says. "We had done a group project and I'd read with my head down, didn't raise my eyes. But now I knew. So they stuck a camera in my face and I was able to speak freely."

In an impromptu press conference in the hallway, Koenderman used the moment to issue a public apology. "I'm sorry for the time that was lost to you. What I did in this case, I would do in any case."

In the next day's newspaper photos, Potkin is invariably smiling. But Barry's face looks wistful and pinched, as if he might be in pain.

One reporter asked Alan how he felt about VJ. He paused before answering. "I got sympathy for the victim. Neither one of us received any justice."

Later he elaborated: VJ had experienced what he called a "heinous thing." Her rapist was still at large, and probably had committed more crimes. Alan felt oddly relieved that she was no longer alive, so she would not have to bear the weight of having helped send the wrong man to jail.

He and Potkin went to Amy Ruth's soul food restaurant in Harlem. His nephew handed him a cell phone, an unfamiliar device. After some joking instruction, Alan used it to take pictures of his family and lawyers.

On his second day of freedom, Alan decided to visit the Innocence Project offices. The staff was celebrating his exoneration, so he joined them. It was karaoke time.

"At first I thought, what the hell am I doing here?" Alan says. "I mean, I got out on Thursday and here it's Friday and I'm out singing with these people. But then they got a room, so it wasn't in front of a whole lot of strangers, more personal. Then I was okay. It just felt good to have the opportunity to do that."

When the music was finished, Alan Newton went home. And at the age of forty-five, he began his life.

"I had no intentions of doing anything. It was summertime. I wanted to go sit in the park. Go to the pool. I needed to get my mind home along with my body."

One morning Alan was returning to his bedroom from the shower when he realized he had brought his toiletries. "In prison, all the showers are always communal. So you take away your stuff. I had to remember I was home now. I could leave my shampoo and nobody was going to take it."

Alan returned to a different world. While he was in jail, the nation had elected four presidents. Apple sold its first personal computer shortly after he was arrested, and now everyone was connected through these odd new entities: Facebook, YouTube, eBay. The stock market had soared from two thousand to eleven thousand and beyond, creating thousands of new millionaires. An antigovernment former soldier blew up a van in Oklahoma City, killing 168. Virginia elected the nation's first African American governor, and New York City its first black mayor. A sheep was cloned. Toyota began selling a car that ran only partly on gas. A new millennium arrived. Massachusetts legalized same-sex marriage. An American cyclist won the Tour de France seven times. The United States invaded Iraq twice, the second time toppling and arresting Saddam Hussein.

The changes in Alan's personal life were equally huge. His mother and father had both died while he was in prison. The company where Alan had worked no longer existed. The giant towers to which he had commuted were destroyed by terrorists. Though he had not been in contact with his former fiancée in years, they did meet after his release.

"She moved on, unfortunately," Alan says. "The time that I had, the distance . . . it was a tough thing for both of us. She moved on. Funny thing, since I was in her bed at the time the crime happened."

Alan's exoneration received considerable local media attention. Mark Cornell, chief executive of the premium liquor distributor Moët Hennessy USA, saw him on the evening news and phoned Noel Hankin, the company's senior vice president for multicultural relations. "He asked me to reach out to Alan," Hankin remembers. "I'd seen it on TV too. I thought, wow. It wasn't just a man being released. Alan also seemed to be very balanced, not bitter, no signs of anger. It was amazing how composed and brave he was."

The NAACP was holding its national conference in Washington, D.C., the following week. Moët Hennessy was sponsoring a dinner for the group's board, and Hankin invited Alan to be his guest.

"I knew that after twenty-two years, it would be a lot for him to travel by himself. So we arranged for his sister to come too. They traveled down by Amtrak, and in a nice Washington hotel I met Alan for the first time."

At the dinner, Hankin had a turn at the podium. He looked out at the crowd—the brain trust of the NAACP, chairman Julian Bond, New York chapter president Hazel Dukes—and he began to tell Alan's story.

"You could see the crowd hanging on every word," Hankin recalls. "And then I introduced Alan. He came up to speak; he handles himself well behind a microphone. He really blew them away."

Hankin, as you might have guessed, has all the attributes of an authentic patriot: In addition to his day job, he is a leader of the New York Urban League, and was a founder of the Thurgood Marshall College Fund. This organization has raised more than $68 million to help some six thousand African American men and women attend historically black colleges and law schools. He told the fund's president about Alan, pointing out his excellent grades before the arrest and solid schoolwork while incarcerated. Soon Alan had a full scholarship to Medgar Evers College at the City University of New York. Less than ten weeks after leaving jail, Alan was a college student. Two years later, when he graduated, the crowd gave him a standing ovation. Hankin threw a party for him that night at company headquarters, with a photo of Alan receiving his diploma enlarged to the size of a poster.

Alan stayed with the college after graduation, recruiting young men to attend and helping them stay enrolled when times are hard. But his sights do not end there. In early 2009 Alan took the Law School Admission Test (LSAT). "I am trying to come full circle. There's a lot of people needing access to decent legal assistance."

So Alan has achieved the clearest sign of a man who is free: He is dreaming again, hopeful for the future and its unlimited potential. He is also showing signs of a person destined to become an authentic patriot.

A few days before the law school exam, he visited the Innocence Project offices again. All down the corridor people called out, "Hey, Alan's here." They left their computers, they came out of their offices. And Alan moved down the hallway, giving and receiving hug after hug.

Freeing Alan Newton does not erase the injustice done to him, Barry Scheck says. Nor does it mean that criminal justice is chastened or reformed. As of this writing, thirty months after Alan's release, the Innocence Project has cleared the names of fifty-three more men. That's about one every seventeen days.

The most recent was Timothy Cole. He was a twenty-five-year-old college student in 1985 when police arrested him for carjacking Meredith Mallin and raping her at knifepoint in a vacant lot outside Lubbock, Texas.

Her rapist smoked constantly during the attack. Cole was a non-smoker with asthma. Mallin's attacker drove the car. Cole's fingerprints were not on the car. Cole had an alibi: His roommate said Cole was studying in his bedroom the whole evening.

Nonetheless, Mallin's identification of him from a photograph brought Cole a twenty-five-year sentence. As he cried later in his cell about being innocent, another inmate overheard. Jerry Wayne Johnson was a heavy smoker charged with two rapes, one of which featured him holding a knife to the throat of a girl as he drove her to a vacant lot outside Lubbock.

Johnson waited ten years, till the statute of limitations had expired on Mallin's case. Then he wrote to the Lubbock court confessing to the rape. When he received no reply he wrote again. No answer. Johnson wrote to the prosecutor in the case, and did not hear back.

Finally, from prison, he wrote to Cole. It was May 11, 2007. Cole's family went to the media, and the news coverage pressured officials to run DNA tests on the rape kit. They found Johnson's DNA, not Cole's. The Innocence Project in Texas filed motions to clear Cole's name, but the Lubbock courts did not act. Finally a state court did, holding a hearing in February 2009. Mallin herself testified on Cole's behalf.

It worked. He was cleared of the crime. But the exoneration arrived ten years too late. Timothy Cole's asthma had worsened in prison, and he died in 1999, after fourteen years in jail for a crime he did not commit—and four years after the actual rapist had first tried to confess.

"Every human being has an innate sense of justice," Barry says. "Every human being is offended at a deep and personal level by these stories. So it has to lead to change. It has to. I have to believe that it will."

He pushes his hair back with both hands. "These men have suffered in ways you and I, as free people, cannot even begin to imagine. I have to believe. . . ." His throat clenches. He takes a deep breath, rubs his face hard with both hands, then holds them up as fists. "I have to hold on tight to the faith that their suffering is not in vain. It must not be wasted. They can instruct us. They can teach us how to achieve genuine justice. They have experienced so much pain."

Barry Scheck lays both hands gently on the table. "I have to believe that their pain has a purpose."

And he weeps.

9

The Win-Win-Win-Win-Win

What's the use of a fine house if you haven't got a tolerable planet to put it on?

— HENRY DAVID THOREAU

What we call Man's Power over Nature turns out to be a power exercised by some men over other men with Nature as its instrument.

— C. S. LEWIS

THE PUPPY DID NOT yet have a name, that rainy day in 1998 when Majora Carter rescued her. This was a true mutt, a street dog of the city whose markings hinted at German Shepherd parentage.

"She turned out to be much bigger than I'd anticipated," Majora remembers. So she named the dog Xena, after the mighty warrior princess who battled evil in comic books and on TV.

Just as Xena the superheroine has the bard Gabrielle as her ally and guide, Xena the dog had thirty-two-year-old Majora feeding her, giving her a warm place to sleep, running her each day around the neighborhood. If these sound like ordinary tasks, however, this was no ordinary community.

Majora lived in the South Bronx of New York City. Within walking distance of her home—and within smelling distance—stood a massive treatment plant that turned sewage into fertilizer pellets.

There was an ordinary sewage plant as well. The neighborhood also had four power plants. It possessed numerous trash facilities serving hundreds of thousands of people. It was home to the largest food distribution center in the world. These industrial uses and others meant sixty thousand truck trips through the neighborhood—noise, traffic, diesel exhaust—every week.

Although you might think no one would want to live in such a place, the community was home to tens of thousands of people, crowded into two thousand per acre. Trapped by an inability both to sell their houses and to afford property elsewhere, they endured one of the lowest ratios of parks to people of any city in the nation. With so much air pollution and so little green space, one-quarter of the children had asthma; in fact, the local asthma hospitalization rate was double the national average. Meanwhile, because there was nowhere decent to walk or jog, the rate of obesity soared to levels exceeding almost everywhere else in the country.

Not surprisingly, people living in such a place suffer other degradations on top of the environmental ones. Unemployment remains high, as does crime. Per capita income is $13,959 a year, making Majora's community the poorest large urban area in America.

And what of pride? And of hope, and of the belief in opportunity that defines the American character? They were buried deep in the hearts of the people. Amid poverty, neglect, and the constantly reinforced message that the neighborhood was fit primarily to be a dump, the community's spirits were every bit as depressed as the prospects for decent jobs.

And yet these circumstances were not dire enough. They could become worse. At the time Majora adopted Xena, her community was also the proposed site for a new facility to handle 40 percent of the commercial waste of America's most populous city. More trash, more trucks, more stench, more erosion of livability, deeper entrenchment of the idea that this area was unfit for decent treatment and its people unworthy of basics such as clean air.

Not, in all, an ideal place to walk a dog. If ever there was a community in America that one ought to escape at all cost, this was it.

Who would be the Xena for the South Bronx? What warrior princess would fly to the rescue?

MAJORA CARTER WAS born in 1966, the youngest of ten children. Her father, an older man who was the son of a slave, had been a Pullman porter. He moved to the South Bronx and worked various jobs before becoming a janitor at a juvenile detention center. In those days the neighborhood was working class, with a mix of races and ethnicities. The primary job for Majora's mother was raising six boys and four girls. Later she worked at a residential facility for mentally disabled adults.

During the family's early years, the urban planner Robert Moses began his landscape-changing work. At one time hailed as a transportation visionary—especially for moving city people efficiently to and from surrounding rural areas—Moses built many highways. One in particular, designed to ferry wealthy New Yorkers from Westchester County to their Manhattan jobs and home again, sliced through the South Bronx like a scalpel through a healthy organ.

Time revealed that Moses' focus on highway endpoints meant that he paid too scant attention to the lands along the way. Speed for some came at the expense of quality of life for others. The highway became a wall that could not be breached. Neighborhoods were broken, air quality fell, people no longer walked to work or shops or church. In Majora's community, white flight turned a vibrant and diverse area into a concentration of low-income families and minorities. Redlining—the practice of banks setting geographic boundaries within which they will not provide loans—completed the fall. Businesses failed, jobs dwindled, people's houses became unsellable.

"My family's property was worthless," Majora recalls, "save that it was our home. Luckily for me that home, and the love inside it—with help from mentors, teachers, and friends—was enough."

A three-bedroom house with ten children meant sleeping three or four to a room. It was a life of hand-me-downs, of always scrimping, of what Majora calls "total poverty . . . There was a crack house across the street."

A series of arsons in the 1970s left indelible images in young Majora's mind: buildings burning on her own block, neighbors going up and down the fire escapes to rescue friends, and most inexplicably to a seven-year-old girl, the fire trucks not coming.

Then her brother Lenny, who had served two tours in Vietnam, returned to the States and the South Bronx—only to be gunned down a few blocks from home. He was shot above his left eye.

So from her earliest days, Majora had one ambition. "I wanted to leave this neighborhood so badly. I lied about being from here. I knew that to be successful, I would have to leave this place."

She may as well have dreamed of growing wings. Escape from the cycles of minimal opportunity is all but impossible, as millions of impoverished people have shown through generations. But it can be done; Colin Powell, the son of immigrants from Jamaica, transcended his South Bronx origins to become the nation's first black secretary of state. For every Colin Powell, though, there are hundreds of thousands in jail, or in virtual prisons of want and despair.

In grade school Majora simply aimed as high as anyone could imagine: She would be a neurosurgeon. "I was fascinated with the nervous system, that the brain had different chambers doing different things."

Teachers spotted her intellectual curiosity, and nurtured it. The best avenue upward was the Bronx High School of Science, which had a challenging entrance exam. Tutors worked with four chosen students, Majora among them, preparing for the test.

"Only one other besides me went in," she recalls. Her expression darkens. "But he got into drugs. He's okay now."

Majora escaped those traps thanks to what she calls "home training . . . I don't remember my parents ever explicitly lecturing me about sex or drugs. But they would see my friends acting up and say, 'No home training, that's why they act the fool.' "

Majora learned about a program that paired poor minority students with first-rate medical schools at a young age, to build connections, to foster ambition, to make the point that dreams like becoming a doctor were not unattainable. "I went to Mount Sinai Medical Center, and to the Albert Einstein school, every Saturday. I did cadaver dissection, testing chemicals on frog hearts. I dissected several cats."

The hands-on experience had a definite outcome, but not what others had expected. "I do not want to do this. Instead I got it into my head that I was going to be an actress. My parents were devastated. They wanted a doctor in the family."

The program's benefactors did not give up on Majora. They connected her with arts colleges; they explained how financial aid works. Still, the diminished sights of Majora's community held her back.

"We had an awful guidance counselor. Horrible, abusive. When one college's financial aid office didn't get my stuff, I knew something was wrong. My father and sister went to this counselor's office. They watched her get the papers. They watched her put it in the mailbox."

Majora was accepted at Wesleyan University and she leapt at the chance. "It was a good arts school. It was just far enough away."

Majora had attained her goal of escaping. Perhaps.

WESLEYAN UNIVERSITY, LOCATED in Middletown, Connecticut, was founded by Methodists in 1831. About 2,700 undergraduates occupy its 360 landscaped acres—almost as many people as occupy 1.3 acres in the South Bronx. Admissions are highly selective, with 65 percent of incoming students ranking in the top 10 percent of their high school class. Incoming SAT scores, in writing, verbal, and math tests, average 700 each. The university offers nine hundred courses, forty-six majors, and two hundred student organizations. Alumni recognized as noteworthy on Wesleyan's Web site include a senator, a governor, investors, film directors, TV news correspondents, editors, a football coach with three Super Bowl victories, writers of works as varied as a Pulitzer Prize–winning biography of Martin Luther King Jr. and the Lemony Snicket children's books. Tuition and fees for the 2008–09 academic year run $51,934, with 42 percent of students receiving some form of financial aid.

In other words, Wesleyan stands firmly among the top New England liberal arts colleges. However, of those 176 notable alumni on the college's Web site, the number of African Americans is four. Wesleyan has recruited students of color since the late 1960s, yet even today only 8 percent of the young adults at Wesleyan are black. In 1984, Majora arrived at a place as different from her home as the Everglades. As with medicine, she soon learned that her theatrical path would not be nearly what she had planned.

"I went right into acting. And discovered that I didn't like being on a stage all that much. I became more interested in making films."

Wesleyan's strong arts curriculum nurtured such notions. Majora first learned the basics of film, then chose it for her major. Social comfort did not come as easily.

"I got good at avoiding the topic of where I was from. To be from the South Bronx meant that you were a pimp, a pusher, or a prostitute. It felt like a stain."

Yet when it came to choosing subjects for her work, there were signs that Majora had not left home quite so far behind. When she took a semester off to work on a documentary, for example, it was *The South Bronx Through the Eyes of Children*. When Majora wanted more film-focused schooling, she took a year off from Wesleyan to study at Brooklyn College.

During that time her father died. Her mother was bereft; they had been married fifty-one years. Majora was home then too, and feeling the loss herself.

"I took a walk around. There was a place I came to, where there'd been a fire. It had broken all the windows, and in the lot on the ground there was a blanket of glass. It was a moment for me. Despite how violent the whole image was, with the light glinting off, it was beautiful too."

At once she had the inspiration for her senior project: a film about a young family from her neighborhood, its unrelenting struggles and its unexpected beauties. It would be called *Broken Glass*.

Wesleyan did not like the idea. "They wouldn't let me bring the school equipment to the South Bronx. They were worried. The police chief wrote a letter, saying, 'I'll be responsible for the equipment.' The answer was no. Instead they gave the gear to a guy who made a film in Manhattan, the guy who later did *American Pie*."

Something in the college's decision caused a change in Majora's direction. An inward reflection began, a period of drift, that took time to resolve. Its first expression was the film she ended up making for her senior project, *The Darker Side of Trust.*

"It was about a woman awakening to trust herself," Majora remembers. It was a silent film.

When Majora graduated from college she was the second person in her family to do so. She went right to work in film, a field that requires a long and sometimes degrading apprenticeship. "I worked for nothing, at way too many places," she remembers. In a hurry for adulthood, she also married right away. She applied to New York University's prestigious film school, and was accepted, but she deferred for lack of money.

Within two years, the marriage was in trouble. "I got married stupidly, when I was young young young." The destination was divorce. Suddenly Majora was without work, housing, a partner. There was only one place left to go. "It was a basic thing: I needed a place to stay. That's when I moved back home."

Majora Carter was thirty years old, and right back where she'd started. "It was horrible. I couldn't believe this was what my life was going to be."

THE WOMAN WHO returned, however, was not the child who'd left twelve years before. Majora had sharper eyes now, especially for seeing the neighborhood's subterranean pride. She began volunteering with the Point—a fledgling group working to revive the cultural life of the Hunt's Point area. "I got involved in public arts projects, and there was a surprise. It connected me with an arts community I hadn't even known existed."

In 1997 Majora learned that the city of New York was developing plans for a new waste transfer station in the South Bronx. It would be massive, handling 40 percent of the city's commercial waste.

"I was blown away. I mean, I remembered when I got back here how everyone had had asthma, which I'd dismissed like it was a hereditary thing or an excuse to get out of gym. But then I saw an adult woman going through an attack. It's a scary, scary thing. And here they were proposing *x* thousand more truck trips through the neighborhood. And I said wait a second. Just wait one second."

Seated at a desk as she speaks, Majora begins jabbing her pointed finger into the tabletop. "There are policies that designed my community, and communities like it, to be the way they are. It's not an accident. This area is zoned M3, which means manufacturing, supernoxious, heavy-use industries. Right where people live. New York City zoning laws are not much changed since the 1970s, so when they were written there was no such thing as a waste transfer station."

Majora was also able to examine the issue from another perspective, one her neighborhood did not share: In her time away, she had seen communities that were green—not in the metaphorical environmentalist sense, but in reality. They had trees, lawns, open spaces. Places to gather, places to rest. She had lived that life, and brought the memory back with her. The question was whether, if she protested the new waste proposal, her neighbors would also imagine that vision.

"This community I'd hated, I just assumed people at some level were fine with living this way, that they didn't much care. I know my parents were more forgiving than I was. They were from the South, and had lived through Jim Crow segregation. So my neighbors, they were so used to having this stuff pushed down their throat. 'Girl, where you been? This is what happens.'"

The waste transfer station felt like a personal insult. Majora says city officials essentially told her, "'It's a poor community, what's the difference?' I was outraged. It propelled me to act. It moved my spirit in a way that I didn't know was possible. And it changed my beliefs. It changed the way I felt about myself and my community."

How to defeat this proposal? How to generate the same insulted feeling among her neighbors? Majora decided to trust her creative side, the actress, the filmmaker. "I'm a different kind of activist. And I'm thankful for that. . . . We did street theater. We went to the steps of a public building and showed how much garbage isn't garbage. We put on rubber gloves and aprons and went through it to show how much could be recycled."

Photos from that time show an attractive woman with dreadlocks who is smiling while she protests. Her energy was contagious. At later events, more people from the neighborhood joined in. "We had a garbage parade, and walked up and down Hunt's Point Avenue. I was wearing a recycling bag, had a hairdo out of Coke cans."

As the community spirit rose, Majora realized that lifting people's hopes was as important as improving their environment—if not more so. With that understanding, she accepted the path before her. "'Okay,' I said, 'this is what I'm doing.' I wasn't going anywhere."

In 1998 Majora founded Sustainable South Bronx—a nonprofit organization whose goal was not merely to oppose bad ideas, but to offer new ones. The idea of sustainability was to make changes that would endure longer than one activist's involvement, one administration in City Hall, one generation in the community. "I wanted to play offense, not defense."

The city showed begrudging respect for her initiative: The Parks Department offered to connect her with a federal grant for green space planning. The size of the grant? Ten thousand dollars.

"I thought it was well-meaning, but naive," she remembers. Given the scale of the problems, what could so small a sum accomplish?

Then came the morning she went jogging with Xena. The dog, though not yet full grown, had a strong will and a stronger pull. As they passed one side street, Xena turned hard. At the leash's other end, Majora had to follow. They headed directly into an illegal dump.

"There were weeds, garbage, trash, things I don't even want to tell you about. But she kept pulling me, dragging me along. We went through all that junk, and lo and behold: There was the river."

The Bronx River is actually the only freshwater river in New York City; the others are estuarial, with a mix of fresh and seawater. Beginning at the Kensico Reservoir north of White Plains, the river flows southward for about twenty-three miles, then joins the East River to spill into Long Island Sound.

Fresh water does not mean clean water. In the 1800s the river received industrial wastes steadily. In the twentieth century, it suffered intermittent raw sewage discharges from communities in Westchester County, as well as the side effects of running beside the Bronx River Parkway.

Where anyone else saw just another illegal dump, however, Majora stood with her dog and envisioned something completely different: a park. A green and clean gathering place, where people of the poorest urban area in America could experience the benefits of nature on a local scale. A park, in a borough that had seen no new green space in sixty years. A park, in a community that had been downstream of the sewage pipes and downhill of the trash bins for generations. A park, because everyone deserves a share in the benefits of a livable environment. A park.

"At that time I knew nothing about zoning, environmental impacts, policies that lead to disenfranchisement." She holds up her fingers to make a zero. "Not a bit. I was not an environmentalist. I just wanted to have something beautiful for me and my neighbors."

In 1962, Rachel Carson's book *Silent Spring* awakened Americans to the damage humanity was inflicting on the planet, and environmentalism was born. The nation already had a strong conservationist tradition, built on the ideas of people as different as Theodore Roosevelt, John Muir, and Henry David Thoreau. For reasons that were social, economic and above all moral, the goal of this ethos was to esteem nature, to respect and preserve it.

Carson's book walked much the same path. Its power, by raising awareness that mankind was poisoning the air, soil, and waters, was in transforming the conservation tradition into something more populist. *Silent Spring* launched a movement that has grown in strength with each subsequent year. Reverence for nature became a political force. The first results were such things as the ban on the pesticide DDT. But much larger government steps followed, such as the Endangered Species Act to protect plants and animals from vanishing because of human damage to the environment.

The biggest effect, though, was on Americans' minds. Even people who have never read Carson's book nonetheless recycle, eat organic food, support bike paths, participate in neighborhood cleanup days. These individual efforts have fostered group behavior too, with organizations formed to protect whales from harpoons, dolphins and turtles from fishing nets, old-growth trees from chain saws, birds from deforestation, butterflies from development, bats from paving, wetlands from farming.

On each step of this long history, from Walden Pond to the latest protests against the environmental dangers of globalized trade, the movement has been about *nature*. Wilderness, the plants, the animals all need and deserve human care and protection. Even today's growing and belated clamor about climate change has concentrated on the natural world foremost: the dwindling of polar bear populations, the shrinking of ice caps, the opening of northern seas, the migration or extinction of species.

Well and good. However, far too little attention has been paid, over all of these years, to the *human* consequences of environmental policy. Certain upsetting incidents remind everyone that people live in the earth's environment too: families forced to move away from the toxic Love Canal, elderly folks who died in a Chicago heat wave one summer, the powerful object lesson of Hurricane Katrina, which hit with such force in part because the waters of the Gulf of Mexico were unusually warm.

But the main focus has been on nature, not humans. People have spoken of canaries in coal mines—the emblematic metaphor of warning of diminishing air quality—without noticing that a portion of humanity was already serving just that purpose.

That is, while the world anticipates the irreparable degradation of nature if policies and practices do not change, there are communities feeling that degradation already, right now, today. Not polar bears—people. Recycling is more than just a pretty idea if you live in the place where trash goes. Likewise the high asthma rates in the South Bronx are a perfectly predictable and logical result of the air quality. The South Bronx is unusual only in degree; the air is bad in similar communities all over the country. Environmental policy is not just damaging birds and trees and whatever fish might survive in the turbid Bronx River. It is harming human beings.

More to the point, the harm does not occur to all humans equally. Race and class are brutally reliable predictors of the quality of a community's environment. If you are poor, if your skin is not white, you are simply much less likely in the United States to enjoy clean air and water and green spaces. It turns out that America routinely, and one hopes unwittingly, commits acts of environmental racism.

Does that sound extreme? The same year Majora formed Sustainable South Bronx, a professor from Clark Atlanta University wrote a paper for the Environmental Racism Forum World Summit in Johannesburg, South Africa.

Robert Bullard, Ph.D., began his remarks by recalling a 1982 incident in Warren County, North Carolina. Fourteen counties in that state had 210 miles of roadsides sprayed with thirty thousand gallons of oil that had been contaminated with carcinogenic PCBs. When the soil was removed in 1982, it went to a landfill just south of Warrenton. The toxic dirt, sixty thousand tons of it, was piled twenty-five feet deep. The local township, population 1,300, is 69 percent nonwhite, with 20 percent of incomes below the federal poverty level. When locals organized and protested the dump, more than five hundred were arrested. Their experience was not unusual, Bullard said:

> The U.S. has some of the best environmental laws in the world. However . . . all communities are not created equal. Environmental regulations have not achieved uniform benefits across all segments of society. Some communities are routinely poisoned while the government looks the other way. . . .
>
> People of color around the world must contend with dirty air and drinking water, and the location of noxious facilities such as municipal landfills, incinerators, hazardous waste treatment, storage, and disposal facilities owned by private industry, government, and even the military.

Soon after the Warren County incident, a federal study found that 75 percent of the commercial hazardous waste landfills in Southern states were located in predominantly African American communities, although blacks comprised only 20 percent of the population.

The problem is not limited to black communities, though. Native Americans bear a heavy burden too. Sixteen reservations have been the target of nuclear waste dump proposals, among 317 reservations threatened by environmental hazards overall. The lands of the Western Shoshone in Nevada have been irreparably damaged by roughly a thousand atomic explosions. To the Shoshone, that makes their home the most bombed nation on earth. Toxins from 648 military installations in Alaska threaten the environmental quality of native people in that state.

The pattern persists whether the communities are rural or urban. More than 70 percent of blacks and half of Latinos in the South Coast Air Basin of Los Angeles live with highly polluted air, while only 34 percent of whites live in such conditions.

The pattern persists offshore too. Even though the island of Vieques, off Puerto Rico, has nine thousand inhabitants, it served as a bombing practice site for the U.S. Navy for sixty-two years.

These examples of environmental degradation, primarily affecting low-income people, do not occur inadvertently. They are the result of decisions, policies, and long-standing habits. As Bullard wrote elsewhere, "In Houston, Texas, the only major American city that does not have zoning, . . . city government and private industry targeted landfills, incinerators, and garbage dumps for Houston's black neighborhoods for more than five decades."

Moreover, Bullard said in the South African address, environmental conditions and economic conditions are connected:

> There is a direct correlation between exploitation of land and exploitation of people. The most polluted communities are also the communities with crumbling infrastructure, economic disinvestment, deteriorating housing, inadequate schools, chronic unemployment, high poverty, and overloaded health care systems.

Consider just one illustration. Childhood asthma, the scourge of the South Bronx, causes 10 million missed school days in America each year. Guess which kids are affected? Asthma causes 1.2 million emergency room visits annually, 15 million outpatient visits, half a million hospitalizations. Guess who?

AS WITH MANY of the other toughest problems of our time, government is either indifferent to the problem of environmental justice, or presents obstacles to its improvement. Local zoning permits allow polluting industries to locate beside low-income neighborhoods.

Regional planning routes trucks through minority communities. State regulations foster NIMBYism; people with political access can count on landfill operations and sewage treatment to happen out of sight and hearing, without regard to whose home may not enjoy a similar distance from the smell. Federal policies direct where highways, rail yards, and other industrial infrastructures are built, and federal agencies issue air-quality release permits for everything from smokestacks to truck exhaust pipes.

Does the free market do any better? On the contrary, protection of property values is a top priority. There will be no landfills in affluent places, nor truck routes through nice neighborhoods. Indeed, from a capitalist viewpoint, poor communities are ideal locations for industries with a large environmental footprint: Land is cheap, influence at city hall is minimal, and protests are generally weak because the residents are woefully accustomed to being trod upon. The free market could not care less who breathes dirty air, so long as it does not increase the costs of doing business.

Thus, if Chicago constructs public housing, it will accept this rationale and economize by building in urban wastelands—like the Altgeld Gardens project, nearly all its residents minorities, which sits within breathing distance of more than twenty heavy polluters. In 2005 those people's risks of pollution-triggered cancer and lung disease were the highest in the nation.

Likewise if Saint Louis builds a school, it may well sit atop a contaminated site. And if it's on the 98 percent black East Side, home to one of the largest hazardous waste incinerators in the world, the children already have one of the nation's highest asthma rates.

Between scholars like Robert Bullard and activists like Majora Carter, change is coming gradually. It begins with calling things by their proper names. The antidote to environmental racism is environmental justice, a notion concrete enough that the EPA has issued a definition of it:

The fair treatment and meaningful involvement of all people regardless of race, color, national origin, or income with respect to the development, implementation, and enforcement of environ-

mental laws, regulations and policies. Fair treatment means that no
group of people, including racial, ethnic, or socio-economic groups,
should bear a disproportionate share of the negative environmental
consequences resulting from industrial, municipal, and commercial operations or the execution of federal, state, local, and tribal
programs and policies.

"We pretty much get an F, as a country, on this," Majora says.
"We've done a miserable job."

The components of environmental justice are many, but three
stand tallest. First, legal avenues must be open to all equally. That
starts with equal standing in the permitting process, equal voice in
hearings, and so on. But equality in the legal process requires attention to details whose primary prerequisite is an attitude among regulators and lawmakers that all people should be included in improving
the environment. Maybe the documents in proposed projects or regulations, for example, should be available not only in City Hall offices,
and not only in English.

The second type of equality is geographic. Undesirable impacts,
from such facilities as incinerators, smelters, refineries, transfer stations, sewage plants, and truck routes should not concentrate in low-
income areas.

The third type of equality is in race and class; no group of people
should endure greater environmental compromise, nor forgo greater
benefits from a clean environment because of skin color or income
level. The lungs of poor people need clean air every bit as much as the
lungs of affluent people.

If you accept that way of thinking, a park in the South Bronx is
not merely a dream, concocted by a headstrong woman and her headstrong dog. For environmentalists who care about the human species,
green space is a necessity, a bare beginning, a down payment toward
many more kinds of environmental and social justice. A park is an
essential first remedy.

As it turned out, those imperatives proved stronger than New
York City's plans for its garbage, or the shortage of money for green
ideas, or the lack of respect for residents of the South Bronx. The

environmental needs of thousands of people had been completely ignored for too long. Majora's park simply had to happen.

HUNT'S POINT RIVERSIDE Park has a fence around its perimeter, but unlike the gray razor wire protecting buildings and parking lots nearby, this one is smooth steel, and painted bright blue. Within, locust trees offer dappled shade for the benches and paths. Here is the only green space on this side of the river as far as the eye can see—and it is not just green. There are daisies, roses, cornflowers, overgrown butterfly bushes with plenty of winged visitors on the purple blossoms. Picnic tables and grills ring a fountain. There's a small amphitheater for musical performances. A dock along the river offers canoe rentals.

Reaching this point took months: hauling away garbage, reclaiming metal, mitigating soil damage, designing and planting and weeding and watering. In other words, it was work.

A major recycling center is located next door, immediately upriver. A bucket loader scoops mounds of plastic onto a barge at the pier, its smokestack belching black with every hoist. But a workman stands at the river's edge, holding a net on a long aluminum pole. Whenever a milk jug or water bottle drops from the barge to the water, he scoops it right up.

How did it happen? Majora leveraged that original ten-thousand-dollar grant three hundred–fold, raising $3 million from the city and others to clean the site, and turn it from trash into treasure.

Sustainable South Bronx, meanwhile, became more than one idealistic woman. It grew into a true community organization, with offices and a growing staff of like-minded thinkers. Renaldo Dasilva had a fast-climbing career with Enterprise Rent-A-Car, but he left that job to join Sustainable South Bronx when he learned about environmental justice.

"That concept was new to me," he says with a grin. "It was like inventing a new wheel."

He'd volunteered for years in community programs, a food shelf. The environment was not a major concern. "I didn't even recycle till I started here. My main thing was at the street level, creating opportunities for people to break cycles. But when you connect the dots of the environment and the economic situation, it was like a light bulb going on."

Sustainable South Bronx drew one idealist after another. Annette Williams had worked at a project that restored decayed parks and gardens. She'd coordinated cleanups along the Bronx River, hauling out tires and trash while planting trees and bushes to stabilize the stream bank. "It was unique because I remembered so many memories there, and to see so many people working together. . . . This river needed us as much as we needed it."

Annette also had fond memories of a Bronx long gone. "Now 233rd Street, that was kind of a 'lover's lane.' I used to walk there with all my girlfriends too. But after Son of Sam, that murderer, you know? You couldn't go there at all. And once we lost it, there was no getting it back."

Majora hired one kindred spirit after another. At one point the press and publicity work required another addition to the staff. The job went to a bearded white man named James Chase—a filmmaker whose role in Majora's life would only grow with the years.

Meanwhile Sustainable South Bronx joined forces with other groups:

- **Mothers on the Move,** which gathers community members on a regular basis to advocate for reducing the smell from the sewage pellet plant, improving maintenance in public housing, opposing local prison construction, and, through the youth division, seeking greater involvement in school policies;
- **Youth Ministries for Peace and Justice,** which develops future leaders through programs such as community wellness, arts and activism, and youth organizing;
- **Rocking the Boat,** which teaches teens responsibility and achievement by building traditional wooden boats and providing on-the-water education.

Leaders of these organizations and others see the situation as something of a chicken-and-egg question, whether Majora's group fostered their growth or benefited from it. The important thing is that it is working, and the park is visible, undeniable proof.

"Most folks have no idea how that park got there," Majora says. "I'm cool with that. What matters is that finally our city determined that we deserved to have something beautiful. And really, what are the things that make people smile? And be proud of where they are?"

By the time the park opened, the waste transfer station idea was on hold. In fact, it never came to pass. The city also had plans for a two-thousand-inmate jail nearby, which at this writing remains likewise stalled.

"New York City wants to spend somewhere around four hundred million dollars to build a jail here on Hunt's Point," explains Rob Crauderueff, policy director at Sustainable South Bronx. "Yet they're saying there's no money to put forward clean tech industry or green jobs development. But which is the better investment? Much of what we advocate is smart economics."

Meanwhile sixty local groups joined to form a powerful coalition, the Bronx River Alliance, to advocate for stronger water protection, more riverside paths, and more parks.

To its credit, the city also embarked on a study of the stench from the sewage pellet plant; early results were inconclusive because the area had so many other sources of bad smells. A group of businesses on Southern Boulevard agreed to tax themselves more highly in order to fund an economic improvement plan. All of this and more, in a place that had been told for two generations that it was a garbage dump.

Majora began to receive recognition for her work. The EPA gave her an award, as did the Fund for the City of New York. The Open Society Institute named her a fellow, and she was an honoree at Court TV's New Chapters in African American History event.

She was, however, just getting warmed up. The work of clearing the site, building the park, and maintaining it gave Majora another idea. If people in the area are chronically underemployed, and if they deserve clean air as much as anyone, why not teach them green skills? If the environment of the South Bronx is going to be improved, why not have local people do the work? How is environmental justice possible without employment opportunity? And how can environmental revitalization contribute to economic revitalization? What about creating a "green-collar" economy?

The answer to all of these questions was Sustainable South Bronx's BEST program: Bronx Environmental Stewardship Training. The intense ten-week course trains applicants from disadvantaged communities in such skills as river and wetlands restoration, water quality testing, hazardous waste cleanup, and proper use of power tools.

During training students receive $350 a week plus subway cards and lunch money—essential support, because the program allows no time for other work. They learn green job skills: landscaping, asbestos abatement, plant and wildlife identification, soil and water quality sampling, and more. The work involves more than textbook scenarios; it's the real thing, from wading in wetlands to donning hazardous material protection suits to climbing trees.

In addition, trainees develop normal workplace behaviors like dealing with a demanding boss, showing up on time, and dressing appropriately. They cultivate life skills they wouldn't otherwise have an opportunity to develop, such as interviewing for jobs, time management, and how to budget better than paycheck to paycheck. At the program's end, graduates receive professional certifications in first aid, field equipment safety, pesticide application, and occupational safety.

BEST brochures actively recruit people with little likelihood of otherwise landing decent jobs: "Individuals with resolved criminal convictions are encouraged to apply." Nonetheless, the program's success rate is astonishing: Of the one hundred and twelve enrollees thus far, three have dropped out. Meanwhile ninety-five have landed jobs and eight went have gone to school.

"We are moving people from welfare to work," Annette Williams says. "They are working with their hands and their minds. They are helping nature and helping themselves. Sometimes there's something they destroyed, someone, or a life with drugs. This restores them."

The need for decent paying jobs is vast. The first BEST semester drew 120 applicants for four positions. The cream of the program's graduates, meanwhile, have stayed on for Majora's next venture, the green roof project.

Here was a way to lower energy costs for building owners, clean the air, reduce a building's impact on climate change, and create jobs.

"It's not a win-win," Majora said. "It's a win-win-win-win-win."

"It's cool, completely cool," explains Dwaine Lee, while giving a tour of a recent green roof installation. These projects replace the typical black tar roof of a South Bronx building with a collection of plants that can grow in the harsh city air. A green roof costs more at the outset, but less over time.

"The chief benefit is the offset to utility bills," Dwaine explains, standing atop a warehouse and office building in the South Bronx. In summer, a black roof absorbs heat, funnels it into the building, and increases cooling costs. In winter, heat escapes through the roof, also at a cost. A green roof has the opposite effect in both seasons. It absorbs heat in summer, reducing cooling needs, and it adds insulation to prevent heat loss in the winter.

That is just the start. A green roof benefits more than the building it sits on. "This roof is taking carbon and particulates out of the air," Dwaine says. "The plant mass cleans the air."

The shallow garden at his feet consists largely of sedum (an ornamental flowering plant), but there are also stands of sage, lavender, mint, and yarrow. "It looks like a regular garden, but it's technically very specific," Dwaine says. "We use a growing medium one-quarter the weight of soil, for example."

A jet leaving LaGuardia airport roars overhead. From the rooftop, the South Bronx appears as it really is: a small residential core surrounded by intense industry.

Dwaine gestures toward the plants. "At one level these are drought-tolerant herbs. The sun hits here hard, with no shade. But the roof has become a mini-ecology too. Local bees discovered it up here, somehow. I've found cocoons for moths and butterflies. We had predatory aphids over there, but then the ladybugs that eat them moved in too."

Green roofs last 50 percent longer than regular ones, lowering building maintenance costs. Growing knowledge of climate change also indicates that dark urban areas become islands of intense heat in summer; green roofs reduce the impact of those islands. But again, that's not all.

"Another great thing is the storm water runoff retention," Dwaine says. Normally rainwater washes dirt off buildings, sidewalks, and streets, carrying it directly into the river. A green roof captures those particles, so water that reaches the river is vastly cleaner. "There's a definite mitigation."

The combination of so many benefits is what makes green roofs worthwhile, Dwaine says. "All of our solutions need to have that multiple bottom line."

There is one more win Dwaine has not mentioned. Talk of bottom lines and mitigation glosses over the fact that he himself is part of the equation. "I grew up in a very, very sketchy area, with extremely shady people. I've been shot, I have a bullet in my leg. Almost everybody I knew had spent time in the penal system."

Problems in his youth followed Dwaine into adulthood. "My good friend Albert just came out after serving seven years. Yeah, and I had two children out of wedlock, two different baby-mamas. I never finished college."

He was drifting, and knew it. "Then one day I heard about this lady and what she's doing in the Bronx. It was so amazing, to see a person of color, someone from my community, doing this. Holy shit, this is what I want to be doing."

He applied to the BEST program and was accepted. "It was intense. Twelve weeks, full-time training program, eight to four every day on top of my job. It's supposed to be all you're doing, but I couldn't afford to stop working—I was working in a hotel then—because I can't give up my job and still pay rent and pay child support. I just kind of bit the bullet. It was like ecological boot camp. We had professors from [the state university] Maritime College coming to teach us water quality sampling and testing. Another college's professors taught us identification of vertebrate and invertebrate creatures.

"It's one thing to sit in a classroom and hear about remediation and take notes about it. It's something else to be in the field, to see the teamwork, to see what it's like to depend on another cat."

Dwaine sets his feet wider, puffs out his chest as he calls up the memories. "It was tough, I was sleeping maybe two or three hours a night. And it was tremendous physical work, clearing half an acre of land of invasive species, for example.

"There were times you'd wake up in the morning saying, 'Man, I can't do it, this is just too crazy.' But this was about finding the bigger goal. I can't even imagine how many lifetimes it would have taken me to be exposed to this. It was a sacrifice I was making, in order to move my life completely in another direction."

Today Dwaine is a field manager for the BEST program. During a tour of the roof, it begins to rain. He does not pause in his speech, but opens his palms toward the sky, catching the drops as if he were a plant himself.

WITH MORE ROOFS installed, with stories like Dwaine's becoming more frequent, with more people awakening to the power of environmental justice, Majora went on the lecture circuit—going to other communities to lift their spirits and ambitions. Recognition began pouring in: honorary degrees, public service awards, serving with former President Clinton's Global Initiative, the National Audubon Society's Rachel Carson Award, a MacArthur Foundation "genius" grant, even recognition of her fashion style in a magazine about organic living. In Majora's current office, the awards occupy a long shelf—but with enough room left over for a Godzilla statue from a friend.

The accolades did not translate into ease or wealth, however. "I've worked a lot and did not take any time off. Look, we do this work and . . . well, you absolutely give up things like sleep."

For moral support she has relied on the "Tini Club," a group of older women seasoned in social justice efforts whose gatherings take place around cold martinis. Otherwise, Majora says, "Your personal relationships suffer. We just saw some friends who'd had a kid. He was walking, talking, had a whole set of teeth since we last saw him.

"I don't know how people have kids and do this. I am not programmed that way. If I had to go home right now and make dinner for my child . . . child? I have a proposal to get out."

Yet the work is rewarding, she says, beyond her wildest imaginings. "There is a Buddhist saying that there are three things everybody needs: someone to love, something to do, and something to feel hopeful about."

The Bronx River, for example. The Westchester communities upstream agreed in 2006 to stop allowing sewage overflows into the river. Herons have returned, which means there's a sufficient supply of edible fish. Two beavers have been spotted; one's named José, after U.S. Representative José Serrano, who Majora admires for his persistent efforts to obtain federal cleanup funds for the river. As one indicator that water quality is improving, river herring reintroduced to the river are now returning each year to spawn.

Majora's sights, and the community's, continue to rise. The Sheridan Expressway, with which Robert Moses divided the South Bronx in 1963—they want it taken down. In its place, local residents want affordable housing and more green space. They want tax credits for businesses that install green roof technology. The Bronx River Alliance is close to establishing its goal of a greenway—ten miles of paths and parks along the river.

Environmental gains have come simultaneously with progress on other fronts: Twenty-five hundred units of affordable housing are under construction. Plans for a new high school are taking shape. Economic development ideas include organizing businesses so that the waste products of one are the raw materials for another. It will take a long time before the work is complete, but the South Bronx is on the move.

"If you devalue people," Majora says, "bad things happen and violence will happen. You create the path to domestic terrorists. But it works in the other direction too. I've seen people's lives change dramatically, once they realize they should have never been considered a throwaway person. So how do you set up a society where everyone thinks they can contribute to it? Can we build our community in a way that acknowledges the beauty of the local? The green economy reconnects people—to one another, to community, to healing the world around them."

In a 2009 interview, Majora described the work's healing effect on her personally. "Today the South Bronx is no longer a stain, it's a badge of honor for me. I believe that where I'm from helps me to really see the world. Today, when I say I'm from the South Bronx, I stand up straight. This is home and it always will be."

THE MEN BOATED down the river and arrived to the stirring drone of bagpipes. They drew up to the dock, and off stepped a slender man in a kilt. He took his place at the head of the gathering. It was October 7, 2006.

Down the hill, then, came the Love Brigade: a procession of African drummers. They marched behind a flag that was red, black, and green, the colors of pan-African pride. The red signifies blood, which all people share and which has been shed to achieve freedom. Black represents the black people, whose connection transcends national boundaries. Green symbolizes nature, the abundant natural wealth of the African continent.

Amid that colorful parade strode a tall woman with dreadlocked hair and a brilliant smile. To the beat of drums she strode past the warehouses, past the vacant lots, past the razor wire, across a dirty boulevard, and into the place of quiet and green, an oasis where there were birds, flowers, friends.

There were also compostable paper goods for the meal ahead, and arrangements to take any food waste to the Lower East Side Ecology Center for composting. The party was to be a zero-waste event.

But first, standing before two clergy and among a mix of races and cultures, surrounded by hopeful people with great shared dreams, Majora Carter and James Chase were married. Behind them, just down the hill, reflecting light like millions of pieces of broken glass, time and the power of change flowed silently on.

IO

***

The Gift Everyone Can Give

The individual is capable of both great compassion and great indifference. He has it within him to nourish the former and outgrow the latter.

— NORMAN COUSINS

MARILYN SOFIA WAS CLEANING up dinner when the pains began in her back and arms. She was fifty-two. She did not know that her heart was right then beginning to die.

It was September 28, 1996. Marilyn and her husband, Jack, were down from Kansas City for the weekend at her parents' place, on Truman Lake in southwestern Missouri. Her folks had moved there in the 1980s when her mother developed emphysema. After she died in 1993, Marilyn's dad refused to budge. Sometimes it was a strain for Marilyn and her sister, taking weekend turns caring for their father as he became legally blind and his dependency grew. Marilyn was already busy raising two kids from a previous marriage, plus helping with four from Jack's first marriage. She also worked full time at Bitterman Family Confections, a candy-distributing company in Kansas City. At work Marilyn eased the stress by indulging her serious sweet tooth.

"I love candy, I'm sorry. That was probably the downfall of my health," she jokes.

That, or the smoking. Marilyn puffed away two packs of Newports every day, enough to give her the classic smoker's hack. "That's why I remember the date of my heart attack so much. Everybody remembers the day they quit smoking."

Autumn in Missouri is Southern pleasant. Although the leaves had begun to turn that fall of 1996, Truman Lake was still warm. By then the children were mostly grown; some had kids of their own. Dinner that night was pork chops, vegetables, potatoes smothered in gravy. Marilyn cooked the meal up at the trailer, then brought it down to the main house.

"Jack and the guys were out fishing," she recalls. "The ones there went ahead and ate, 'cause you never know when they're fishing what time they'll be in. Well, when I came back to the trailer I just didn't feel right."

Her sister Wanda strolled up the hill. A nurse, she took one look at Marilyn, and she said, "We're going to the hospital."

It was eighteen miles to the nearest emergency room, in Clinton. The pain spread into Marilyn's jaw. "Now I know that that's where women feel it."

The ER doctor in Clinton immediately diagnosed a heart attack. "It's kind of shocking. I just said, 'Okay, can you fix it?'"

First the doctor gave her pain medicine. Then he asked which of the region's medical centers she preferred for treatment. "I said Saint Luke's right away. I'd heard so much about their Heart Institute."

That meant air transport. While they waited, Jack arrived. "He was pretty worried." But he was not allowed to ride along; there was only room for Marilyn, the pilot, and a nurse. Jack would have to drive the hundred miles to Kansas City. It was her first realization that an illness could also be hard on those who are well. "That would be worse than riding in it," she says, "standing there watching it take off."

Marilyn had been in a helicopter once before, for a tour over the lake. This time there was no sightseeing. The flight took forty minutes. The doctor on duty at Saint Luke's said Marilyn's arteries were too small for bypass surgery, but he would perform an angioplasty. That procedure involves making an incision in the thigh, into which doctors insert a slender tube with a camera attached. They snake the tube through the blood vessels until they see the blockage in an artery supplying blood to the heart. Then they inflate a tiny balloon to open the vessel, and—in Marilyn's case as for many patients—place a springy wire-mesh tube called a stent to keep the artery clear in the future. Although the procedure is serious, it also has a high success rate; about 2 million stents are placed in Americans' blood vessels every year.

Marilyn had so many clogged arteries, the doctors saved some to open the next day. Before they could begin the next angioplasty, though, Marilyn went into cardiac arrest. Her heart stopped.

"I was just lying there watching the monitor, and the next thing I knew someone was on my chest. They had to use the paddles. And the next thing I knew after that, I was in the intensive care unit."

Marilyn spent a week there. One day a doctor came in and told her she would not be going back to work.

"I was crushed," she says. " 'We can't survive,' I told him. I was making good money."

But she had the support of family. "Everybody pitched in. We all got closer." Her grandson Chris, six at the time, caught Jack at a quiet moment and handed him a ring. "Take and give this to Grandma, 'cause this is my lucky ring," Marilyn recalls him saying. "It was a little cheap ring he probably got out of a gum machine, oh yes. But I wore that ring quite a while, till I got out of danger."

Chris's baby brother, Brian, too little even to afford a gumball ring, later gave Marilyn a rock for luck. "I still have that rock. It was on my desk and now it's on the bookcase. And just to be safe I have a little note with it, 'Don't throw away.' "

Marilyn came home from the hospital with a walker and the prospect of a long recovery. "Some people get a rush from their arteries getting cleaned out, feeling stronger, but not me. I couldn't hardly walk, and I was weak. A gal came in three times a week and exercised my leg and stuff. I was determined to graduate to a cane. Still, I didn't drive for about a year."

Meanwhile the plant where Jack worked as a welder closed, and he was out of work. "Can anything else go wrong?" Marilyn asks.

Jack made ends meet by working two jobs, days at the Manley Popcorn Company and nights at General Motors. "You worry about finances," Marilyn says. "We paid the house off, paid the van off. That way whatever happened we wouldn't lose them."

He landed a secure job after that, with Mills Banks—a company that used his welding skills, and better still, showed great flexibility when Jack had to leave for caregiving duty. That necessity came often, as Marilyn landed back in the hospital several times. Doctors told her to try the cardiac rehabilitation program. "I thought, 'I need to do that.'" Her motivation was as much mental as physical; she signed up for the 5 P.M. class, while Jack was at work, to force herself to drive.

She also began studying the heart and her condition. The news was not encouraging, so Marilyn agreed to participate in an experimental drug trial. "It improved my ejection factor, how much it pumps and everything."

The trial disqualified her from being on the list of potential heart transplant patients. In 1998 Marilyn was visiting a friend in the hospital when she began having difficulty breathing. Someone called a nurse, who put a stethoscope on Marilyn's back and sent her straight to the emergency room. She was suffering from flash pulmonary edema, in which lungs rapidly fill with fluid.

"Oh, God, it was horrible," she remembers. "You can't breathe. You're just drowning. You could hear the water in your lungs when you try to breathe. It was really scary."

She recovered, but had a repeat episode in February 1999. She told her daughter-in-law to take her to the hospital immediately. "She was scared to death. So was I, and I knew what it was this time. She pulled into the ER and was just laying on the horn till someone came out with a wheelchair."

The third episode of edema hit two months later. At that point the medical team began moving Marilyn toward the idea of a heart transplant. Her heart would be removed, and some stranger's heart put in its place. For her to live, that stranger would have to die. Before Marilyn could formally become a transplant candidate, though, she had to undergo screening of her health otherwise. The process uncovered a lump in her breast. "That held things up. Luckily it was benign, 'cause otherwise I would have been in big trouble."

She was in big trouble anyway: Her cardiologist, writing a letter to qualify Marilyn for disability insurance payments, said she would live about six to twelve more months. Now, as she went on the list for a donated heart, doctors told her how long the wait typically lasted: six to twelve months.

MICHAEL BORKON WAS born and raised outside of Cleveland, where he grew up a star athlete indifferent to academics. But his world changed on December 3, 1967. That was the day Dr. Christiaan Bernard of South Africa removed the heart of twenty-three-year-old Denise Darvall, who had died in a car accident, and transplanted it into Lewis Washkansky.

"I was so blown away by that," Borkon recalls. "It was like putting a man on the moon."

It put a young man on a path, as well. Borkon was a freshman at Case Western Reserve at the time, but he soon accelerated his education. He applied to the early-admission program in the medical school at Johns Hopkins University: Students complete college and obtain an M.D. in one fast-track swoop. The university accepted him, and he was off to Baltimore.

"I was in heaven from the day I got to Hopkins until the day eighteen years later when I left," he says.

Borkon can rattle off the names of his mentors and teachers, many of them leading surgeons in the country. He remained at Hopkins for his internship and residency, leaving only for a stint at the National Institutes of Health. Other paths beckoned—in research, in obstetrics—but he kept choosing surgery, and remained fascinated by the heart.

"There's something very personal for a physician who can really put his hands on somebody and make them better. This field offered the best medically intellectual challenge, with the hands-on opportunity to deal with patients. There is nothing like the reward."

Recently Borkon saw a brain for the first time in years. "It was just not that impressive. It just sits there. And a liver, well, a liver looks the same in a body as it does at a meat market. But the heart? That is a moving, active, beating organ."

The training had unforeseen dimensions. For example, Borkon had to learn how to approach the families of people who were dying, to ask if they might be willing to donate the patient's organs. It was the beginning of his appreciation for what the donor family experiences, and the possibility of finding something positive amid the sorrow.

"I have seen so many tragedies," he says. "Innocent victims, people who died young, people who died violently. You cannot eliminate grief, but there can be a sense of directed purpose."

Borkon finished his training and joined the faculty at Hopkins. He co-wrote research papers, participated in twenty-five or thirty transplants, and taught. It was rewarding, he recalls, and it was exhausting.

"I was on a collision course. With research, teaching, and operating, there wasn't enough time left in the day. I was going to lose my family. We decided to make a change."

It was 1987, and the Heart Institute at Saint Luke's Hospital in Kansas City was looking for a transplant surgeon. "There is a normal desire to go off on your own, being able to run with a program. Plus Saint Luke's has such a central focus on the patient."

Twenty years later, having held some three hundred hearts, Borkon starts each transplant the same way. "It begins with a prayer. The donor is a very precious and sacred resource. It is an absolutely sacrosanct experience where you must preserve the dignity of the patient and the wishes of the family."

Still, the surgical team retrieving a heart receives what Borkon called "rock-star convenience: We are the last to arrive and the first to leave."

The team—with a surgeon, a resident or surgical fellow, a technician, and a representative of the regional organ bank—arrives when the donor's body is already open. The patient has been pronounced dead, and the family has likely gone home. Borkon rarely meets them. "Anonymity is best."

While his crew scrubs, the liver team is busy with its procurement. "We don't like the word *harvest*," Borkon says. Finally the heart team approaches the donor body. By then the breastbone is opened, and Borkon calls the recipient's surgical team to describe the heart's condition. "We like a heart with a very strong beat, with all chambers moving. There are many ways of assessing—an electrocardiogram, measurements of the pressures inside—but you can look at the heart and pretty well tell. If it was a car accident, it will look pretty bruised up. If it was a gunshot or a head wound, it will look strong."

The team saturates the organ with a cold chemical solution that preserves the glucose—food energy—still in the muscle. As the heart cools, beating stops. "Then the heart is cut out in a predictable way," Borkon says: seven incisions to slice away veins and arteries. It takes two or three minutes.

Borkon calls ahead with the news that the surgery is over. Then the team and heart are airborne as quickly as possible. "Timing is everything. We are racing the clock."

A heart can recover after as long as four hours outside of a body—but the longer the delay, the greater the risk. In times past, the organ recovery team would also conduct the second operation, but now, in the interest of speed, two teams are usually involved.

The recipient's surgical team personnel mirrors the donor's, and after anesthesia the preparation is similar too: the incision, opening the sternum. The patient is connected to a heart-lung machine, as in cardiac bypass surgery, to circulate the blood and maintain breathing. At that point the team removes the diseased heart.

"Then we take the donated heart out of the bucket," Borkon explains. "There is a lot of sewing. It's not very sophisticated. Other surgeries require greater skill, actually. Then we let the heart get new blood flow."

And if such a word is allowed in the surgical theater, that is when the miracle occurs. All by itself, as it warms up, the heart begins to beat.

"It's really cool," Borkon says. "There's nothing neater in the world. Our hearts *want* to beat. There are few things that are as exciting. Maybe the birth of my first son. And then, going out to tell the family their loved one has a new heart? I cry almost every time. I try not to let the family see. But I tear up."

His emotions regarding the donor families may run even stronger, Borkon says. At a recent annual organ-bank picnic, he was asked to speak. "It was hard, though. I had to follow a ten-year-old boy whose dad was a donor. He gave me tremendous inspiration. And when a donor family thanks you, it's humbling. What can you say? You just stand there in awe."

Tara Diane was born in Carthage, Missouri, on December 6, 1985. Her mother and father did not have jobs or stable housing. When Tara was a newborn, the young family lived with Tara's grandfather, Bob Bricker, and his second wife, Charlotte. There were difficulties almost immediately.

"It was the 1980s and drugs were everywhere," Charlotte says. "I had the police come to my house. It got so we couldn't leave the baby. We came home one time and the baby was screaming, and her mom was in there asleep."

When Tara was a few months old, her parents moved out. Her mother "would be gone for weeks, and then call and ask for money, and not even ask about the baby."

Bob worked in tool and die manufacturing, everything from parts for the space shuttle to back supports in car seats. Charlotte worked nights in a cheese factory. Together they raised the baby through infancy, at which point they sought and received temporary legal custody, Charlotte says.

Meanwhile Tara's mother divorced, and later remarried. "She's sober now," Charlotte says. "She is a good mom to two daughters."

Charlotte and Bob's home in Carthage is immaculate, from the neat gardens out front to the spotless kitchen counters. A coffee maker is nearly always on, to satisfy Charlotte's caffeine habit. Bob is an involved grandparent who does things such as taking a grandson to an evening hunter safety class. Charlotte and Bob have been married for thirty-nine years.

Asked the effect of parental turmoil on the toddler in her care in the 1990s, Charlotte picks at a placemat and sighs. "Part of Tara's problem was knowing all of this, and understanding what had happened."

One day Tara's mother "called out of the clear blue and asked us to adopt Tara. She was four."

For Bob and Charlotte, as grandfather and step-grandmother, it was a straightforward decision. "She lived in our home. We loved her dearly. I couldn't have loved her more if I'd given birth to her."

There was a legal process. "We had to run an ad in the paper, but no one came forward to contest it." After a six-month waiting period, "They had to do a home study, even though she already lived here. Bob had no patience with that, but I told him, 'Look what you get in the end.'"

Tara's mother signed the adoption documents, and the little girl went with Bob and Charlotte to court. "She understood it all. She was thrilled, didn't bother her a bit. We asked if she wanted to change her last name to ours and she said yes. For court, I brought along a coloring book—animals. They pull the shade and lock the doors so no one can see in. During the whole thing she just sat with her coloring books and she colored. . . . When we walked out of there, she was ours."

Tara called Charlotte "Mom" and Bob "Papa." And so she grew up in Carthage. She went to Hawthorne Elementary School, which Charlotte had also attended, as had Bob's father. In the summer she went to nearby Christian camps. Tara did not have hardy lungs, fighting numerous allergies and bouts of bronchitis and pneumonia, but otherwise she enjoyed youthful good health. Tara was fond of cats, and devoted to the family dachshund, Snickers. When he died and Bob buried him in the backyard, the next day Charlotte found Tara stooped over the grave with honeysuckle flowers, arranging them on the freshly dug earth.

Most of Tara's life was happiness, though, an innocent Midwestern childhood. She loved the color purple. In a photo from 1987, Tara is the little girl in bright red shorts, a floating balloon knotted around her index finger.

"She was just silly," Charlotte remembers, "a very bubbly personality, very outgoing."

Tara had a sentimental streak too. There was a girl in her class whose mother had died. A few days before a school event, Charlotte recalls, Tara asked, "Would it be okay if I brought her over and you help fix her hair and do that special stuff to get ready that you do for me?"

Tara went off to Carthage Junior High, where she flourished. In school photos she wears a winsome smile, year after year, and behind her glasses Tara's eyes are bright. She was a standout flute player in the school band. She taught herself to speak Spanish and sign language. She was an honors student, and won awards for her grades.

Such recognition caused more embarrassment than pride, though. Tara was a T-shirt-and-jeans girl, sometimes fighting with Charlotte when urged to dress up. Nothing irritated her more than being called a preppie. She had a herd of friends who kept the phone busy after school, including one quiet boy who sometimes received extra attention.

As she grew, Tara's sentimental ways developed into an adolescent conscience. One night when she was eleven, she and Charlotte watched a TV show about organ donation. The program described the many body parts that a person could donate. Tara told Charlotte she was amazed. "If I ever died," Charlotte recalls her saying, "I'd want to do that, I'd want somebody to live because of me."

Tara drew the line at skin transplantation, though. "That would be gross."

Tara's developing sensibilities also surfaced in a journal she kept for school. "What do adults know about our age?" she asked in an entry from November 1998. "They didn't grow up in this age."

What are society's problems? "Number one, our government is messed up. Number two, schools aren't good enough for us. Number three, people think they know what we are going through. Personally, I can't wait to die. Then I won't have to put up with this world any longer."

The sentences are written in the flowery but tidy hand of a fourteen-year-old girl. In the margins, a teacher's note replies: "I hope your mood improves. Try concentrating on the good things in your life. Things will get better."

In other words, it seemed to be merely a moment of teen angst. And Tara otherwise appeared happy. She turned fifteen. The family celebrated Christmas. Tara won the distinction of being chosen to represent her school in a music competition in Oklahoma in a few months, and the other musicians in the trio were among her best friends. She went to the ninth-grade sweethearts dance on Valentine's Day, and it was one occasion without a fight over attire. In a family photo from that night she wears a dark velvet blouse, a lighter skirt with a pattern of daisies.

But American teenage life was not all flowers in early 1999. The carnage at Columbine was weeks away. Locally there had been a rash of suicides, with fear of copycat incidents.

On March 9, Charlotte remembers, Tara had a headache and her grandmother brought her aspirin at school. They hugged. Otherwise it was an ordinary day for a busy teenager. "She'd been upset the night before because she'd had to give a speech and she didn't feel prepared, she'd had to change topics. She couldn't get enough time on the computer for it. So she wound up preparing a speech about hair spray. I don't know if she gave that speech or not. . . . The band and singing teachers saw her after school, she was her bubbly little self."

By then Charlotte had a day-shift job, so she and Bob were both at work when Tara came home from school. Bob was due at 5 P.M. to take her to the trio's rehearsal. Later phone records revealed that Tara tried calling many of her friends during that alone time. But it was a busy weekday. Her friends all had after-school activities. No one was home.

Tara opened Bob's locked gun cabinet and got herself a pistol. Leaving no doubt about whether she was in earnest, she loaded the gun with a hollow-point bullet to inflict maximum internal damage. At some point she had written numerous notes—to friends, siblings, Bob, and Charlotte. On a sheet listing the people she wanted to serve as pallbearers, there is that tidy handwriting again, two misspellings properly corrected. She wrote detailed instructions, down to what she should be dressed in for her funeral: the same outfit she'd worn to the sweethearts dance three weeks before.

Tara was careful to spare her face any damage. "She put it right there," Charlotte says, placing a pinkie behind her right ear.

"She shot herself at about ten of five," Charlotte says. "She did it in the living room. My husband found her. He thought she had a nosebleed, she'd had lots of allergies, but she wasn't responding. He called an ambulance. She was still breathing. The police came too, and they were the ones that found the gun."

As Charlotte relates the events of the day, her hands fidget, her face reddens. Driving home from work that evening, she saw a rescue helicopter flying low over the neighborhood. When she came down the street, she could see a police car in the driveway. "I thought it was my husband. The police officer got in front of me so I couldn't see the couch. There was a lot of blood on it. Bob came out of the bedroom and told me. Of course I was screaming, totally out of it. And then we prayed, all the way to Joplin."

Doctors at the hospital there described the extent of damage, explaining that Tara would not recover. "I said, 'Just let us spend some time with her.' And I sat and held her hand. If she'd ever got sick with a cold, she'd say, 'Mama, will you hold my hand?'"

Charlotte could think of no reason for Tara to shoot herself. "It was shattering. Later I asked all of her friends, 'Did you guys know?' Nobody did. She'd joked with one friend, one time, 'I'm going to kill myself,' but they just laughed and blew it off."

Later Charlotte read Tara's journals. Aside from that one November entry, there were no signals of distress. Trying to imagine every possibility, Charlotte asked a nurse to give Tara a pregnancy test. It came back negative.

Then a local minister and family friend approached and asked Bob and Charlotte what they thought about donating Tara's organs and tissues. Her blood type made her a universal donor, so her organs could work in people of every other blood type.

"My husband at first said no. He couldn't bear to think of what they would be doing to her, to her body." But Charlotte told him about that TV show years before, and what Tara had said. "He said, 'I don't want to sit down with anybody and do this long, lengthy rigmarole.' We decided what we wanted them to take. The corneas of her eyes would help somebody to see. Kidneys are always important. Her liver. Her lungs, but they turned out to be too damaged from her allergies. Her heart. I would feel a lot better if her heart was still beating in someone else. She'd still be alive, to that extent."

The family held an all-night vigil at Tara's bedside. In the morning the medical team briefly disconnected her from the ventilator, to gauge if there was any brain activity. She didn't move, Charlotte says. "She didn't even gasp for air. I put my arms around her head, gave her a big hug. You can just tell when there's no life there."

With Tara reconnected, they consented to the transplants. Then a bustle of activity began. "Lots of people had to be notified. The team came in for her surgery. The coordinator said he would be with her through the whole procedure, and would call us when it was done.

"We did get some comfort, because some people were going to be living that day because of Tara. We said our good-byes, and you have to walk down that hallway. That is the hardest thing I have ever done in my life."

Charlotte's sister-in-law delayed her on the way home, forcing her to stop for breakfast. Only later did she learn that the delay was deliberate, to give Bob time to remove the couch before she arrived. But there was no avoiding the soul-searching that lay ahead.

"I know what guilt I went through, even though it probably wasn't justified. Could you have done this? Could you have done that? It's something you go through, part of the grieving process."

The crowd for Tara's funeral was huge. Charlotte had a mission that day. "I had a job to talk to as many of those teenage kids as I could, to let them know that what Tara did was not right, that there are other ways, other resources to get help."

Once the busy time had passed, once she'd tried to unravel the mystery of Tara's suicide as much as possible, Charlotte found her thoughts turning to the people who had received the organ donations. What were they like? Who were these people?

THE HEART TRANSPLANT has been around for decades, but for many years its success rate was limited. Surgery was not the problem; the challenge was managing the body's instinct to reject foreign tissues. Medicines that harness the immune system remained fatally crude. Lewis Washkansky survived his transplant for only eighteen days. His new heart beat well, but antirejection medicines compromised his immune system and he died from pneumonia. Of the 170 patients who underwent successful heart transplant operations before 1971, 146 died similarly.

The breakthrough was cyclosporine, a drug that suppresses the immune system in a more controlled fashion. Suddenly people with all kinds of transplants were surviving far longer. Today 94 percent of the people who receive a kidney from a deceased donor survive for the long term. With organs from living donors, the survival rate is 98 percent. Liver transplant results are nearly as remarkable, with 89 percent survival rates.

Organ transplants, bone grafts, bone marrow transplants—these formerly miraculous and desperate measures are developing into routinely successful interventions. In 2004 Americans received 7,500 transplanted corneas, with a 95 percent success rate. Leukemia patients underwent 2,500 bone marrow transplants. In 2005 the United States saw 28,000 organ transplants, 44,000 grafts, and 1 million transplants of tissues such as skin.

Unfortunately, this train of astonishing achievements pulls a caboose of disappointment. As medical science's ability to perform successful transplants grows, so therefore has the population of people who potentially could benefit from donated tissue. Meanwhile trends in illness also heighten demand. For example, the type 2 diabetes associated with obesity can lead to kidney failure. As obesity grows as a public health concern, the demand for donated kidneys likewise climbs.

The result is that the nation's waiting list for organs is now more than 103,000 names long. The number of donors, after averaging about six thousand a year in the early 1990s, rose to fourteen thousand donors in 2003—and there it plateaued. Now more than half of the candidates for transplants wait longer than a year. During that time their health will decay, while their capacity to recover from the severity of transplant surgery diminishes.

The cost of keeping them alive will rise too. Dialysis for kidney failure patients, for example, runs about sixty thousand dollars a year.

But of course the people who pay the greatest price are those whose illness will not wait. Each year some seven thousand people on the candidate list die before an organ becomes available for them. Another fifteen hundred to two thousand people, when their matches come, are simply too sick to survive a transplant. So in 2004, for example, 3,886 kidney patients died awaiting an organ. Another 1,811 liver patients, 483 lung candidates, and 457 heart transplant patients all died, unable to survive the delay. Ten percent of the people on the heart waiting list were younger than eighteen.

Why is there a shortage? Many people are unwilling to be organ donors because they succumb to myths:

- **That a person identified as a potential donor will receive less lifesaving care.** Not true; donated organs are only recovered from the body of a person who has already been declared dead.
- **That only young people can donate organs.** Not true; nearly one-third of organ donors are older than fifty and almost 10 percent are over sixty-five. The organs of a middle-aged person have tremendous value to someone on the verge of dying.
- **That churches oppose organ donation.** Actually, most major religions support organ donation and consider it an act of profound charity.

Myths aside, the *reality* that poses the greatest obstacle is that most people don't ever think to arrange to donate their organs and tissues. More than 2.3 million people die in this country every year, and many take perfectly good organs with them.

They could help people replace skin damaged by burns. They could give the gift of sight, by donating their corneas. They could relieve people from dialysis, by giving a kidney. They could rescue people from the many ailments of liver failure. And making perhaps the ultimate gift, they could provide another human being with the life-giving pulse of their beating heart.

Perhaps this organ is more than a part of the body. Perhaps it is a metaphor, a symbol for the capacity we all have to make America a more compassionate nation.

If that's so, then who in this troubled land needs the lifesaving thoughtfulness that organ donation exemplifies? Perhaps more important, who needs the healing power of being generous, the gratification of giving to others for their benefit without expectation of recognition or personal reward? Who needs the pleasure of giving?

The answer is obvious: everyone. Every person in this country needs to know the warmth of doing something for others. Everyone needs to learn the benefits of personal sacrifice: Generosity is its own reward.

This is a fundamental tenet of authentic patriots. The power of an individual to improve all of society is greater in a land of liberty than anywhere else. Likewise, the need for that power is greater in a democracy than anywhere else.

Tara and her family are authentic patriots of the first order. They did not have the benefit of a medical degree, like Jack McConnell, or a law degree, like Barry Scheck. They did not have the unique blend of experiences, in the privileged world and in the environmentally abused world, which enabled Majora Carter to see her community's problems and act on them. They did not have the singing experience and the pulpit that Reverend Christopher Moore used to start his choir.

Moreover, the projects these people built required stamina, charisma, persuasiveness. Not everyone has those talents in abundance. Plenty of good people are also disinclined to surrender the life they have built in order to serve others. But donating organs requires no special talent, no sacrifice of family or career. All it takes is the most important thing: generosity.

And everyone is capable of that. If the gift is made at death, all organ donation requires is forethought—to tell family members or make arrangements. From that modest effort, goodness flows in many directions: The recipient enjoys extended life of higher quality. The donor receives a peace of mind that comes from knowing life will conclude with a good deed. For the donor's survivors there is a leavening of sorrow, a sense of positive purpose. And for everyone involved, there is the unexpected knowledge that death can be cheated by a heart that gives.

Tara and her family completely fit the mold. Granted, they did not have the grand mission of some authentic patriots. What they did have, though, was a sense of themselves as more than independent beings in this culture. They understood the connectedness that enables a society to thrive, the power of common purpose. Even in the darkest of hours, they thought of others, and seized an opportunity to do good. It lightened their grief. It also offered the deeper lesson that a person does not need special credentials to become an authentic patriot. All it takes is an exertion of will on behalf of others, on behalf of a larger good.

The impact of one family's generosity extends in all directions. "We know of people who have signed up to become donors because of Tara," Charlotte says. If we want to restore a nation adrift, what better place to begin, quite literally, than with our hearts?

MARILYN SOFIA WAS on her way to the lake for the weekend. It was early March 1999, but her energy was flagging even as spring gained momentum. She carried a beeper in case a heart became available, but she did not expect to be contacted for months, if ever. The beeper didn't work down at the lake. Before she was out of range, though, a Heart Institute coordinator called.

"She said, 'Your heart's coming in,' Marilyn recalls. "I said, 'I don't think I'm ready for this.' She said, 'You better get ready. I want you here in an hour.'"

Jack drove "like a madman," Marilyn remembers. "I said, 'If you kill me before I get to the hospital, I will haunt you forever.'" But her nerves felt electrified. "I don't remember walking into the hospital or nothing. I told them, 'Just give me something please, to calm me down.'"

On March 9, 1999, Marilyn received Saint Luke's Heart Institute transplant number 189. Her surgeon? Dr. Michael Borkon. Her heart? Tara's heart.

"I remember that case," Borkon says. "It was very sad. It was very happy."

Marilyn's memories are less clear. "I woke up and I thought they didn't even do nothing. I didn't feel any different. But then I felt good. And my grandson came in and he said, 'Grandma, you've got color.' I wasn't pale and white anymore."

Marilyn was walking within hours. "My boss came up to see me, and I was sitting in a chair talking on the phone, and he said, 'I don't believe it.'"

Marilyn does not know what became of her diseased heart. "Some girls I've heard have held them, but not me." Asked to describe her scar, Marilyn promptly pulls down the collar of her turtleneck. A thin white line runs from the notch of her neck down to her sternum. "I wear it with pride."

She immediately began a cocktail of antirejection drugs, which can cost some patients up to twenty-five hunded dollars a month. Marilyn has been lucky, needing less medicine and thus avoiding serious side effects (the leading antirejection drug, for example, is a known carcinogen). Noting that she also has been spared any rejection episodes, she knocks her knuckles on a table. "I have been very, very fortunate."

After she returned home, the implications of the transplant weighed on her. "Some people have trouble with it. Somebody had to die so you could live. But you know, that person was going to die anyway. Still, you're always curious about who this person was. A guy or a girl? Everything."

Marilyn decided to try a service in the donor program, in which recipients can write to the donor's family. Letters are screened for revealing information, to protect the privacy of both sides. After a year, if everyone agrees, the program will provide contact information so the families can meet. For Marilyn, writing the first letter proved daunting enough.

"It took me a while. I had written it umpteen million times in my head. It's so hard, because you're so happy, but they're going to be sad. You don't know what to say or how to say it. How do you say thank you to somebody for a gift like this?"

In July, four months after the transplant, her family was heading to the lake once again. "What if something happens when I am out of town?" Marilyn worried. She went out and bought a card—and then a second one in case she made any mistakes with the first. And she sent it off.

"I WAS IN so much grief then," Charlotte says, remembering that summer. "I thought I was losing my mind. For a long time I couldn't even go in Tara's room. I just closed the door."

She knew only the barest details about where Tara's gifts had gone—corneas to a woman in South Carolina, heart and kidney to people in Missouri. The regional organ bank would deliver letters from Charlotte to the organ recipients, but there was no guarantee that any of them would respond. If the transplants failed, the patients might not even be alive.

In fact, the cornea and liver recipients never did answer Charlotte's letter. But the heart and kidney patients "responded immediately," she says. "I was thrilled to get an answer back."

Charlotte and Marilyn exchanged letters for a year. Each keeps the other's correspondence in a special folder. Marilyn unfolds the mail with tender care. "We got important stuff right here."

Finally the organ bank allowed them to share phone numbers. "That was the hardest phone call," Marilyn says. "I really wanted to do it, though."

It took a few messages before they connected. "There was not a dry eye," Marilyn says. "She was on one phone, he was on another. They did not tell me yet how Tara died."

The women spoke several times, but Bob hated driving in Kansas City traffic, so no date was set for a meeting. He and Charlotte meanwhile met with the kidney recipient, at a restaurant in central Missouri.

"On the way up it was quiet," Charlotte recalls. "So many things going through your mind. We got there first, and we'd told them what was happening. They had a quiet table for us, said we could stay as long as we liked. There on the porch, as soon as I saw this truck I knew it was them. Oh, we had great big hugs and tears, lots of tears."

All the recipient knew was that the donor had been a fifteen-year-old girl. Delivering the news of how Tara had died, "That was a hard thing to tell."

All the while Marilyn noticed certain changes in herself, and wondered whether they had any connection to Tara. "You have different cravings, that you didn't have before. Cereal, stuff I never ate. Then I bought a new car. Well, I'd always driven vans. But I got a Kia Sportage, four-wheel drive, and purple. Purple. I don't know if it was me who bought it, or Tara."

One day a co-worker of Charlotte's was headed to Kansas City, and she decided to come along. She called Marilyn. "I said, 'You're not getting out of town without me seeing you,'" Marilyn says.

"We pulled in their driveway," Charlotte says. "There was this pretty little purple Sportage, and I just burst out in tears because that was Tara's very favorite color."

* * *

TARA'S FRIENDS HAVE graduated from college now. Bob and Charlotte attended several of their weddings. Tara's best friend is in music school in New York City. "You've got to go back to work," Charlotte says. "You've got to go back to life."

The kidney recipient was a hunter, like Bob, and they became great friends. Then he developed cancer, and died four years after Tara. Bob and Charlotte get together with Marilyn and Jack often, for special occasions or visiting at the lake. Birthdays are still hard; Father's Day is tough for Bob.

Always, though, the grief is eased by Tara's gifts. "Most people, if they're like I was, have heard about organ donation but never really thought about it," Charlotte says. "But if they knew what donation does for people? Even though you went through a lot of grief and heartache, that made other people happy, and you get their love back tenfold."

IN 2006 TARA'S sister Laura married. Bob and Charlotte invited Marilyn and Jack. They said yes, but worried that it could be awkward.

"We kept a low profile," Marilyn remembers. "Then this girl came up and said, 'Are you the one that's got our peanut's heart?' I said yeah."

Bob started introducing Marilyn to everybody. "I met grandmas and grandpas, uncles and aunts and cousins." The strangers could not help themselves, giving her hug after hug. Marilyn was amazed. "I guess they just feel like there's still a part of Tara they can love."

They are not alone. To this day Charlotte has a special way that she hugs Marilyn, every time she sees her: Her left arm goes firmly around Marilyn's back, pulling her close in a sincere embrace. But then Charlotte places her right hand flat on Marilyn's chest, against the ribs, about where the scar is. There, under her palm, eight years after Tara's life ended, she can feel her daughter's heart. It is still beating.

PART THREE

Authentic Patriotism: Five Elements

II

Element One: Doing Good, Saving Money

If not us, who? If not now, when?

— Robert Kennedy

Democracy must be something more than two wolves and a sheep voting on what to have for dinner.

— James Bovard

IMAGINE THE BOY, ARRIVING at Rikers Island for the first time. He's eighteen. He is not connected with any school. He reads at a sixth-grade level. He has no employment history, and no income. Survey statistics say in his short life he has already experienced either homelessness, parental incarceration, parental death, mental illness, violence, abuse, or several of these combined. Poverty is all he knows. His only role models—occupying that status because of their power and money—are drug dealers. So he dances around the edge of the functioning world, and eventually finds himself in trouble with the law. Maybe he was trying his hand at dealing. Maybe he stole something to afford drugs. Maybe he was just young and foolish.

So he lands at Rikers Island, a 413-acre jail that sits in the East River of New York City. The landmass is insufficient for this largest penal colony in the world, however, so Rikers also includes two former Staten Island ferries converted into extra jail space, as well as a barge refitted to hold eight hundred beds. The entire facility pens fifteen thousand inmates at a time, most of them awaiting trial and unable to post bail. Other inmates are serving short sentences, typically a year or less. Over the course of a year as many as 130,000 people might live on the island, 90 percent of them coming from the same tough, poor neighborhoods of New York City.

Rapid turnover in population actually makes Rikers Island a more dangerous place. Jails with longer-term residents achieve a tense equilibrium, with friendships, pecking orders, even communities forming. In short-term situations everyone is perpetually on guard, and in order to avoid looking weak, completely unwilling to ask for help. The atmosphere grows even more charged considering the rate of mental illness among inmates on the island—estimated in one study at 20 percent.

Rikers Island is a massive enterprise, with a staff of almost twelve thousand and an annual budget approaching $1 billion. There are gyms, churches, a hospital, a power plant. There is also the nearly constant roar of jets, taking off or landing at nearby LaGuardia Airport. To boys standing behind razor wire or sitting in their cells, all those sounds of people freely coming and going must be almost like rubbing it in.

The newly arrived boy is not an angel, but neither is he necessarily a permanent threat to society. Fewer than one-quarter of Rikers inmates are charged with violent crimes. Most are decidedly small-timers. But they are placed in this harrowing environment, where even misdemeanor suspects are subject to strip searches, and where the history of assaults by other inmates and even guards is long and bloody.

How is this boy to survive? There is only one way: by adopting the prison culture, first mimicking and then embracing the violent ethos, the poses, the talk, and the attitude. And after his case comes to trial and he is found innocent and released, or is found guilty and placed on probation, or is sentenced to his short stint, what becomes of him then?

The answer is grim. Upon release none of the young inmates are enrolled in school—that's zero percent. He often doesn't have a place to go or a place to live. He doesn't have a job. And now that he has been educated in the criminal way of life, and learned to depend on those studies to survive, the result is predictable: 70 percent of adolescent inmates released from Rikers Island wind up back in jail again.

The next time it's a longer stay, though, because the offense is worse or the record is lengthening. The life of a criminal gradually becomes familiar, almost normal. Thus does the nation's jail population continue to grow.

Yet for some boys, the story is not quite over. A different path lies before some people like him, thanks to Friends of Island.

This organization, formed in 1990, intervenes during the boy's first incarceration, with the explicit goal of preventing future arrests. The boy receives schooling and job training at the island. He is linked with resources that can support him after he is released—a school, food stamps, health care, a potential job. Friends of Island does not necessarily create new programs, but rather directs the boy to services he did not even know existed, much less that he could qualify for.

It's a classic authentic-patriot enterprise—founded by Barbara Strove-Grodd and Norma Green to fill an obvious human need. The idealism of this project is obvious and unapologetic.

The unexpected thing about Friends of Island is that it works. The boy develops sufficient skills to function independently. He passes a high school equivalency exam. He gets a job. He avoids going back to jail.

The benefits of that rescue are many: The city endures less crime, and instead of being a drain on taxpayers the boy becomes a contributing member of society. Some Friends of Island clients thrive so well in a constructive setting, they go on to serve as mentors—their voices of hard experience preventing others from following the downward path.

These are the kinds of human benefits that make Friends of Island laudable, and that characterize the work of authentic patriots. But actually the most important lesson about Friends of Island is not humanitarian. It is *economic*.

THE BEST IDEAS for lifting society often win praise because they are the right thing to do: We should provide health care to the sick regardless of their ability to pay, we can't have genuine justice without preventing wrongful convictions, we must find a cure for ALS to alleviate its victims' suffering. As a result, people tend to think of social initiatives like those we've been discussing as noble causes, an outstretched hand or a tin cup rattled, so we write a check or give an hour and then feel good about ourselves.

That notion is entirely too misty-eyed. The reality is that doing good often makes excellent economic sense. And funding these programs is less about philanthropy than it is about investing.

Friends of Island demonstrates this logic impeccably. Housing an inmate at Rikers Island costs north of eighty thousand dollars a year. Helping a first-offense boy to salvage his life has an average cost of about seventy-five hundred dollars. Of the adolescents who participate in Friends of Island programs, the portion who return to jail is 5.2 percent—a long, long way from the 70 percent reincarceration rate of teens who don't receive that help. Current enrollment in Friends of Island programs stands at nearly five hundred students. If those adolescents each avoid as little as one year in jail, every investment of $3.75 million avoids the expenditure of $40 million. That's just for the current class. The long-term economics—many years of Friends' classes of boys avoiding decades of imprisonment—are even stronger.

Even if you are a throw-away-the-key hawk on criminal justice, and believe that the primary purpose of jail is punishment, you have to concede that vast sums of taxpayers' money can be saved by preventing that boy from going back to prison. And again, that is above and beyond the crimes not committed, the years not squandered in incarceration, and the near impossibility of achieving productive adulthood with a prison record.

Not every program or service makes such direct economic sense. But if your notion of social activism allows a view one or two steps removed from the immediate problem, it's striking how frequently the economic argument is every bit as strong as the humanitarian one.

There are roughly 1.6 million nonprofit organizations in the United States. Obviously not all of them are great. Some may be inefficient, some redundant. Yet these companies enjoy exemption from paying taxes that for-profit businesses must pay. With that special status comes a responsibility to perform at a deserving level. It is easy to become passionate about this or that idealistic endeavor, but those sentiments will never be enough. The urgent task of restoring a nation adrift requires hard thinking, a cool assessment of an organization's worth. One of the clearest tests is whether the enterprise makes economic sense.

Think back to Volunteers in Medicine. People can argue about whether health care is a right, a privilege, or simply a service that the world's richest nation ought to provide each citizen. Regardless, let's agree that everyone ought to have access to basic medical treatment. That's the humane purpose. What about the economics?

At first blush, the clinic represents a new cost on society. There's a building to construct, heat, light, and equip. There's an administrative staff to pay. There are medical supplies to purchase. But a view only slightly broader shows that the economics are not so simple.

Before the first clinic opened, Jack McConnell said, every year the Hilton Head hospital lost about $1.8 million to free care. That is, people arrived at the emergency room, the hospital provided care to them, and the patients had no money to pay for that treatment. Sometimes they arrived bleeding, or in labor, or in some situation that clearly required emergency care. But often the situation was much less dire. People had fevers, toothaches, minor ailments. They came to the ER simply because they lacked a regular doctor; they had no place else to go.

When the Volunteers in Medicine clinic opened, the hospital's free-care costs plunged. There were still heart attacks and babies born, but nonurgent problems no longer reached the ER. They were solved in the clinic.

Again, it's easy to see the human benefits. People receive care before their illnesses become advanced. They don't miss days of work. They don't spend hours waiting for care in a busy emergency room. They don't suffer the humiliation of receiving treatment they know they can't afford. They don't wonder if being poor will result in their receiving lower-quality care.

But the economic arguments are equally strong. The Volunteers in Medicine clinic costs $800,000 a year to operate. According to

Jack—and he would know because he sat on the hospital's board of directors—once the clinic opened, the hospital's bad debt bill fell by $1.3 million. In other words, entirely in addition to the gain in people's health, doing the right thing saved the local economy $500,000 a year.

The Chicago Children's Choir makes economic sense too. It serves as the primary performing-arts education organization for Chicago's public schools. Its programs costs far, far less than what the city would have to spend to provide a comparable curriculum itself. Meanwhile, between performance income, revenues from CD sales, and other sources of cash, the choir only has to raise about $500,000 a year to operate. That's a pittance given the importance of its lessons of self-improvement for singers and racial harmony for audiences.

Over and over, the ideas with the strongest humanitarian argument also have the clearest economic justification. It doesn't matter what realm of society is involved. Science? Finding a cure for ALS would end the need for costly support services and personal care for people afflicted with the disease. Moreover, the Project ALS collaborative approach is making greater progress, and faster, at a much lower cost than the old funding methods. Collaboration also benefits researchers working on related diseases such as Alzheimer's and Parkinson's.

Law enforcement? Preventing errors in criminal justice would save millions in legal fees, prison costs, squandered investigative efforts, and ultimately, restitution payments to people who have been wrongfully convicted. Alan Newman sued the city of New York for $50 million—not only for his wrongful conviction, but also for failing to find the evidence that cleared him. Obviously avoiding such suits makes financial sense for any jurisdiction.

The environment? Sustainable South Bronx offers an economic justification as strong as any. It trains people who have been on welfare or in jail and enables them to land decent jobs. Instead of causing a drain on society, with the cost of their incarceration or social services, BEST graduates become contributing, taxpaying members of society. Their training costs about seven thousand dollars; their subsequent jobs start at about twenty-five thousand dollars a year and run up to sixty thousand dollars. In the longer term, better air quality will mean fewer asthma attacks, missed school days, and hospitalizations. Moreover, a community that shares in the benefits of clean air and green spaces loses some of its reasons for violence and self-destruction, at the same time it regains its dignity and sense of worth.

Organ donation? A liver transplant costs about seventy thousand dollars. But dialysis for a person awaiting a transplant can run sixty thousand dollars a year. (And the vast majority of the 250,000 people currently on dialysis have their care paid for by the federal government, and thus by taxpayers.) A transplant pays for itself—entirely in addition to the life saved—and starts saving money in about twenty months.

THERE IS A danger in overemphasizing the economic benefits of humanitarian work: The overall gains are broader, the motives nobler, the purposes greater than any cost-benefit analysis can express. Economics is only one aspect of society.

Think of it this way: If you hire someone to plant a garden at your house, that expenditure is measured positively in the gross national product. But if you dig the dirt and plant the seeds and weed and water the plot yourself, the economic contribution is measured as much smaller—and the pleasure you received from the project does not count at all. If some weeks later you take a friend to a restaurant for dinner, that counts positively in the GDP. But if you have that friend over to your house, and serve food from your garden, your contribution to the economy is nearly zero.

The fact that great social initiatives make sound economic sense, therefore, should in no way eclipse their primary reasons for being: to help address human needs.

Yet the simplest financial justification is also the most sensible human reason as well—the avoidance of larger and more costly problems. It is cheaper to keep a boy out of jail. It costs less to treat a poor woman's high blood pressure than it does to provide her with a triple bypass later. Societies that are not adrift abound in policies geared toward prevention. We vaccinate toddlers to avoid later health problems. We try to teach teens about responsible sexual behavior. After a certain age we tell women to receive an annual mammogram and men to have an annual prostate exam. We encourage seniors to get a flu shot each fall. This thinking is not limited to medicine either. We are quite accustomed, after all, to seeing a traffic light turn yellow.

It is interesting to ponder, then, what needs exist today that could be eliminated by shifting the idea of philanthropy from an act of generosity to a method of investment. What problems could we prevent? What money could we save? What fires could we avoid needing to put out?

What kind of America could we create?

12

Element Two: Doing Good in Place After Place

These are times in which a genius would wish to live. It is not in the still calm of life, or the repose of a pacific station, that great characters are formed.

— ABIGAIL ADAMS, FIRST LADY 1798–1802

THE OFFICES OF THE Majora Carter Group are located in a bright blue building, above an auto parts store in the South Bronx. Visitors are greeted at the door by a large, friendly, skeptical dog. Xena gives each guest a thorough inspecting sniff before stepping aside to clear the stairway.

Upstairs the windows have rainbow-colored curtains. The office decor is Spartan, bare tables and plastic chairs. Majora, emerging from a meeting dressed in jeans and high heels, smiles and chirps, "How art thou?"

By late 2009 the days of her leadership at Sustainable South Bronx have passed. A handpicked successor now runs the show, a few blocks away, while Majora uses this office as a base for taking her talents on the road. She is in demand as a speaker. She has sat on panels with Nobel Peace Prize–winner Desmond Tutu, appeared with folksinger and activist Pete Seeger, took a climate-action cruise with former president Jimmy Carter.

"I am having a blast," she says. "At Sustainable South Bronx I was getting incredibly burnt out. I participated in a leadership development program and realized it was time for me to go. Time to take the lessons that I'd learned, and sometimes created, and help communities around the country and around the world to create a green-collar economy."

Occasionally the achievements she describes have a slightly surreal sound: "We've had incredible success with people who did armed robbery, when we get them into horticulture."

But the fact remains: Other communities need environmental justice, cleaner air and water, job opportunities for people presently without options. Majora is finding these places all over the country.

"Kansas City has a Black Heritage District that includes a grand theatrical restoration, and it's located right beside a black community that cannot afford to attend. So there was a $2 billion bond issued for storm-water management, and we're working with architects to create horticultural supports. It will help with storm water, help with climate change, and put people to work."

In one corner of North Carolina, her group is helping Elizabeth City State University anticipate the impact of climate change. "This is the area in the U.S. most threatened by sea-level rise, except for New Orleans and the Everglades. It's a fascinating place, mostly poor but with pockets of serious wealth. Elizabeth State is a black college on the water. They sought us out."

A few miles south in Durham, Majora is working with local officials to develop green-collar jobs with a focus on energy efficiency. There's also a similar potential project in the Northeast. "I met with the mayor of New Bedford, Massachusetts, and he has great plans—energy efficiency programs, but only for owner-occupied homes. That's your green-collar training and a housing stability program all in one."

The point is that the issues Majora faced in the South Bronx, and the solutions the community found, can be replicated elsewhere. Her ambition is to accomplish precisely that.

Here is a second indicator of whether the nonprofits in this country can contribute to restoring a nation adrift: Can they be duplicated? Will the ideas work in more than one location?

Majora's new venture shows that the idea of a developing green-collar economy meets this test. Quite apart from her efforts, plenty of other people are building on the green-collar idea. Richmond, California, operates a program in solar panel construction and installation, investing $1 million a year to train low-income people in these skills. Chicago has a fifteen-year-old program that teaches participants landscaping and tree pruning. In recent years the project has grown to include recycling computers, plus household toxins such as paint and motor oil. Of the program's 265 participants thus far, nearly two-thirds have found jobs as landscapers, arborists, and the like. Oakland, California, established a $250,000 Green Collar Job Corps to teach unemployed people how to install solar panels, insulation, and green roofs.

In fact, if Sustainable South Bronx has a sibling, it would have to be Oakland's Green For All. Founded by activist and author Van Jones, Green For All has a mission of battling pollution and poverty simultaneously. There is a Green For All Academy, though its purpose is more policy- and advocacy-oriented than the hands-on training of the South Bronx. There are Green For All projects in Philadelphia, Atlanta, Seattle, Pittsburgh. A pilot project in Newark is winterizing the homes of senior citizens, which lowers their heating costs and builds the skill base of local workers.

Quite apart from the welfare-to-work dimension, green roofs have grown in popularity around the world. In Chicago there is an extensive garden on the roof of City Hall. In San Francisco bus shelters have miniature gardens on top. In Dearborn, Michigan, a Ford factory with a 10.4-acre roof now uses sedum plantings to reduce storm-water pollution. The Fairmont Waterfront hotel in Vancouver harvests sixteen thousand dollars' worth in fruit and produce annually from its rooftop garden. Germany offers incentives for building owners to install green roofs. The Hakutsuru Sake company grows some of the rice for its products atop its Tokyo office. In parts of Switzerland, any new building with a flat roof is required to have greenery on it.

The popularity of green-roof technology results in part from a growing understanding about the benefits, but word has spread more quickly and passionately because of green job initiatives. The point is that the ideas of Majora Carter are larger than her charisma, and even—with the organization flourishing after she has left—her leadership.

It's a surprisingly reliable indicator of how strong the case for a social or civic initiative really is: Can it be duplicated?

Sometimes an idea works in one place because there are unique conditions or some special person—a brilliant leader, a generous philanthropist—without which the program would fail. But the best initiatives of authentic patriots can succeed almost anywhere, because the logic behind their existence is so persuasive that it transcends the conditions at the founding location.

Volunteers in Medicine began thanks to the vision and determination of one man. He had the professional clout of a physician, he had a career's experience in solving complex problems, he had strong personal motives, and he happened to live in a community with plenty of affluent retired people. Hilton Head provided an ideal laboratory in which to test the idea of a free clinic staffed by retired professionals.

But since then Volunteers in Medicine has grown miles beyond Jack McConnell's considerable charm, and the pocketbooks of one county in South Carolina. Today the organization boasts seventy-eight clinics in twenty-two states, with many more facilities in the works. Indeed, are there any cities in America, or any rural outposts, that would not benefit from a Volunteers in Medicine clinic? Plain evidence exists today that in one community after another, there is sufficient generosity to launch the clinic, buy or build a facility, equip and staff it. Amy Hamlin, executive director of the Volunteers in Medicine Institute, says the primary barriers to more clinics are not financial. Just as Jack overcame South Carolina's hurdles with doctor licensing and malpractice insurance, each potential new clinic must contend with its state's obstacles to free care provided by retired doctors and nurses. Today there are seventy-eight examples of how those barriers can be broken, and how Jack's model makes sense in place after place. One day there will be one hundred and seventy-eight.

It's true of the Innocence Project too. Nearly every state now has a legal clinic that focuses on criminal cases in which DNA evidence could provide conclusive proof of innocence or guilt. The state groups, who form a national association called the Innocence Network, meet annually to share strategies and successes. The speakers always include several exonerees, whose stories reinvigorate everyone's passion for justice.

More important, the majority of states have begun to acknowledge the implications of sending so many innocent people to jail. Undisputed wrongful convictions have occurred in thirty-one states. The best of them have learned from what those cases say about criminal justice. Now twenty-seven states have laws to compensate people who have been unjustly jailed. Some are negligible; New Hampshire pays a flat twenty thousand dollars regardless of how long an innocent person was behind bars. Some are creative; Vermont gives the exoneree ten years of free participation in the state employees' health plan. Some consider the whole damage a wrongful conviction has caused; Texas pays fifty thousand dollars per year of incarceration, plus accrued unpaid child support.

Meanwhile nine states have mandated that police interrogations of suspects be videotaped, so there is a record of the conditions under which any person confesses. Four states passed laws that require the preservation of biological evidence for decades, with several other states poised to follow suit. Forty-six states enacted statutes to deal with evidence that develops after a conviction. Ten states passed reforms in eyewitness identification procedures.

All these efforts have been bolstered by substantive research, for example by the California Commission on the Fair Administration of Justice. Using diverse and experienced legal experts, the commission has developed a thorough list of ideas for improvement—from how witnesses should be shown photos of suspects to how judges should instruct juries, from treating jailhouse informants with appropriate skepticism to adopting best practices in handling biological evidence.

The most far-reaching reform was the Innocence Protection Act, which enjoyed bipartisan support in Congress and which President George W. Bush signed into law in 2004. The act provided funds to clear the nation's backlog of three hundred thousand rape kits whose DNA has not been tested, increased appropriations to improve the quality of legal counsel for suspects facing the death penalty, improved the quality of DNA labs, and raised funding for victims' assistance programs. One indicator of the Innocence Project's impact on that law is the Kirk Bloodsworth Testing Program provision. It provides funding so states can conduct postconviction DNA testing like the kind that freed Kirk from death row. The influence of the Innocence Project continues to extend nationwide.

There does not have to be visible policy transformation, however, to know that an authentic patriot's idea will work in more than one location. As the vocal performance on Martin Luther King Jr. Day amply demonstrates, a choir comprising a city's best voices, without regard to race or class, makes great music wherever the singers happen to live. Christopher Moore's idea and passion have proven infectious: In addition to Chicago and Boston, Detroit has launched a diverse children's choir as well. Is there a major city in America that could not build a comparable choir, with similarly elevated musical standards and social goals? Is there a major city that does not have a need for the kind of healing and celebration a children's choir provides?

Even Project ALS fits the pattern, proving that duplication is a sign of an idea's merit. In this case, it's not that other groups are working to cure the same disease. But organizations seeking cures for other illnesses have embraced the innovations of private funding and collaborative research. And they are seeing comparably stunning results.

The best example may be the Christopher and Dana Reeve Foundation, which they founded after he became paralyzed in 1995. The foundation's goal is to enable people with spinal injuries to walk again. As with ALS, motor neurons are involved. As with ALS, stem cells offer hope of a cure. And as with ALS, modern medicine has made negligible progress. A broken spine still means a lifetime in a wheelchair or in bed.

The Reeve family declared that prognosis unacceptable. Their foundation has raised millions of dollars for research in spinal care and recovery of function. Just like Project ALS, the foundation requires its researchers to collaborate in the interest of speed.

The results are nothing short of astonishing. The foundation has gathered many of the best minds on stem cells internationally, to determine the state of research and to identify urgent gaps in knowledge. Meanwhile the foundation has awarded more than $12 million in "quality-of-life" grants to organizations that help people who are paralyzed. These programs range from tutorials in skin care for paralyzed lower extremities to films that help kids reckon with their parent's paralysis.

Most remarkable of all, though, is the success of "activity-based recovery." This is an extreme form of physical therapy, in which people who cannot walk—who in fact have been told by doctors and health insurers that they will never walk again—prove them wrong. First they are strapped into a reclining bicycle, which moves their legs in a circle for them. Later they are supported by a sling above a treadmill, while a therapist on each side moves their legs in a steady gait. Gradually—the process can take years—the spine relearns walking. It is an incredibly slow, labor-intensive, expensive treatment. But it is working. People are walking again.

The Reeve Foundation not only funds research into this method, it fosters communication between labs, medical centers, and fitness facilities across the country. In other words, just as with Project ALS, the progress for patients is a direct result of the collaborative model—which itself is a direct outcome of private financing toward finding a cure.

Replication works. Remember Dr. Harold Freeman's navigators for cancer care of the poor? More than three hundred hospitals use this idea today.

SO: IF AN idea is good enough to make economic sense, and if it is strong and flexible enough to work in multiple locations, it has the essential attributes to contribute to restoring a nation adrift.

But all of these endeavors, and their kind, bring another benefit that has gone unmentioned. It is greater than the humanitarian good that social activism accomplishes. And it is stronger than the economic dividends that investing in human capital yields. Although this gain has not been declared directly in this book until now, it has been a silent force in every example. And if this element can become widespread in our society today, if it can flourish, that change would create the largest positive outcome of all.

13

Element Three: The Real Gold

Ask not what your country can do for you. Ask what you can do for your country.

—JOHN F. KENNEDY, 1960

Here may we be reminded that a man is most honored not by that which a city may do for him, but by that which he has done for the city.

—VAN WYCK BROOKS, 1940

Men and women are born to put more into their country than they take out of it.

— GUY EMERSON, 1920

It is now the moment when by common consent we pause to become conscious of our national life and to rejoice in it, to recall what our country has done for each of us, and to ask ourselves what we can do for our country in return.

— OLIVER WENDELL HOLMES, 1884

IF THERE IS A PINNACLE in the United States for retail commerce, it must be Fifth Avenue in New York City. There are contenders: Rodeo Drive in Los Angeles, Worth Avenue in Palm Beach. But Fifth Avenue boasts an unrivaled collection of stores, high-end hotels, and higher-end merchandise. Jewelers cluster at Forty-seventh Street. Ten blocks north at Fifty-seventh, the fashion industry holds court. Here Trump Tower stands, all glitter and gilt. Here the fabled Plaza Hotel cocks an eyebrow at Central Park.

And if there is a centerpiece to this display, it stands seven stories high at 754 Fifth Avenue: Bergdorf Goodman. Here one can purchase pink platform sandals for a thousand dollars, handbags that cost more than some cars, sunglasses for $700, or a few ounces of cologne for $950. For those whose purchasing exertions bring fatigue, or whose lunch date commands a fresh appearance, all it takes is a ride in the elevator to the penthouse, where the John Barrett Salon caters to every whim of vanity.

It is here, at the top of the top of the top, that Mercedes Shapiro works her magic. It is here too that the soul of the place is revealed, the innate inner desire to do good that even all this commerce cannot suppress.

Mercedes Shapiro is no hair stylist, though, nor a lowly fingernail buffer. Mercedes is a makeup artist of the first degree. Need a blemish concealed? A ready flush to the cheek? An eyebrow shaped into a curve that conveys the perfect blend of intelligence and flirtation? Mercedes will see to it with warmth and humor and competence. A thirty-minute makeup job may set you back three hundred dollars.

But when Mercedes steps away from her spot in the salon, leaves her window with the park view, and sits down to discuss her work, her conversation is the opposite of name dropping or catty chatter. Instead she talks about the time a young woman was about to appear on a national television show. But the client was unable to come to the salon. So Mercedes, whose round-trip commute in those days already occupied two and half hours, made a house call. She hauled herself and her equipment down to Chelsea. And there she was introduced to Jenifer Estess.

"It was different right from the start," Mercedes remembers. "Her room was crowded all the time, because Project ALS had its office right in there. I saw right away I'd have to get on the bed with her. But she was great. She told me, 'I want my lips to look just like yours.'

Then I was working away and she asked me if I would scratch her nose. That's when I really realized. It broke my heart, and I left there feeling very sad."

Mercedes sent a bill, as usual. "They called me, said, 'Do you mind doing it for ALS?' I thought about my people here—some are good but some are pretty completely self-absorbed. I tore up the invoice. After that I was always doing it for free. Jenifer would get an interview on *Larry King*, or the *Today* show, or there'd be some Project ALS event, and they'd call me.

"Sometimes I'd get all the way over there and they'd say, 'Jenifer doesn't feel good.' But still I was always glad they asked me. I mean, don't get me wrong. It was hard to go over there. She was sick and never getting better. She might be a little depressed, but she'd snap right out of it. Then they'd prop her up and I'd go to work. Jenifer deserved to look her best. A woman is a woman until the day she dies."

ALS usually emaciates its victims, and Jenifer often said she was the first person ever to gain weight with the disease. Just her luck, she joked.

"So she always had a turtleneck on," Mercedes says. "She never wanted to look in the mirror when I was done either. She trusted me."

Jenifer's sisters canceled her last appointment. "She was done. It was too much work. Doing TV, getting her out of bed and dressed, it was a half-day thing. So no, we didn't really get to say good-bye. But hey, I do the sisters sometimes, even now."

Mercedes' free services for Jenifer were not her first experience in helping others. In her twenties, she participated in a local hospital's cuddle program: Premature infants gain weight faster if they receive human touch. Jenifer's death did not mark the end of Mercedes' volunteering either.

"For the last four years I've done the Sloan-Kettering prom. I do the makeup on the kids with cancer. Once there was this little Indian girl, she was so cute, but she was too weak to go to the prom. I walked outside thinking, 'Today is the most beautiful day, and that kid is in the hospital.' But we helped her out, we even put rhinestone tattoos on her. And she got up and got dressed and she went. This kid was so hip, so beautiful."

"Look." Mercedes places her palms together as if in prayer. "A lot of people in America are spoiled. Their computer games and TV, it's out of control. The other day I saw a kid, had to be six years old, standing at the curb with his arm up hailing a taxi.

"But I believe everyone's important. The mailman's important. The milkman's important. Everyone's the same. So we have to do our part. We have to help. And I think it feels better to do it than any amount of sacrifice it takes."

And then she blushes. "It's not like I go around telling anybody. It's just that I feel sad, but I feel good. And it is the best kind of good."

ALL OF THE elements for constructive social change can be found in Mercedes' modest self-description: an awareness of the need, the capacity to contribute, and the understanding that it does the heart good to treat others well. Service is its own reward. A person need not create Project ALS or any of these other great ventures in order to be an authentic patriot. All it takes is individual initiative, a belief that people can accomplish more today than government or the free market, and a willingness to get involved.

That last element can take wonderfully unique shapes, depending on what a person has to offer. Carmen Landreth was born of an Italian father and Spanish mother, and raised in a multilingual household. In her long marriage, her executive husband was posted to twenty-four different foreign assignments. In each place, her first task was to find a charity and volunteer.

"When we would go overseas, I used to go down in the lobby and see these women not doing a damn thing. 'Why don't you go to the consulate,' I'd say, 'and see if you can do anything?' They'd say, 'We can't do that.' I'd answer, 'Well, I did. I have an orphanage, and I wouldn't give it up for anything.'"

When Carmen's husband retired, they chose Hilton Head, and he died a decade ago. Now eighty-eight, Carmen is a regular volunteer at the Volunteers in Medicine clinic. Two afternoons a week, she stands by the front door and goes wherever she's needed. Her job? Translator.

"Latinos I adore, because they have a feeling for their family. These are people with no money. But as little as they make, they always send some to their mother or father." The clinic serves a crucial purpose, she explains: Latinos tend to avoid the emergency room not only due to the cost but also to avoid drawing attention to themselves. "Here the immigration crackdown is not our concern. Helping people is."

Carmen has Bell's palsy, so one side of her face is fallen and motionless. But the other side is bright and expressive, and as she greets patients and families, her accent is intact too. She credits her volunteer experience with energizing her days, and with giving her life meaning.

"The old ladies where I live now, they don't ever do anything but complain and go to the doctor. The whole world has changed, you know. I lived in great years. The world is struggling today because it's selfish, everything is money. It makes me sad. In a way, I'm glad I'm old because I won't see the rest of it."

As long as her energy lasts, though, Carmen intends to spend it giving. "I have three children and six grandchildren, in Texas and California and Virginia. But I'm staying right here for Thanksgiving and Christmas. If I'm with strangers for the holidays I tolerate it better. At Thanksgiving, I'm going to a restaurant to help serve food for people who can't afford to buy a dinner. Same thing at Christmastime."

Over the years, Carmen says, she learned that volunteering was the opposite of what she'd thought. "They are doing me a favor, rather than me doing one for them. It's not a sacrifice. They help me, because I get to help."

The gratification of helping can take many forms. One surprisingly common version is a desire to make something positive out of grief.

December 15, 1989, was a Friday, and an overnight snowstorm closed schools for the day. For Marcia Schoenfeld of Kansas City, a second-grade teacher, that meant a snow day with her young son and daughter. Steve, her husband of seventeen years, waited until the roads were clear before heading to work. A type-A guy like Steve—small-business leader, board director of community groups, active member of his synagogue—would not let weather keep him home, Marcia said. Besides, he had errands to do for his brother's thirty-fifth birthday party that night.

Steve's precautions were not enough. His car spun into another lane, an eighteen-wheeler went into a skid beside him, and they collided. Steve had an internal head injury.

Marcia woke the kids and hurried to the hospital. "He didn't look that injured. But when he came in one pupil was dilated, an indicator that something's not right."

The family kept a close vigil over the weekend, and then Steve's other eye dilated. "I knew that was bad," Marcia says. By Wednesday an electroencephalogram confirmed there was no brain activity.

"That means there is no chance for healing," she says. "Brain death doesn't get better. Brain death is dead."

Marcia knew that Steve wished to donate his organs; they'd discussed it in the car one time. She also had the authority to make that decision. Still, she held a family meeting: parents, siblings, a rabbi. "It was really important to me to have everyone on board. Everyone said okay. I was lucky."

She signed the papers with a nurse in the ICU. "Then I peeled my kids up off the floor and went home."

Even though Marcia knew she was doing what Steve wanted, still she felt some guilt. "My head knew he had died, but my heart was like, 'You left him there to die alone.'"

The hospital declared Steve dead at 11:05 Thursday morning, on December 21. With holidays looming, Marcia decided to hold visiting hours the next day. The funeral director said that would be difficult, because Steve had not arrived from the hospital until 4 A.M., seventeen hours after his death.

"I had a lot of questions about what took so long," she remembers. "I never sat with anyone. No one asked if I had any questions. I had no time or energy to ask them. But I didn't forget."

What Marcia did instead was get involved. It started the following summer, in a class required for renewing her teaching license. One presenter was from the Midwest Transplant Network. "I went up to her afterward; I had a lot of questions. She very kindly gave me her card. Then, close to the one-year anniversary, I came to visit and got my questions answered."

Steve's liver went to a fifty-eight-year-old steelworker. His kidney went to a seventy-two-year-old man. His heart went a thirty-two-year-old father of two. Both corneas were transplanted too.

It was just the closure Marcia needed: "To know that Steve is still contributing to this world, that people wake up every day and give thanks that he lived, that is huge."

In March the network was conducting nursing education, and a staffer called Marcia. "He said, 'We were wondering if you could give the donor family perspective.' I said, 'Yeah, sure.' Then I hung up and wondered, 'What exactly do you want me to do?'"

Marcia told her story. She did it so well, the network asked her back. She contributed to nurse training for a year and a half. The work grew on her; she changed her day job to half-time so she could volunteer more. She joined the program that helps support donor families, which lasts up to two years after the patient's death.

"Last year we had a hundred and sixty-eight organ donors, plus six or seven hundred tissue donors, and that's a lot of new families." Now they are Marcia's full-time job. "I'm so glad it is different now. We work hard to help families get as comfortable as they can. We want to make it the best possible experience under the worst possible circumstances."

Marcia does not think of herself as an authentic patriot. She dismisses any talk of initiative or heroism; for her, organ donation is all about alleviating grief about Steve. But she admits that her appreciation of the difference a donor can make—and that she can make by helping donor families recover from their loss—fills her with energy and purpose.

"I love it here, and I'm thinking this place is *so* about life. Sure, it's just an office with cubicles. But I finally understand the miracle of it all."

ONE OTHER COMMON element among people who participate in authentic-patriot endeavors is how the work grows on them. They start out in the smallest way, but somehow their contribution expands, gradually occupying a larger role in their lives and their personal contentment.

By all outward appearances, Rob Kaplan had little reason to look

for greater fulfillment. A senior director at Goldman Sachs investment bank, he had ample professional challenges and spectacular
monetary rewards. With a sideline as a senior lecturer at Harvard
Business School, he suffered no shortage of intellectual engagement
too. He'd done philanthropic work, for example with the TEAK Fellowship, which helps high-performing students from low-income families gain admission to top colleges.

But that effort changed in focus and intensity in 1999, when he
met all three Estess sisters. "I had no interest in medical research," he
remembers, "but with their story and their situation, you can't help
but be intrigued. Here they are with this tough, tough challenge, and
they essentially took matters into their own hands."

They asked him to join the Project ALS board. Rob declined, instead offering to serve as a free consultant for one year. He brought
fiscal discipline, expanded the medical advisory board, contacted
new potential donors. And found himself more engaged every day.

"Shoot, I've been chairman of the board ever since. And when
Jenifer died, I felt a moral obligation to Valerie and Meredith to make
sure that Project ALS did not go away."

His first discovery was the limitations of the traditional ways of
addressing difficult issues. "The problems of the world are not going
to be solved by the government. In the next twenty years, it will be
individuals."

Rob's second discovery was the reward of participating in solving those problems. "Making money in business is challenging. If it's
the only thing you do, though, it's not enough. I felt I could possibly
have a huge impact, maybe bigger than at Goldman Sachs, in the
nonprofit world. It's true too. It's a great feeling. You can move the
mark."

Now Ron is practically evangelical about the benefits of social action. "If you leave it to somebody else, or think it's somebody else's
job, it won't get done. Step up. Take ownership. Have a passion. Medical research is certainly my passion now.

"So what are you good at? What does the world need? We're all
lucky to be here, we all receive enormous benefits from living in this
country. All of us can pick something where we have a real passion. If

you get involved, you are going to make a huge difference. Better yet, you'll get much more back than you put in. Much, much more."

Seeing a need, sharing a capability, making a commitment. From an investment banker to a health-center translator, the recipe for people committed to constructive social action remains the same. And from these attributes comes the benefit of giving, the discovery that helping others—however much it demands in time or money or heart—repays far more than it costs.

Virtually every American is familiar with the lines from John F. Kennedy's inaugural address, about people asking themselves what they can do for their country. But few people know what the young president said would be the benefit of acting on the answer to that question: "a good conscience our only sure reward."

What he meant is that serving others deepens life and lifts the spirits. It provides a kind of connection and healing that is essential to restoring a nation adrift. It reveals to people their inner wealth. This change will take more than a few people's actions, of course. But as more people begin with themselves, they help contribute to the larger element discussed in the next chapter.

Authentic patriots do not set out to change the world; they set out to solve a problem. But eventually and incrementally, their perspective shifts. They discover that work of this kind fills life with meaning, connections, shared concern. Their initiative becomes a calling. They discover the sense of purpose and sense of belonging that comes when a person attains Kennedy's "good conscience." While helping others change bad situations, they see the biggest transformations occur within themselves. The ways in which their lives and their hearts are enriched and enlarged, these are the real benefits. This is the real gold.

14

Element Four:
A National Movement

Many men go fishing all of their lives without knowing
it is not fish they are after.

— HENRY DAVID THOREAU

Don't say you don't have enough time. You have exactly
the same number of hours per day that were given to
Helen Keller, Pasteur, Michelangelo, Mother Teresa,
Leonardo da Vinci, Thomas Jefferson and Albert Einstein.

— H. JACKSON BROWN JR.

You and I have a rendezvous with destiny. . . . If we
fail, at least let our children's children say of us we justified our brief moment here. We did all that could be
done.

— RONALD REAGAN

ONCE UPON A TIME David Goggins weighed 280 pounds. He
was a powerlifter, a Navy SEAL who never ran more than short
distances, an American stationed in Iraq. It was 2005, he was thirty,
and he already had a tour of duty in Afghanistan to his credit.

When Goggins' stint in the giant sandbox was up, though, he remembered one operation in particular. A mission to save SEALS by
helicopter from a dangerous situation went awry, and eleven soldiers

died. In response Goggins set out to fund-raise for the Special Operations Warrior Foundation, which gives college tuition to children of special operations members who die on duty.

How would he raise the money? By running. But David Goggins was no Saturday-morning-10K kind of guy. He entered only the hardest races, the longest and most demanding. While ninety pounds melted off his frame, he put one foot in front of the other to train for and complete a marathon. Later he ran a hundred miles in nineteen hours. Then he completed a double Ironman distance triathlon (that's a 4.8-mile swim, a 224-mile bike, and a 52.5-mile run). He ran a one-hundred-mile race considered one of the toughest ever, sponsored by the Hawaii Ultra Running Team (H.U.R.T.).

David was just getting started. He ran the grueling Badwater Ultramarathon, which begins in Death Valley (282 feet below sea level) and concludes 135 miles later atop Mount Whitney (8,360 feet above sea level). He competed in the Ultra Centric run, covering a record-setting 203.5 miles in forty-eight hours. Yes: That's one man, two days, two hundred–plus miles.

By late 2008 Goggins had raised three hundred thousand dollars for the foundation. That feat, and his ability to withstand pain, make him an exceptional human being. What he is doing, though—running to raise money—is not unusual at all. In fact, if there is any place in America in which sweating for a cause has become completely ordinary, it is in endurance sports.

The role model is the Race for the Cure, now better known as the Susan G. Komen for the Cure. Nancy Brinker launched this grassroots campaign to raise money and awareness in 1982, after her sister Susan died of breast cancer. To date the race and its related fund-raising efforts have invested $1.2 billion in research, education, and support.

It is a staggering sum, amassed one runner and one mile at a time. More important, this race has provided inspiration. All over the country now, on nearly any Saturday morning, thousands of runners line up in fund-raising races of one kind or another—5Ks, 10Ks, half marathons, marathons, triathlons—all for some purpose in addition to the athletic competition.

How does it work? Either the entry fee is higher than for a purely recreational race, or the runners have cajoled friends and colleagues into sponsoring them. Both ways, millions of dollars move from wallets to causes, carried there on runners' feet.

Even races that did not begin as fund-raisers have evolved in that direction. The New York City Marathon began in 1970 with 127 athletes in a quirky run around and around Central Park. By 2008 an astonishing 37,899 people participated in the run through all five boroughs of the city. More to the point, in just that year's marathon they raised $18.2 million for charity.

The point is this: In the subculture of endurance sports, social action has become the *norm*. It is as ordinary as starting guns and finish lines. Just imagine how American culture would be improved if this norm reached into other parts of society. The idea is spreading, in subtle and diverse ways. There are signs that a growing number of Americans understand the need for renewal of our common purpose.

"Service learning," for example, has become standard practice on college campuses. Students are encouraged, and at some schools required, to perform community service. It may seem contradictory to mandate that young adults volunteer to do good works. But the requirement reflects a belief that addressing social needs is an essential part of the intellectual growth and character development that is the mission of higher education. The idea is for students to develop a sense of purpose beyond their studies—and as with distance runners, it is fast becoming a new norm.

California State University Monterey was a bellwether in treating social responsibility learning as seriously as classroom learning; it was the first public university in the country to require service. A school department helps students find all kinds of tasks, from mentoring local kids to building community gardens in a nearby Chinatown.

Across the country at Columbia University, engineering students worked in 2007 to design a better walker for people living in Harlem's largest nursing home. In so doing they fulfilled a degree requirement well outside the traditional engineering academic path.

"We obviously want to create engineers and applied scientists who are technically adept, but also effective in this global society," said Jack McGourty, the university's associate engineering dean. That effectiveness requires more than competence in handling equations, structures, and systems. "We want to create students who are socially aware."

Colleges' attention to developing student consciences is not in the least unusual. Tulane University operates a Center for Public Service to engage undergraduates with the needs of New Orleans, and presents the prestigious Jim Runsdorf Excellence in Public Service Student Award to students who show exemplary social responsibility.

At Rice University in Houston, the latest strategic plan explains why service learning is important there:

> While the value of undergraduate research is well established and widely understood, there is a growing consensus in higher education that the benefits of research are enhanced when research intersects with real-world experience through service learning and community based research. Indeed, the complex challenges facing our world will be solved by students who have such real-world experience: students who understand the potential and limits of knowledge they are given in the classroom; students who are capable of applying standard theories in nonstandard settings in search of creative solutions; students who can tackle open-ended and ambiguous problems that require original thought and analysis; and students who can effectively communicate what they have learned in their research to academic, professional, and lay audiences alike.

In other words, the lessons of social responsibility are essential to success in the world today. New York University has taken this idea even further, with the Catherine B. Reynolds Foundation Program in Social Entrepreneurship. Along with scholarships, the program helps students develop skills and networks to cultivate world-changing ideas into actual solutions. Their teachers are some of the best social entrepreneurs in the country. Competition for a spot in the program is intense.

Programs like these send out ripples too. For example, five years ago Columbia engineering majors began working with students at nearby Frederick Douglass Academy on a robotics project. Since then, average SAT scores at the high school have risen two hundred points. Now Frederick Douglass students are performing their own service, by mentoring in local elementary schools. Ripples indeed. No wonder 68 percent of high schools either offer or endorse service-learning programs, and the number continues to rise.

Obviously the education leaders of America did not invent service learning, any more than marathoners invented fund-raising. But increasingly, these subcultures have embraced an old-fashioned idea: The truly educated person of letters, just like the true athlete, excels in the moral and civic realm as much as in the classroom or on the track. The fully developed citizen is engaged and developed.

Another generation of Americans has been working from that theme for years, quietly but with admirable persistence. They too represent a subculture in which acting with authentic patriotism is the norm.

Who? The fraternal groups. The Benevolent and Protective Order of Elks, with roughly a million members, awards almost $3.7 million in college scholarships each year. The Loyal Order of Moose, also a million strong, has provided housing and schooling for more than eleven thousand orphans since 1913. The 375,000 members of Shriners International—they're the ones who show up at community parades wearing funny hats and riding on miniature fire trucks—fund twenty-two pediatric hospitals. Since the Shriners started their work in 1922, they have helped 865,000 children. Rotary International, with 1.2 million members, merges business networking with civic activism to support disaster relief and the eradication of polio, and to provide the generous Ambassadorial Scholarships. Those awards have enabled forty-seven thousand students to study in foreign lands, and to bring their cultural lessons home.

The largest of all such fraternal organizations is the Lions Club, with 1.3 million members in 205 countries. Since Helen Keller challenged this group in 1925 to serve as "knights to the blind in the crusade against darkness," Lions clubs have raised hundreds of millions of dollars to prevent blindness, restore vision, and provide services to people who have lost their sight. Lions also work on programs for children, from running camps to providing immunizations to sponsoring Boy Scout troops. Local Lions clubs also pair with clubs in other countries, thereby building international friendships.

People unacquainted with fraternal groups tend to dismiss them. But there is no denying the impact of the social service norm in their subculture, nor the fact that they have improved millions of lives.

Social activism does not always occur in such structured ways. Sometimes it arises simply when people understand the degree of need. That inspiration was clearly at work in the nation's response to Hurricane Katrina. While government's preparation for a storm of that magnitude was insufficient, its response to the developing tragedy inadequate, and its efforts to rebuild the Gulf Coast sluggish, individual Americans showed none of these failings. Hundreds of thousands of people opened their homes and their wallets, and even more gave of their time. In the year following Katrina, 550,000 people volunteered to help rebuild and repair the Gulf states. When it became clear that the work was not finished, volunteerism not only did not wane, it grew: Six hundred thousand people helped in the second year after Katrina. That is the sustaining power of work with a common purpose.

SOME OF THE most inspirational stories come from individuals who saw a need, responded, and suddenly found themselves atop a groundswell of social and civic engagement. They weren't part of a large organization; they simply had a good idea, a commitment to making a difference, and a way to apply those values in a local way. How local? How about a single tree?

Luna was, it must be said, no ordinary tree. Of the stands of thousand-year-old redwoods that once grew a high canopy over northern California, logging had removed the vast majority. Luna stood in a rare grove that had not been cut—but lay in the path and plans of Pacific Lumber, a division of the $2.2 billion Maxxam, Inc., of Houston.

The surrounding area in Humboldt County had already been logged. On December 31, 1996, a landslide in the town of Stafford buried homes in mud up to seventeen feet deep. Town residents, and an independent investigator chosen by Governor Pete Wilson, theorized that clear-cutting had at least contributed to the slide—and may have caused it.

Beyond those material concerns, people opposed to the logging had other arguments. The forests had stood since before white men came to this continent. The trees were ancient beings. It was the responsibility of humans to protect these living treasures.

Ecological activists had tried negotiating with timber companies to protect the trees. They had tried working through government, via regulation and legislation. They had tried marches and protests. Nothing had worked. Some of the more committed opponents of logging embarked on a new strategy. A group would approach timber workers and attempt to talk them into putting down their chain saws. During the distraction, other activists would climb some of the trees. The loggers would be forced to stop. This was radical action, genuine civil disobedience, the redwood equivalent of lying in front of bulldozers.

Julia Hill knew nothing about these actions, nor even the trees. She'd grown up in Arkansas a preacher's daughter, a youth she calls "a bit aimless." But in 1996 her small car was hit by a truck, and during her yearlong recovery, Julia decided to change priorities. She would live more for the present, and make sure every moment counted. She would travel the world, concentrating on places with deep spiritual roots. She healed, and dreamed.

When neighbors announced they were driving to California and needed someone to help share gas costs, Julia's journey began. She arrived in Humboldt County, and after wandering through the trees at Grizzly Creek Redwoods State Park, decided to stay. Julia hurried home, sold nearly everything she owned, bought a sleeping bag and tent, and returned to California.

She went directly to local forest-protection activists and offered to volunteer. At first they turned her aside, but she persisted. One of them asked her name, and when she said "Julia," he asked if she had a forest name. Everyone has a forest name, he explained. A bit embarrassed, she revealed a childhood nickname, Butterfly. She was in.

A few days later a group member known as Almond asked if there were any volunteers to sit in a tree they had named Luna. Julia volunteered but he demurred; it would be a long sit, perhaps five days. He needed someone with more experience. But it was November, the weather turning chilly, and volunteers were in short supply. Julia insisted; Almond relented.

In late 1997, Julia Butterfly Hill climbed into Luna for her five-day stay. She was twenty-five. She had no experience as an activist, or even as a tree-sitter. But she did have two things that made all the difference: a sense of her personal power, which every American possesses, knowingly or not, and a will of steel.

Right away there was a powerful rainstorm. Winds swayed the platform that hung eighteen stories up. A wildly flapping tarp prevented sleep. By day five, Julia Butterfly was more than willing to climb down, take a hot shower, and sleep under a roof. But the next day she returned. Five days into that second sitting, she developed a kidney virus that sent her shaking and feverish back to the ground. But by then her bond with the giant living thing had roots of its own.

Three weeks later, carrying a backpack stocked with supplies, she returned to Luna. This time Julia Butterfly intended to stay longer, because the ground organization was spending too much effort moving people up and down the tree and not enough effort on outreach. On December 10, 1997, with Almond to keep her company, Julia Butterfly climbed Luna for the third time.

Almond left on January 4 after nearly a month. But Julia Butterfly stayed. To leave the tree was to surrender it to cutting; loggers had begun work in the immediate area. She found herself in conversations with them—arguments, really, shouted from tree to ground and back.

Days became weeks, and then months. All that time she lived on a platform 180 feet from the ground, fashioning a kind of nest among tarps and containers. The tree thrashed in winter storms and the windy onslaught of El Niño. Julia Butterfly endured helicopter harassment, a ten-day siege by company security guards that left her without food supplies, frustration as negotiations to protect the forest limped and stalled, and oceans of solitude.

But she stayed in that tree. And as long as she did so, Luna remained uncut. The media took notice; Julia gave interviews by cell phone. Celebrities such as the musician Bonnie Raitt rallied to the cause. Public pressure grew on the timber company.

Not everyone approved, of course. Julia Butterfly was breaking the law. She was trespassing. She threatened to hurt the local economy, because nearly everyone either worked for Maxxam directly or relied on the company's well-being for their jobs.

But there is no denying that as she persisted, Julia Butterfly's civil disobedience acquired a greater character, an emblematic power. This young woman had no job, no home, no money, no family nearby, no political power, no corporate backing, no media training, no experience. Yet she was preventing an irreversible action, thwarting a huge company, stalemating a legal process, stymieing the tough loggers at the foot of her tree, and through it all, raising concern for old-growth forests to a national level of awareness.

One person. Thomas Jefferson would be proud.

In another country, Julia Butterfly might have been arrested. Or starved down. Or shot. But in this nation, with its founding faith in the power of one person, the nobility of every human being, something else happened: The protestor became a hero, the public learned something, Luna remained standing. The tree-hugging hippie became an authentic patriot.

On December 18, 1999, after Maxxam signed an agreement to spare Luna and the surrounding redwoods, Julia Butterfly Hill climbed down the tree. Her feet touched earth for the first time in 728 days.

ONCE YOU BEGIN noticing social engagement, you see it everywhere. It is a quiet but powerful force, working diligently away. Here are examples just from my immediate circle of friends:

Kathryn Blume was an actress based in New York who performed largely in regional theater companies. She was also a longtime part-time activist, volunteering to work information desks at folk festivals and trying to incorporate her politics into her art. In early 2003, in the lead-up to the invasion of Iraq, she became increasingly agitated. What happened next is something opponents and supporters of that war alike can admire, because it is full of authentic patriotism.

In January Blume and her friend and fellow actor Sharon Bower learned that a New York group, Theater Against War, planned to perform the play *Lysistrata* on March 3. Written by Aristophanes in 411 B.C., the comedy tells of a plan the women of Athens hatch in order to end the Peloponnesian War: They will refuse to have sex until the men stop fighting. Of course the men protest, and many women struggle to keep their pledge of chastity too. But the women rally one another, uphold their vow, and the men soon negotiate a peace. The play is hilarious, unapologetically naughty, and rich with an antiwar message.

Blume and Bower launched a Web site, the Lysistrata Project, which encouraged other theater companies to perform the play on March 3. They found translations and adaptations of the play, which they added to the site for easy downloading. A group in Seattle announced it would do the show. Then Austin, Texas, actors declared they would perform *Lysistrata* as well.

A movement began. Screen actors Kevin Bacon and his wife, Kyra Sedgwick, agreed to play Aristophanes' frustrated husband and celibate wife in a production at the Brooklyn Academy of Music. National media took notice. Theater companies in more cities, and even other countries, arranged their own performances. The Web site kept track as new productions joined the groundswell, and by mid-February they numbered in the hundreds.

When March 3 arrived, Aristophanes' ancient antiwar comedy appeared in all fifty states and fifty-nine countries—Japan, Great Britain, Canada, Iceland, Singapore, Australia, Italy, Cuba—and Greece, of course. Even in Iraq, only days before the U.S. invasion, a group staged a public reading.

In all there were 1,029 performances. The shows raised awareness, and brought in a hundred thousand dollars for peace-oriented charities. The play also tickled the funny bones and sparked the consciences of audiences, who collectively numbered 225,000. Blume later wrote a one-woman show about her crazy two months running a global movement from her apartment laptop, *The Accidental Activist*, which she performed across the country for several years. A film about the project, *Operation Lysistrata*, won numerous awards and showings internationally. The freedom of expression that is part of what makes

America great was put to meaningful purpose by a citizen's creative expression of independent activism. That's authentic patriotism, and it all started with two women and one good idea.

GEOFF GEVALT WAS a lifelong newsman, worked mostly at papers in Massachusetts and Ohio. He was on a team in Akron that won a Pulitzer Prize for its work on race relations. He was later the managing editor of a midsize paper in Vermont, where his responsibilities included a weekly page of creative writing by local teens.

When he learned that only 48 percent of the state's tenth-graders could meet the federal standard for writing competence, he decided to take a leap into the public good. Resigning from the newspaper, he founded the Young Writers' Project (YWP)—with the goal of enabling elementary and high school students to express themselves, receive feedback, and establish a creative community.

The project made one strategic decision, and moved onto the Web. It was a perfect move, because the Internet lends itself to populist ideas so readily, and because that is where people under eighteen spend their free time. Also, young writers could post their work anonymously, which made the act of sharing fresh writing less risky. Their fellow writers could answer with candid but supportive responses, secure in their own anonymity.

The idea took off. The YWP's online enrollment has nearly tripled every year. Students post work in progress, school assignments, and their best creative efforts. They receive feedback on all of it, from professionals, from top writing students at local colleges who work as mentors, and above all from one another. The tone is one of fellowship. YWP members police the site themselves, creating an atmosphere of respect rare on the Internet.

Top student work appears several times a week in newspapers across the state. An annual anthology showcases the best of the best. But publication has become almost a secondary benefit. The real gains have been in the poorest towns, rural farming areas, and mountain outposts, where children of families with next to nothing are discovering the power of their ideas and the reinforcement of their worth— because someone is paying attention.

A professional research study is under way to assess the project's progress toward academic goals. So far, schools that have embraced the YWP as a way to teach writing have seen leaps in standardized-test scores. When one school contemplated cutting its YWP involvement, students went on their own initiative before the school board to protest—and won.

But the writers don't treat the project like homework; they treat it like self-expression. Site traffic actually rises on weekends and during vacations. And the community of YWP readers continues to grow: A short story contest led to collaboration with composers and the Vermont Symphony Orchestra. An invitation for writing about winter led to staged reading by professional actors with the Vermont Stage Company.

As students write and read, they learn more about one another and they develop a sense of empowerment and validation. They discover that they have something valuable to say. They prepare for greater success in the workplace, and more effective participation in democracy.

As for Geoff, he has watched the decline of the newspaper industry with dismay. But he has little time to dwell on the concerns of his former profession. There are new schools wanting online classrooms, new poetry and fiction contests, a program to help Somali refugees learn to write their stories of hardship and perseverance. One person, one idea, and thousands of lives changed for the better.

AS THESE STORIES show, people do not typically choose to become authentic patriots. They simply adopt a certain attitude about their role in society, and then the need comes and finds them—and does not let go.

For example, there's Bill McKibben. A college professor who'd written books about man's relationship to nature, he tried an experiment in 2006. To draw attention to the issue of climate change, McKibben decided to walk from Ripton, Vermont—starting at the cabin where the poet Robert Frost had lived—to the shores of Lake Champlain in Burlington. Inviting others to join him, McKibben made the trek over the Labor Day weekend.

It wasn't far, only sixty miles or so. But along the way he spoke at schools and churches, held rallies, and urged folks to join the walk. They did so, in droves. At its peak the crowd numbered more than a thousand people.

In many ways, McKibben is still on that walk today. The media attention was considerable, the symbolism of walkers crowding a roadside conveying the message that America must wean itself from the gasoline-powered car. Six months later he was on the Interfaith Walk for Climate Rescue, across Massachusetts. Again there were rallies, again the media showed up. When it came to climate change, walking was educating.

One month later, on Earth Day 2007, McKibben's growing organization helped energize over a thousand global warming–related events. A movement had begun. And the author had become an activist.

Today McKibben has less time for writing than ever. He runs 350 .org, a climate-change group busy on three continents. The number 350 is based on what he calls a "red line" for global warming: James Hansen of NASA, one of the world's top climate scientists, published a paper in 2008 that defined the sustainable level for carbon dioxide (in parts per million) in the earth's atmosphere:

> If humanity wants to preserve a planet similar to that on which civilization developed and to which life on Earth is adapted, paleo-climate evidence and ongoing climate change suggest that CO_2 will need to be reduced from its current 385 ppm to at most 350 ppm.

Through 350.org, McKibben now speaks all over the world about these issues, participates in climate treaty negotiations, shepherds activists in Europe and Africa, and above all urges Americans to consider their role in protecting the environment.

"We make up four percent of the world's population, and we produce twenty-five percent of the carbon output," McKibben says. "We need to do the moral mathematics."

On October 24, 2009, 350.org called for an international day of action on climate change. Groups gathered at more than fifty-two hundred events in 181 countries and on every continent—even Antarctica. One highlight of the day was the idea for churches to ring their bells

350 times, combining a clarion call about climate change with a reminder of the sacred value of a living planet.

The ancient philosophical text *Tao Te Ching*, written by Lao-tzu in the sixth century B.C., says: "A journey of a thousand miles begins with a single step." From a weekend walk to an international movement, Bill McKibben embodies that lesson.

WHAT DO JULIA Butterfly Hill, Kathryn Blume, Sharon Bower, Geoff Gevalt and Bill McKibben have in common? They identified an urgent need. They saw that government was doing an insufficient job. They observed that the marketplace was indifferent to the issue. And they decided to do something about it.

Their kindred, in projects large and small, are all over the country:

- Talia Lehman, an eighth-grader in Waukee, Iowa, responded to Katrina with a treat-or-treat coin fund-raising the following Halloween. Thanks to exposure on the *Today* show, she raised $10 million. Next she created the RandomKid program, whose Web site teaches kids how to build their own successful programs. Among the site's projects are clean water for African villages (involving kids in seven states) and building a school in Cambodia (thanks to children in forty-eight states and nineteen countries). When enough funds are raised, kids get to name the school.

- Talia is not the only youngster to take the world of need by storm. In 2006 Rachel S. Rosenfeld was an eleventh-grader in Harrison, New York, who developed a stomach illness that kept her out of school for the academic year. During that time she read about a Cambodian girl, nearly her age, whose only hope for avoiding a life of prostitution was in obtaining an education. But there was no school in her town. Rachel wrote letters requesting contributions, raising both $52,000 and greater awareness of the plight of Cambodian girls. The World Bank and Asian Development Bank followed her lead with additional funding. In 2007 Rachel cut a wide red ribbon at the opening of the three-hundred-student R. S. Rosenfeld School in Siem Reap Province.

- Wendy Kopp was a senior at Princeton University when she wrote a thesis about connecting graduating seniors with schools most in need of teachers. She raised $2.5 million while still twenty-one years old, and in 1990 placed five hundred young men and women in six communities' schools. Since then fourteen thousand new teachers have gone to work in twenty-nine communities. They reach four hundred thousand students a year, 3 million since the program began. In 2008 Teach for America, the program Wendy founded, brought thirty-seven hundred new teachers to communities as varied as New York City and Indian reservations in South Dakota. Research has found that students with faculty from Teach for America make greater gains than those with ordinary teachers, especially in math. Meanwhile the program is becoming an ever more desirable way of starting a career. In 2007 Teach for America received 24,700 applications, including 11 percent of the seniors at Yale, 10 percent at Georgetown, and 9 percent at Harvard.
- Littleton Mitchell rose to prominence during the civil rights movement as head of the Delaware chapter of the NAACP. But as that movement diminished his work did not end. He led the desegregation of hospitals, hotels, movie theaters, golf courses, fire departments, cemeteries, and more. He also worked to eliminate discrimination in employment and housing. A fellowship named for him provides support for Delaware graduate students to learn leadership and social responsibility.
- Daniel Zilka runs the American Diner Museum, an organization that pays homage to the classic diners of the country. He also runs the New Hope Diner Project, which engages teen offenders in the Rhode Island juvenile detention center in the restoration of diners around New England. Once construction is done, the kids learn to cook, handle the cash register, even manage the business. For many, it is their last chance to step off a path that otherwise could lead to criminal conduct as an adult.

- Each year Jim Keane, a state representative in Montana, asks for ideas for bills from the high school in Butte. Students propose up to seven, and he picks the one most likely to succeed. Students research why the bill ought to pass, testify before lawmakers about what they've learned, and follow the bill during the legislative session (with a little friendly lobbying). When the 2006 bill passed, the governor signed it into law in a ceremony at the high school. Today a copy of the bill sits in the school's awards case, beside the athletic trophies.

- J. B. Schramm worked as an admissions counselor at Harvard while a graduate student there, and he witnessed the university's struggle to recruit low-income applicants. Top students from impoverished communities go to college, but kids with middling grades do not even apply. Later he worked at a teen center in Washington, D.C., and experienced the other side of the equation: Those middle-tier kids had no one counseling them about how to choose a college, how to find financial aid, or even how to apply. He created College Summit, to assist teens who might otherwise have gone directly from high school to a lifetime of low-wage, low-skilled jobs. Since its founding in 1993, College Summit has helped thirty-five thousand twelfth-graders reach for college, while also training ninety-five hundred teachers, guidance counselors, and others who can influence students. In Saint Louis schools that adopted the College Summit approach, 20 percent more teens enrolled in college. In West Virginia, schools using Schramm's method outperformed the rest of the state by 13 percent.

- Eloise Cobell is the great-granddaughter of Mountain Chief, one of the great Indian leaders in U.S. history. She is also a tireless and effective advocate for the Blackfeet Nation. Many Native Americans remain locked in poverty because they have no access to capital—loans that would enable them to buy a tractor to improve their farming, or a cooler for a grocery store. As a result businesses on the reservations often starve, though just outside the reservation white-owned businesses are thriving. While cattle ranching with her husband in northern Montana,

Eloise led the effort to create the Blackfeet National Bank—the nation's first bank on a reservation and the first owned by a tribe. Then, to help cultivate businesses that would use that bank, she took charge of the nonprofit Native American Community Development Corporation. Now economic growth occurs on the reservation, and the Blackfeet share in building one another's prosperity. Eloise is also the lead plaintiff in a 1996 case claiming U.S. government mismanagement of oil, timber, and other royalties on Indian land. Eleven years into the case, a federal judge ruled that the government committed an "irreparable breach of fiduciary duty." Cobell's goal is to see the billions of dollars that the government received for oil and timber leases properly paid to the Indians who own the land.

- David Joyce was the new president of Ripon College in Wisconsin when facilities managers approached him with a perennial problem: There were not enough parking spaces on campus. He challenged them to find alternative solutions. "We are not paving over any more prairie," he said. The result was a program that gives a free bicycle to every incoming student who promises not to bring a car to campus. Almost two hundred first-year students signed up for the program—decongesting the college's roads and parking lots, while also teaching fitness and sustainability. Other colleges have since followed Ripon's lead, from the University of New England in Maine to Emory University in Georgia to Saint Xavier University in Chicago.

Sometimes people who launch a new initiative have already enjoyed huge success in some other endeavor, but did not lose their conscience along the way:

- Gerald Chertavian served as a Big Brother after college, and wrote about his experience in his application to Harvard Business School. He went to Wall Street, then built a $20 million communications company with 130 employees in the United States and Europe. He sold the business in 1999. But Chertavian did not pull the ladder of opportunity up after him when he was done climbing it. Instead he created Year Up, a program that provides college-level courses to low-income teens so they can pursue careers in high tech. Students go to class, connect with mentors, and even get paid for their intensive work. The results: 100 percent of students land internships—every one of them—and 87 percent find jobs within four months of completing the program. Year Up now operates in five states and Washington, D.C.

- George Weiss took a different approach to the same problem. He was a nineteen-year-old college sophomore in Philadelphia when his fraternity hosted a dozen low-income children for Christmas dinner. It was his introduction to the potential these children possessed, and they became friends. When they graduated from high school, a rarity in their community, they credited his role modeling. Years later, when he had amassed a fortune in money management, Weiss went to one of Philadelphia's toughest neighborhoods and made an offer to a group of 112 sixth-graders: If they made it through high school, he would pay their college tuition. That challenge led to offers in four other cities, plus the creation of Say Yes to Education. Say Yes provides students with help in overcoming social, medical, financial, and academic obstacles. Today the program offers everything from social work to scholarships, after-school tutoring to summer schooling. And hundreds of young men and women have received a college education they would never have believed within their reach.

- Country music star Dolly Parton created the Imagination Library in her eastern Tennessee home county of Sevier, with the intent of teaching young children about the importance of books. The beneficiaries are eligible from birth to age five. They receive one book every month for free, starting with *The Little Engine That Could* and finishing with *Look Out Kindergarten, Here I Come*. The Library now operates in 732 communities in forty-three states, providing 420,000 children with a book every month. In 2007, with partnerships ranging from the United Way to the Governor's Books from Birth Foundation in Ten-

nessee, and with support from local communities, the Library
mailed some 4.5 million books.

These are just examples, and there are many, many others. Geof-
frey Canada has devoted twenty years to the Harlem Children's Zone
Project, a meshwork of support services for a blighted hundred-square
block area that aims to provide a safety net so strong, no child can fall
through. Taste of the Nation, founded by Bill Shore, organizes benefit
meals annually in fifty-five U.S. cities, involving ten thousand chefs
and restaurants, and in its twenty-year history has raised $70 million
to fight childhood hunger.

Always, at every level, the work of authentic patriots begins with
one committed person.

Here's a sweet one. Each year in this country, about twenty thousand children in foster care fall out of that system because they reach
eighteen and their services cease. They can lose school funds, financial support for the family that took them in, and more. Mary Louise
Hartpence worked many years for the state Human Services Department in Oklahoma City. When she died in 1983, she left her three-
hundred-thousand-dollar estate to establish an education fund for
these foster kids. So far, 208 children have received scholarships, 5
received associates or technical degrees, 25 earned bachelor's degrees, and 11 went on to graduate school in law, medicine, dentistry,
and more.

It goes on and on and wonderfully on. The United States is now
home to 1.6 million nonprofit ventures. Not all are devoted to social
responsibility, and not all are expertly run. Still, there's no denying:
Millions of people are actively engaged in making America a better
place. And millions more people are the beneficiaries of those good
deeds. The importance of these organizations has increased so
dramatically—because of growing needs, and because of insufficient
responses by government and the marketplace—that their reach has
extended into the for-profit world. If the public leads, eventually some
businesses will follow. A growing number of companies now form
and operate with social responsibility as their credo.

The forerunner in this movement arguably was Ben & Jerry's ice cream. Although the company makes a luxury food, and a highly caloric one at that, for many years social responsibility has been as important as profit. The corporate mission statement explicitly affirms that Ben & Jerry's "seeks to meet human needs and eliminate injustices in our local, national and international communities by integrating those concerns into our day-to-day business activities."

That pledge has meant limiting the gap in pay between top executives and the lowest-wage earners. It has meant minimizing manufacturing waste and needless packaging. It has meant diverting 7.5 percent of pretax profits into a nonprofit foundation.

It has also meant being dismissed in the Me Generation business climate of the 1980s, even though in that era Ben & Jerry's doubled in size each year. The merging of principles and profit worked. In 1988 Ben & Jerry's won both the Corporate Giving Award from the Council on Economic Priorities *and* the Small Business of the Year Award from the federal Small Business Administration. For the White House ceremony with President Reagan, Ben donned a borrowed Italian waiter's jacket and Jerry wore his only suit.

The moment seems almost quaint to recall, as if the company were a relic of a more innocent time. And yet the success of Ben & Jerry's provides an example.

With the deregulation of long-distance calling, a company named Working Assets began offering phone service with a social mission. Every bill automatically took 1 percent for donation to nonprofits. The company later expanded to cell phone service and credit cards—each swipe of the card leads to a ten-cent donation. The company actively solicits customer nominations for where the money should go.

Nearly all the beneficiaries are liberal causes: the Brady Center to Prevent Gun Violence, the National Coalition to Abolish the Death Penalty, the Sierra Club. But liberal and conservative alike can be impressed by the results: Since its founding in 1985, Working Assets (now called Credo) has given away more than $60 million.

The most fully evolved example of this business model, though the founder once called it "a joke that got out of control," is Newman's Own. Granted, it helps when you launch a business if the founder is one of the more appealing and famous people on the planet—the late

Paul Newman, aka Butch Cassidy, aka Hud, aka Cool Hand Luke. Newman's Own started with salad dressings, then moved into cookies and organic products, and now offers a broad line of food items. All profits go to charity. The goods are pricey, honoring the unapologetic corporate motto: "Shameless exploitation in pursuit of the common good."

It works. The Newman's Own Foundation has given away tens of millions of dollars in the United States and fifteen other countries. The foundation's first Hole in the Wall Gang Camp for children with cancer opened in 1988. Now there are eight camps in three countries, serving thirteen thousand kids a year.

Working in the realm of social responsibility does not mean that businesses enjoy freedom from ordinary market concerns. If anything, the issues are multiplied. A company not only has to worry about making a profit, it also must satisfy scrupulous scrutiny of its practices. Newman's Own conducted a long deliberation, for example, over whether to package its salad dressings in glass or plastic. That meant researching which plastics could be recycled, whether glass or plastic was recycled at a higher rate, what the fuel savings would be from shipping products in the lower-weight container—and oh yes, what degree of certainty there would be that packaging would not affect the flavor.

Paul Newman's smiling face appears on every label, beside that of his daughter Nell for items in the organic product line. But the wise old actor never forgot what deserves top billing on the products' marquee: Each container trumpets the amount of money raised thus far. At this writing, the labels proclaim donations of $265 million.

BEN & JERRY'S, WORKING ASSETS, and Newman's Own are familiar American brand names. They have lots of company today, as social responsibility has taken a firm hold in many businesses. These endeavors far exceed normal corporate generosity, in which a company gives money to some charity in order to gain goodwill and a nice tax deduction. Socially responsible enterprises make changing the world their organizing principle.

Consumer support for this concept is so strong, some companies profess civic responsibility while actually making negligible contributions. Apparently there are sharks in all kinds of waters. Manipulation of consumers does not mean that authentic-patriot ideas are wrong for the corporate world, only that just as in any other corner of capitalism, let the buyer beware. If anything, these scoundrel companies provide more proof that capitalism does not meet the social and human needs of our time.

The fact that companies designed to serve as authentic patriots succeed can be attributed to one reason only: the hunger of American consumers for products and services that reflect their values, or that uphold the importance of a social contract based on values beyond profit. Just like the endurance athletes, therefore, just like the service learners and fraternal groups, the public's appetite for products from socially responsible companies reflects much more than a passing phase. We are talking about a new, emerging cultural norm.

We have seen how government, for all its strengths, responds insufficiently to the human needs of our time. We have witnessed how the marketplace, while enriching some and creating prosperity for many, displays capitalism's inherent indifference to human, nonmarket concerns.

Yet there stirs in the American breast today an energy, an idea, and a potential. There is a word for this powerful animating spirit, and that word is *greatness*. It is the greatness of the authentic patriots, displaying all the nobility and power that the nation's Founders believed every person possesses, which enables them to start and succeed and spread their missions. It is greatness that inspires other people to follow that lead, as donors, as volunteers, as supporters. These are the elements to restore a nation adrift.

Can you feel it? In your neighborhood? In your community? In your own heart? Can you sense, if not greatness, then the potential for greatness? It is there, stronger and more needed and more effective every day.

And for this greatness to renew America, only one final element is missing.

15

Element Five: Everyone an Authentic Patriot

I preach to you, then, my countrymen, that our country calls not for the life of ease but for the life of strenuous endeavor. The twentieth century looms before us big with the fate of many nations. If we stand idly by, if we seek merely swollen, slothful ease and ignoble peace, if we shrink from the hard contests where men must win at hazard of their lives and at the risk of all they hold dear, then the bolder and stronger peoples will pass us by, and will win for themselves the domination of the world.

Let us therefore boldly face the life of strife, resolute to do our duty well and manfully; resolute to uphold righteousness by deed and word; resolute to be honest and brave, to serve high ideals, yet to use practical methods.

Above all, let us shrink from no strife, moral or physical, within or without the nation, provided we are certain that the strife is justified—for it is only through strife, through hard and dangerous endeavor, that we shall ultimately win the goal of true national greatness.

— THEODORE ROOSEVELT

PICTURE GEORGE WASHINGTON, ON the December day in 1783 when he stepped down as general and presented his sword to

Congress. While the world reeled from his humility, Washington climbed on a horse with an escort of a single companion, and rode hard so he would be home by Christmas Eve. But the word *home* is an understatement for his relationship with Mount Vernon. He grew up there. He would die there. During the Revolutionary years, he had been able to spend only a few nights there—a handful in November 1782, a short spell in September 1780. All the time Washington was leading the troops to victory, he was also a man who wanted to go home.

Picture John Adams in February 1778, climbing the gangplank of a ship bound for France. He is traveling as an envoy of the colonies, at that point not a nation but rebellious subjects of Great Britain. Adams' task is to persuade Paris to loan millions of dollars so the rebellion can pay its army and begin to build a navy. The ship he boards is not outfitted for passengers. Between rough winter seas and King George III's mighty naval patrols, crossing the Atlantic in that era is more dangerous than parachuting from a plane today. His only companion is his son, John Quincy Adams. John the elder will not see his wife for eighteen months, his personal finances are a mess, and he may die from British cannons on the sea. He goes anyway.

Picture Thomas Jefferson in his Monticello home in 1782, mourning the death of his beloved young wife. He has left public life completely, calling his sorrow "a stupor of mind." He destroys all of their letters. He climbs on his horse each day for rambling rides, headlong, running from his grief. He shuts himself up in his library for hours of solitude. On her deathbed Martha begged him not to marry again, and the widower keeps that promise all his days. And yet, eventually Jefferson rouses himself, and in twenty years he is president. He buys the Louisiana territories from the French for a pittance, doubling the size of the new nation and thereby establishing the independent, pioneer spirit that characterizes Americans to this day.

These are our role models. And the country in which we are privileged to live is our inheritance from them. What they have entrusted to us is much more than acreage and commerce, natural resources and national boundaries. They have handed down a sacred idea of what a human being is, and how humanity can best protect and provide for itself.

The men and women of that era risked their lives for these ideals because it was necessary. Today the imperatives are less elemental to the nation's existence. But that does not mean that Americans can afford to risk nothing, contribute nothing. A democracy without an engaged populace is like a monarchy without a king.

The question today, in our nation adrift, is what level of participation makes sense—given our busy lives, our economic realities, our contentment with a certain level of comfort. We cannot all quit our jobs to launch some new philanthropic endeavor. Nor are we all capable of coming up with an initiative that will succeed. The projects you've read about here are the result of enormous effort by truly unusual people.

But leaders cannot exist without followers. For every new campaign from some social entrepreneur, many more volunteers stuff the envelopes. For every dream some civic activist pursues, many more people write checks to make it possible. For every inspiring speaker standing at a microphone, there are countless people who have scheduled the event, brought in the podium, and set up the chairs. For every celebration, someone filled the balloons.

If you speak with these people—the Mercedes Shapiros, Carmen Landreths, and Marcia Schoenfelds—they say the same things leaders do: They are not giving, they are receiving. Helping others gives their life greater purpose. They are humbled by the need they see, and gratified to be able to do something about it.

The emotions these people feel are not secrets or illusions. They are real, they endure, and they are attainable for every person in America. What this nation most needs is identical to what her citizens also most need—the reinvigoration of common purpose.

But how much is enough? If the revolutionaries had to risk their lives, what level of effort is appropriate on our part? To find an answer, let's try a brief thought experiment.

Imagine three hours a week. That is, imagine people setting aside three hours out of every week for work on a project that offered no benefit to themselves—only to others. That is a far cry less than risking life and property. It's one evening a week without television. It's Saturday morning, or Sunday afternoon. The time need not conflict with family, because the whole family can take part. Imagine if everyone in America between the ages of ten and eighty gave that small slice of their week. What could come of those three hours?

The first benefit would be a rapid reduction in the issues facing this nation. Well-meaning groups, perpetually desperate for help, would find themselves with the welcome challenge of coping with a flood of it. The most persistent problems—hunger, illiteracy, homelessness, isolation, race relations, crime, decaying schools, teens at risk, struggling families, lonely elders, dirty air and water—would all diminish.

The second benefit would be the economic rewards. If there are 250 million Americans between the ages of ten and eighty, their three hours would equal 19 million new jobs in the nonprofit sector. That's larger than the population of New York State, more than that of Washington, Oregon, Nevada, and Montana combined—all doing good works on others' behalf. What problem does America face that would not be obliterated by that army of caring? It seems a potent force compared with one night a week without TV.

The third thing that would happen is that ingenuity and creativity in human services would explode. One reason the U.S. economy has lost global preeminence is that the brightest young people no longer follow traditional career paths—construction, manufacturing, professional services—but choose the vastly more lucrative path of finance. When managing money transactions is rewarded much more handsomely than making things, actual objects, no wonder the quality and uniqueness of American goods suffer.

Likewise, if more people participate in the nation's common purpose, the power of initiative and invention grows correspondingly. There's no ceiling: What about putting the kitchens of schools, which are idle every night, to work for people who are hungry? What about using those classrooms, empty on weekends and in summer, to help the 42 million Americans who cannot read? What about making some connection between the hundreds of thousands of houses now empty due to foreclosure and the 750,000 Americans who are homeless tonight? What about finding new ways to use the Internet to make government more visible and accountable? If the creative energy that has fueled this nation's economy since its birth were to shift to human needs, it is hard to conceive of any limit to what the American people might accomplish.

And that leads us to the fourth outcome, which may be the most important of all. This benefit is the transformation of the people who join that army of caring. By investing three hours a week, each one of them begins to belong to this nation in a new way. And the nation belongs to them in a new way too—as their inheritance, as their responsibility, and as the source of the deep gratification they feel from participating in something larger than themselves.

Those emotions are contagious too. If more people joined in working with others, it would rebuild America's broken sense of community. It would reconnect us, rededicate us, remind us of how rich in resources and enterprise we are. And in so doing, it would restore the nation's soul.

Is three hours too much? Is life too busy, making ends meet too challenging, juggling family too stressful? If so, then try one: One walk for hope, one rally for a cure, one run for something good. Go to one meeting of a local legislative body—a zoning panel, school board, PTO, board of selectmen—and see if you think you might be able to contribute. Volunteer for one small project with a short time horizon. Just once, give blood.

Then pay close attention to how you feel afterward. Are you part of a new community? Do you feel like those sacrificed minutes or hours gave your day greater meaning? Do you find yourself wanting to tell people about your experience? Did you learn something about a problem you didn't know existed? Does your conscience feel a little bit fulfilled?

If the answer to these questions is no, then we are all in trouble. In fact, our nation adrift would be facing the worst possible circumstance: that we are getting used to it.

But if the answer is yes, and if you find yourself thinking about doing it again—one more meeting, one more walk—it's easy to know what you ought to do next.

THE IDEA OF America, in large measure, is about individualism. Freedom means the liberty to vote as you wish, worship as you are inspired, live where you choose, speak as you feel, make a living in your own fashion, raise children as you will, choose a lifestyle that reflects your values.

That idea has accomplished incomparable things. The diversity of democracy and the restless energy of capitalism have combined to create a courageous, frontier mentality, whether the new territories are the upper Missouri River in the time of Jefferson or the moon in the days of Kennedy or the virtual landscapes of today.

But this independent spirit is not the only one. The American idea is also about unity. It includes interconnectedness, the shared endeavor of making this democracy work. The Founders were mindful of unity, and demonstrated its importance by naming the new country the *United* States. They made it iconic by putting *E pluribus unum*—from many, one—on our new currency. They began the Constitution, "We, the people . . ."

The people have forgotten. Independence has overshadowed unity. Common purpose has been usurped by isolation. License has displaced liberty. Our family members no longer live near one another. Our transportation is solitary, as are an ever growing portion of our entertainments. Our cities and towns have sprawled into countryside, disconnecting us from centers of shared activity and interest. We live in less community every day.

These are hardly new phenomena. They are so much a part of our culture they hardly bear mentioning—except for one thing. Simultaneous with these changes in how people relate to one another, more and more Americans have said their country is headed in the wrong direction. People say they lack connection. They feel a void in their hearts.

If you multiply that void by the millions of people who feel it, then you arrive at a sum so high it explains completely why we are a nation adrift.

Are we ready for an America that is a second-tier nation? It would not be a complete tragedy. We would still have beautiful landscapes, and pockets of vibrancy in our cities. What we would not have, however, is common purpose, a resolve to attain greatness. We would permit continued decay, and the worsening of problems we could have solved. We would see an ever smaller portion of people enjoying

America's benefits, and an ever larger portion falling behind. In all, we would be accepting something far less than the Founders' sublime vision of the nobility of every human being.

As we've seen, government cannot bring that vision into reality. Yes, it has an essential supporting role. Poverty would be worse without food stamps, Medicare, Section 8 housing vouchers. Environmental degradation would be more severe without clear air and water laws, land conservation, the inspiration of national parks. Prosperity would be less secure without a strong national defense.

But it is not enough. Government is not nimble. It is rarely inspiring. It is not responsive. It does not lead, but rather follows the public's guidance as expressed through clamor and votes.

We know too that the free market has its purpose. It sustains people through jobs, and enriches those who are able to invest in successful enterprises. Capitalism has turned a wilderness into a massive economy and thirteen colonies into a global power.

But this also is not enough. Too many people are being left by the wayside, their wages too low to support a family. Too many people lack access to decent schools, safe housing, basic health care. Too few people are sharing in the gains of American capitalism, with a growing portion of society falling further behind.

If government and the free market cannot do the job of lifting this nation, of leading it through the twenty-first century with lofty goals and a sense of common purpose, then the task falls to the citizens of this land. How we respond will be the measure of the character of this people and this age. Will we watch passively as the problems of our time worsen before our eyes? Will we persist in allowing the degradation of humanity's noblest dream?

At least for some, the answer is no. For some, the answer is to participate, to be part of the solution, to take responsibility for the well-being of this nation and her people. We have met a few of these authentic patriots; there are thousands more, all over the country, doing amazing things simply because they believe in those old, radical, original ideas: We are all equal, every person can make a difference, everyone is needed for the nation to thrive, and no one has the power to stop progress toward a common purpose.

These ideas have a name, in the word's original meaning: *patriotism*. People working to solve their nation's toughest problems are demonstrating deep and active love of country.

AMERICA IS IN many ways a microcosm of the world. The people of this land come from all lands. We are a nation of immigrants. And thus, to a certain extent, if America does not work, then the world does not work. Since this nation is governed by the collective will of her people, if America is broken, then humanity is broken. If America cannot rise in common purpose to overcome its greatest hurdles, then humanity is incapable of doing so as well.

If you see a man with difficulties nonetheless making his way through life, if you see a woman with challenges reckoning with those woes, if you witness this struggling up close, it affects you. It humbles you. It causes you to reflect upon your own good fortune. It diminishes your swagger and enlarges your heart.

And if you have an opportunity to serve this man, to place yourself deliberately in a position of serving this woman, and they allow you to help, it will heal and fill and strengthen your conscience. It will deepen your life, your appreciation for its blessings, and your awareness of your existence belonging to a larger purpose.

What this experience can do for you individually, it can also do for a nation. What you learn, society can learn. The ways in which you are enriched, so too may a country be enriched.

That was the original idea, after all. America would embrace all who came, in order to fulfill the potential within every human being. In so doing, it would build a nation of conscience to serve as a beacon to the world. It is an idea of breathtaking ambition. It is also a statement of bold hope: that this place would endure simply because innately, *inalienably*, people are that good.

Are we that good? Certainly the authentic patriots are. Whatever their personal foibles, their sacrifice for the betterment of fellow citizens shows what we are all capable of doing. What are the elements of their success? Authentic patriots prevail because they have a good idea that benefits others instead of themselves. Whether as founders, leaders, or volunteers, they devote time and energy to that idea. They discover that the humanitarian mission also makes economic sense. They realize that the idea works in more than one location. They attempt to nurture a culture of involvement. They see their work as part of a larger national endeavor. And they do not stop. It becomes a way of life, a more fulfilling and satisfying and meaningful way to live.

There is only one remaining element, one asset that remains uninvested. If you believe America is a nation adrift, if you believe government and the free market cannot by themselves assure a nation's greatness, if you believe the United States deserves to fulfill its lofty promise to the world, and if you accept that authentic patriots are showing the way toward these goals, there is only one step left: Be one.

For the sake of the nation, your neighbors, your family, yourself: Be one.

To Learn More, to Do More

There is nothing more common than to confound the
terms American Revolution with those of the American
War. The American War is over, but this is far from the
case with the American Revolution. On the contrary,
[only] the first act of that great drama is closed.

— BENJAMIN RUSH, PHILADELPHIA, JULY 4, 1781

IF YOU WOULD LIKE to learn about ongoing authentic patriotism,
please visit www.authenticpatriotism.com. The site will provide
regular updates of people making a visible difference across the country. You'll also find an opportunity to comment about authentic patriots you encounter or civic improvement efforts you discover.

If you admire authentic patriots enough to want to *be one*, please
also visit www.B1campaign.com. There you will find a directory of
thousands of nonprofit ventures working on problems that government and the free market have not solved. The organizations are
arranged geographically, to help you find projects in or near your
community.

If you are already involved with an organization that is making
a difference, please come to www.B1campaign.com and let us know.
We're always interested in adding to the list of agencies looking for
help. And we hope to provide many people with new ways to enrich
their lives as volunteers.

Sources and Resources

He was so learned that he could name a horse in nine languages; so ignorant that he bought a cow to ride on.

— BENJAMIN FRANKLIN

Full references for sources given in short form in the notes below may be found in the bibliography that follows.

Notes

PART ONE: A NATION ADRIFT

CHAPTER 1: A Human Benefit

3 *The young doctor* Interviews with Dr. Harold Freeman are supplemented by his remarks at the Robin Hood Foundation's Heroes' Breakfast (Nov. 29, 2007), and personal background material from an interview taped by Chicago-based History Makers (May 2001).

CHAPTER 2: No Longer the Fringe

12 *to measure a country's drift* This paragraph relies on numerous sources: Laurence O'Sullivan, "U.S. Energy Sources and American Use of Energy," *Energy Conservation* (Sept. 9, 2008); Bill McKibben, remarks, Charlotte Congregational Church, Charlotte, Vt. (April 2009); Felicity Barringer, "U.S. Given Poor Marks on the Environment," *The New York Times* (Jan. 23, 2008); National Sentencing Project; World Health Organization; Judith Mackay, *The Penguin Atlas of Human Sexual Behavior,*

(New York: Penguin, 2000); Judith Mackay, "How Does the United States Compare with the Rest of the World in Sexual Behavior?" *Western Journal of Medicine* (June 2001); David U. Himmelstein et al., "Market-Watch: Illness and Injury as Contributors to Bankruptcy," *Health Affairs*, 2005 (Web exclusives W5-63 and W5-66: available at http://content .healthaffairs.org/cgi/reprint/hlthaff.w5.63v1.pdf); "The Plight of the Underinsured," editorial, *The New York Times* (June 12, 2008); Annie E. Casey Foundation, *The 2007 Kids Count Data Book* (available at: http:// datacenter.kidscount.org/databook/2008/Default.aspx); Jared Diamond, "What's Your Consumption Factor?" *The New York Times* (Jan. 2, 2008); Bob Herbert, "A Dubious Milestone," *The New York Times* (June 21, 2008); Christian E. Weller, "Economic Snapshot for June 2008," Center for American Progress (available at: http://www.americanprogress.org/ issues/2008/06/econ_snapshot.html); Pamela Paul, *Pornified: How Pornography Is Transforming Our Lives, Our Relationships, and Our Families* (New York: Times Books, 2005); Commonwealth Fund, "National Scorecard on Health System Performance," (November 2007; available at: http://www.commonwealthfund.org/usr_doc/site_docs/slideshows/ NatlScorecard/NatlScorecard.html).

14 *Oil-rich nations* The correlation between oil revenues and political repression is advanced by Thomas Friedman in "The First Law of Petropolitics," *Foreign Affairs* (May/June, 2006).

14 *a trip he and his wife took* Friedman's observations about the Singapore airport and the Berlin train station appear in "Who Will Tell the People?" *The New York Times* (May 4, 2008).

14 *The world's tallest building* Fareed Zakaria's list of areas in which other nations have the biggest or best appears in "The Rise of the Rest," *Newsweek* (May 12, 2008).

CHAPTER 3: The Need for a New Way

20 *day before his inauguration* The story of Herbert Hoover warning Franklin Roosevelt about the banking crisis, and details about the Reconstruction Finance Corporation, come from Rohatyn, *Bold Endeavors*.

22 *President Lyndon Johnson's War on Poverty* Discussion of the War on Poverty draws on Paul Krugman's "Poverty Is Poison," *The New York Times* (Feb. 18, 2008).

22 *various special interests* The tally of daily spending on lobbying comes from the nonprofit, nonpartisan Center for Responsive Politics, "Washington Lobbying Grew to $3.2 Billion Last Year, Despite Economy"

(Jan. 29, 2009; available at: http://www.opensecrets.org/news/2009/01/washington-lobbying-grew-to-32.html).

25 *the federal treasury was indebted* The tally of the national debt comes from Ed Brillig, "The U.S. National Debt Clock," October 27, 2009 (http://www.brillig.com/debt_clock).

29 *how economic gains are shared* Data about the portion of national income that has gone to top earners, as well as analysis of government policy exacerbating the polarization of wealth, comes from an editorial, "It Didn't End Well Last Time," *The New York Times* (April 4, 2007).

29 *this trend had vanished* Data about the growing polarization of wealth comes from Barbara Hagenbaugh, "Nation's Wealth Disparity Widens," *USA Today* (Jan. 22, 2003). Her report cites as its source a survey on stock ownership by the Federal Reserve Bank.

29 *A man in his thirties today* Robert Reich, "Totally Spent," *The New York Times* (Feb. 13, 2008).

29 *The smaller the income slice* Chye-Ching Huang and Chad Stone, "Average Income in 2006 Up $60,000 for Top 1 Percent of Households, Just $430 for Bottom 90 Percent," Center on Budget and Policy Priorities (July 29, 2008; revised Oct. 22, 2008; available at: http://www.cbpp.org/cms/?fa=view&id=69)

29 *fifteen thousand families in the top 0.01 percent* "Good Times at Sotheby's," editorial, *The New York Times* (May 11, 2008).

30 *Today 19 percent of American children* Dan Frosch, "Study Shows Colorado Has Largest Rise in Child Poverty," *The New York Times* (June 11, 2008).

30 *not limited to children* David Baer, "State Handbook of 2006 Economic, Demographic, and Fiscal Indicators 2008," AARP Public Policy Institute (April 28, 2008; available online at http://www.aarp.org/research/ppi/econ-sec/income/articles/d19014_fiscal.html). Deborah Thorne, Elizabeth Warren, and Teresa Sullivan, "Generations of Struggle," AARP Public Policy Institute (June 2008; can be downloaded at: assets.aarp.org/rgcenter/consume/2008_11_debt.pdf).

31 *growth in corporate earnings* Aviva Aron-Dine, "Share of National Income Going to Wages and Salaries at Record Low in 2006," Center on Budget and Policy Priorities (revised March 29, 2007; available at: http://www.cbpp.org/cms/?fa=view&id=634).

31 *more than 13 million Americans* Christopher Rugaber, "Meltdown 101: Unemployment by the Numbers," Associated Press (March 7, 2009).

32 *McMansions will continue to rise* The size of an average home, in 2006 and 1976, comes from the U.S. Census Bureau.

32 *one-third of their income* Eric Belsky et al., "Measuring the Nation's Rental Housing Affordability Problems" (Cambridge, Mass.: Joint Center for Housing Studies at Harvard University, June 2005; can be downloaded at: www.jchs.harvard.edu/publications/rental/rd05-1_measuring _rental_affordability05.pdf).

32 *the number of homeless people* National Coalition for the Homeless.

33 *where labor costs are cheapest* Sharon Otterman, "Outsourcing Jobs," Council on Foreign Relations (Feb. 20, 2004); Daniel Drezner, "The Outsourcing Bogeyman," *Foreign Affairs* (May/June 2004); and Pete Engardio et al., "The Future of Outsourcing," *BusinessWeek* (Jan. 30, 2006).

CHAPTER 4: Founding Principles

36 *they had a larger purpose* Discussion of the culture and issues in revolutionary America relies upon Bailyn, *Ideological Origins*, and Wood, *Radicalism*. Wood's book provides the quote from Dr. David Ramsay on subjects and citizens, the comment from the royal governor of Georgia, George Mason's contribution to the Constitution of Virginia, and the writings of Thomas Hutchinson and Montesquieu on the virtues of economic stratification.

38 *the Church of George III* Information on the power and influence of the Anglican Church comes from Kowalski, *Revolutionary Spirits*.

40 *the king sent warships* David McCullough describes England's navy arriving in New York Harbor in *1776*.

PART TWO: AUTHENTIC PATRIOTS

CHAPTER 5: Seven Steps to a Cure

52 *Jenifer quoted West Side Story* Three Sisters: *The Search for a Cure*, HBO (2003). This program also supplied me with Jenifer's U.S. Senate testimony, including her description of being unable to hold a cup of coffee and her desire to be "jumping on them."

53 *hardly an urban sluggard* Jenifer Estess, *Tales from the Bed*. The narrative of Jenifer's early illness—the day with severe wind, her diagnosis, the suggestion to go to Paris, the quotation "I started taking the whole thing personally," the Thanksgiving dinner scene, her description of the news conference, her pneumonia and subsequent near death—all derive from this book.

55 *known as Lou Gehrig's disease* Data about the prevalence and course of ALS comes from the Project ALS Web site, www.projectals.org.

57 *Politics have presented an impediment* See Union of Concerned Scientists, "Restoring Scientific Integrity in Policymaking" and "Scientific Integrity in Policymaking" (2004; both available at http://www.ucsusa .org/scientific_integrity/abuses_of_science/investigations_and_surveys/ reports-scientific-integrity.html), plus an unbylined Associated Press report, "Scientists Rally Around Stem Cell Advocate Fired by Bush," *USA Today* (March 19, 2004), and President George W. Bush, remarks issued from his ranch in Crawford, Texas (Aug. 9, 2001).

59 *an orphan disease* See the Web site of the National Organization for Rare Disorders, www.rarediseases.org.

61 *how most medical research funding occurs* "Refusing to Die," unbylined article in *Forbes* (April 16, 2001).

65 *the research involved collaboration* Scott Hensley et al., "Stem-Cell Test Restored Motion to Paralyzed Mice," *The Wall Street Journal* (July 25, 2001).

66 *Missouri lawmakers killed funding* Andale Gross, "Stem Cell Movement Suffers Delays in Missouri," Associated Press (July 24, 2007).

74 *I hope all of your wishes* Lewis Cole died on Oct. 10, 2008. He was sixty-two.

CHAPTER 6: "The Noblest Question in the World"

82 *that American colonists were indifferent to slavery* See Bailyn, *Ideological Origins*, and Wood, *Radicalism*. The quotation from John Allen's pamphlet comes from Bailyn's book.

100 *The condition of minorities* "The State of Black America," The National Urban League (2007).

101 *A higher percentage of blacks are convicted* See Marc Mauer and Ryan King, "State Rates of Incarceration by Race and Ethnicity," The Sentencing Project (July 2007).

101 *the prison population reached a record* Solomon Moore, "Justice Dept. Numbers Show Prison Trends," *The New York Times* (Dec. 6, 2007).

101 *blacks receive higher-priced mortgage loans* See the National Community Reinvestment Coalition's study, "New Data from Federal Reserve Suggests Least Well Regulated Mortgage Companies Issued Riskiest Loans" (Sept. 11, 2007). The study analyzed 2.3 million loans in 380 U.S. metropolitan areas. Based on 2005 data, blacks were twice as likely to receive expensive loans. While the disparity between blacks and whites existed at all income levels, it was more severe at higher incomes.

101 *the present rate of incarceration in America* Bureau of Justice Statistics, "Prison and Jail Inmates at Midyear 2006" (available at: http://ojp.usdoj .gov/bjs/abstract/pjim06.htm).

101 *the rate in South Africa during apartheid* March Mauer, "Americans Behind Bars: The International Use of Incarceration, 1992–1993," The Sentencing Project (Sept. 1994).

102 *unequal nursing home care* David Barton Smith et al., "Separate and Unequal: Racial Segregation and Disparities in Quality Across U.S. Nursing Homes," *Health Affairs* (Sept. 2007). Smith and his colleagues researched 7,196 nursing homes with 838,000 residents, just under half of the nursing home population nationally.

102 *The Jena Times in Louisiana* Amy Waldman, "The Truth About Jena," *The Atlantic Monthly*, (Jan./Feb. 2008; available at: http://www.the atlantic.com/doc/200801/jena6). Additional details about Mychal Bell I have relied upon Sean Callebs, "Jena 6's Mychal Bell: Pressure Led to Suicide Try," CNN (Jan. 15, 2009).

CHAPTER 7: A Culture of Caring

117 *the nation's second-largest barrier island* Details of the history, demographics, and geography of Hilton Head and Beaufort County come from www.hiltonhead.tv.com and *Island Real Estate Magazine* (Down South Publishers, Nov. 2007).

118 *Median household income* The U.S. Census Bureau (2006), which also supplied house price information.

119 *in a privately published memoir* Jack McConnell, *Circle of Caring: The Story of the Volunteers in Medicine Clinic*, printed with a grant from the Robert Wood Johnson Foundation (1998).

121 *the cost of a General Motors car* Blake Fleetwood, "52% of Americans Disgusted with Health Care Costs," *The Huffington Post* (Oct. 25, 2006; available at: http://www.huffingtonpost.com/blake-fleetwood/52-of-americans-disgusted_b_32495.html).

121 *The United States spends the most* Details about American health care—per capita spending, infant mortality, etc.—appear in "National Scorecard on Health System Performance," the Commonwealth Fund (Sept. 20, 2006; available at: http://www.commonwealthfund.org/Con tent/Publications/In-the-Literature/2006/Sep/U-S--Health-System -Performance--A-National-Scorecard.aspx).

123 *The potential for an encore career* Susan Felt, "Author Sees Career Encore for Boomers," *The Arizona Republic* (July 20, 2007) and Jane Brody, "In

Act 2 of Life, Doing Work That Matters," *The New York Times* (July 8, 2008).

CHAPTER 8: Until Proven Innocent

141 *His inmate number* Chrisena Coleman, "Making Most of 2nd Chance," *The New York Daily News* (Sept. 24, 2006).

144 *we learned about Marion Coakley* Scheck et al., *Actual Innocence*. This book provided me with Coakley's story, as well as background about Scheck, Neufeld, and the project's founding.

148 *James Watson and Francis Crick* Discussion of the evolution of DNA evidence relies upon numerous sources, particularly: Edward Conners et al., *Convicted by Juries, Exonerated by Science: Case Studies in the Use of DNA Evidence to Establish Innocence After Trial*, U.S. Department of Justice, Office of Justice Programs, National Institute of Justice (June 1996); and Karen Cormier, Lisa Calandro, and Dennis Reeder, "Evolution of DNA Evidence for Crime Solving—A Judicial and Legislative History," *Forensic Magazine* (June/July 2005).

151 *A police sergeant's reply* Jim Dwyer quotes Sergeant Patrick J. McGuire in "New York Fails at Finding Evidence to Help the Wrongfully Convicted," *The New York Times* (July 6, 2006).

157 *March 5, 1770* The story of the Boston Massacre and the subsequent legal case relies on several accounts, notably McCullough, *John Adams*.

164–165 *A group of scholar-attorneys* James Liebman, Jeffrey Fagan, and Valerie West, "Broken System: Error Rates in Capital Cases, 1973–1995," Columbia Law School, Public Law Research Paper no. 15 (June 12, 2001; available at: http://www2.law.columbia.edu/instructionalservices/lieb man).

165 *did not trouble Justice Antonin Scalia* Adam Liptak, "Consensus on Counting the Innocent: We Can't," *The New York Times* (March 25, 2008). The opinion of Justice David Souter appeared in the same article.

166 *On six separate occasions* C-SPAN live coverage (Feb. 11, 2000). Former Florida Supreme Court chief justice Gerald Kogan made his remarks about death penalty errors at a news conference in Washington, D.C., at the introduction of the Innocence Protection Act. U.S. Senator Patrick Leahy's comments come from the same coverage of that event.

168 *The United States incarcerates more* Adam Liptak, "Inmate Count in U.S. Dwarfs Other Nations," *The New York Times* (April 23, 2008).

Additional information comes from Liptak's "U.S. Imprisons One in 100 Adults, Report Finds," *The New York Times* (Feb. 29, 2008).

171 *Charles Chatman* "More Than a Steak Dinner," editorial, *The New York Times* (Jan. 10, 2008).

171 *Alan was still in handcuffs* While nearly all of Alan Newton's story comes from interviews and court documents, the narrative of the day of his release is supplemented by Leonard Greene and Lukas Alpert, "Freedom Tastes Sweet: Cleared Man Leaves Prison After 22 years," *New York Post* (July 7, 2006); Tamer El-Ghobashy, "Whole Lot of Catching Up to Do on All Fronts," *New York Daily News* (July 7, 2006); Chrisena Coleman and Corky Siemaszko, "Not Bitter, But Filled with Joy," *New York Daily News* (July 7, 2006).

175 *The most recent was Timothy Cole* Innocence Project documents, plus Wade Goodman, "Family of Man Cleared by DNA Still Seeks Justice," National Public Radio (Feb. 5, 2009).

CHAPTER 9: The Win-Win-Win-Win-Win

177 *when Majora Carter rescued her* Personal interviews of Majora are supplemented by profile information and comments in her presentation at the TED conference (www.TED.org); remarks on *This I Believe*, National Public Radio (Jan. 1, 2009); Marguerite Holloway, "The Green Power Broker," *The New York Times* (Dec. 14, 2008); "Majora Carter: The Green Thumb," *Vibe* (Aug. 8, 2007; available at: http://www.vibe.com/juice07/2007/08/majora_carter_npg/); Andrea Doyle, "Majora Carter, Not Your Ordinary Environmental Leader," Professional Convention Management Association (Dec. 2006; available at: http://www.pcma.org/Convene/Issue_Archives/December_2006/Leading_by_Example-Carter.htm); Karen Breslau, "Bringing Cleaner Air and a Bit of Nature Where It's Really Needed," *Newsweek* (Dec. 25, 2006); Marisol Bello, "Cities Cultivate Two Types of Green," *USA Today* (Dec. 12, 2007); Susan Piperato, "Green the Ghetto," *Yoga+* (March/April 2008; available at: http://www.himalayaninstitute.org/YogaPlus/Article.aspx?id=2348).

177 *No ordinary community* Sources for the condition, incomes, and environmental status of the Bronx include: "Communities of Color and Solid Waste Management," a map prepared by the Municipal Art Society, using data from the New York City Department of City Planning and from New York Lawyers for the Public Interest (2007); Luis Mostacero, "Hunts Point Has to Hold Its Nose," *The Hunts Point Express* (Dec. 2006); "Hunts Point On Parade," a series of articles in *The Hunts Point Express* (June/July 2008); and the U.S. Census Bureau.

181 *Wesleyan University, located in Middletown* Data on admissions, resources, and tuition at Wesleyan University comes from the school's Web site, www.wesleyan.edu.

185 *The only freshwater river* Sources for the history and condition of the Bronx River include: "Herring Fish Restored to Bronx River in New York City," Wildlife Conservation Service (April 6, 2007; available at: http://news.mongabay.com/2007/0406-wcs.html); "Natural and Social History," Bronx River Alliance (available at: http://www.bronxriver. org/?pg=content&p=abouttheriver&ml=9); "The Bronx River Watershed Assessment and Management Report," Westchester County Department of Planning (Oct. 2007); Memorandum of Agreement establishing the Bronx River Watershed Coalition (Jan. 2006; available at: www.hudsonwatershed.org/plans09/bronxriver.pdf).

188 *a professor from Clark Atlanta University* Robert D. Bullard presented "Poverty, Pollution and Environmental Racism: Strategies for Building Healthy and Sustainable Communities" at the Environmental Racism Forum World Summit on Sustainable Development in Johannesburg, South Africa (July 2, 2002).

188 *a 1982 incident in Warren County* Division of Waste Management, North Carolina Department of Environment and Natural Resources, "Warren County Landfill Fact Sheet" (2009).

188 *commercial hazardous waste landfills* General Accounting Office, "Siting of Hazardous Waste Landfills and Their Correlation with Racial and Economic Status of Surrounding Communities" (1983; available at: http://www.gao.gov/products/121648).

188 *Native Americans bear a heavy burden* See Valerie Taliman, "Stuck Holding the Nation's Nuclear Waste," Race, Poverty and the Environment foundation Newsletter (Fall 1992), and Winona LaDuke, "All Our Relations: Native Struggles for Land Rights and Life" (Boston, Mass.: South End Press, 1999).

189 *South Coast Air Basin of Los Angeles* Eric Mann, *L.A.'s Lethal Air: New Strategies for Policy, Organizing, and Action* (Los Angeles: Labor/ Community Strategy Center, 1991).

189 *In Houston, Texas* Robert D. Bullard, *Invisible Houston: The Black Experience in Boom and Bust* (College Station: Texas A&M University Press, 1987).

189 *Childhood asthma* From the Web site of the Centers for Disease Control (available at: www.cdc.gov/nceh/ashtma_old/ataglance/default.htm).

190 *the Altgeld Gardens* Michael Hawthorne and Darnell Little, "Chicago's Toxic Air," *Chicago Tribune* (Sept. 28, 2008).

190 *if Saint Louis builds a school* "Citing History of Explosions, Releases of Poisonous Gases and Injured Workers, Watchdogs Urge Regulators to Close Toxic Waste Incinerator," *Sierra Club News* (July 21, 2003); this article notes that 63 percent of the 62,982 people who live within three miles of the incinerator are African American, and 19,000 are children; "Illinois Hazwaste Incinerator Permitted Despite Explosions, Fires," *Environment News Service* (Sept. 15, 2008) notes that the incinerator had been operating without a permit since 1995, and had accrued more than $3 million in fines.

199 *water quality is improving* Details on the successful spawning of river herring and the naming of the beaver come from "Herring Fish Restored to Bronx River" at mongabay.com (see note for page 185, above).

CHAPTER 10: The Gift Everyone Can Give

205 *on December 3, 1967* Interviews with Michael Borkon, M.D., supplemented by "Cut to the Heart: Pioneers of Heart Surgery," *NOVA*, Public Broadcasting System (April 1999).

213 *The breakthrough was cyclosporine* This drug is defined in Taber's *Cyclopedic Medical Dictionary* (16th edition, 1989), as well as PDR.net, the online version of the Physician's Desk Reference.

213 *people with all kinds of transplants* Numerous sources provided me with information about transplant success: interviews with Jeffrey Reese, M.D., transplant specialist and chief of surgery at the Veterans Administration Hospital in Kansas City; the United Network for Organ Sharing, which maintains data on every U.S. organ donation and transplant conducted since 1986; the Organ Procurement and Transplantation Network, which maintains the hundred thousand person–plus national patient waiting list; and the National Survey of Organ and Tissue Donation Attitudes and Behaviors, from the Health Resource and Service Administration, U.S. Department of Health and Human Services (2005).

PART THREE: AUTHENTIC PATRIOTISM: FIVE ELEMENTS

CHAPTER 11: Element One: Doing Good, Saving Money

223 *He lands at Rikers Island* "Block 9000, Block Group 9, Census Tract 1, Bronx County, New York" from the U.S. Census Bureau; Graham Rayman, "Rikers Island Fight Club," *The Village Voice* (April 8, 2008); Benjamin Weiser, "Lawsuit Suggests Pattern of Rikers Guards Looking Other Way," *The New York Times* (Feb. 3, 2009); Friends of Island Academy.

CHAPTER 12: Element Two: Doing Good in Place After Place

232 *building on the green-collar idea* Marisol Bello, "Cities Cultivate Two Types of Green," *USA Today* (Dec. 12, 2007).

233 *green roofs have grown in popularity* Verlyn Klinkenborg, "Up On the Roof," *National Geographic* (May 2009).

CHAPTER 14: Element Four: A National Movement

247 *David Goggins weighed 280 pounds* Matthew Dale, "When Ironman Isn't Enough," www.ironman.com (Nov. 13, 2008; available at: http://ironman.com/events/ironman/worldchampionship/in-awe-of-the-sports-elite-athletes-for-david-goggins-ultramarathons-are-much-more-of-a-challenge), and Peter Flax, "The Warrior: David Goggins," *Runner's World* (Dec. 2008).

248 *Race for the Cure* See www.komen.org.

249 *The New York Marathon began* See the race's Web site, www.nycmarathon.org, and George Vecsey, "Marathon Remains on Right Course," *The New York Times* (Nov. 4, 2008).

249 *Across the country at Columbia* Marc Santora, "At Columbia, Students Mix Studies with Volunteer Work, for Credits," *The New York Times* (Sept. 11, 2008).

252 *no ordinary tree* The narrative of Luna's rescue relies on Julia Butterfly Hill, *The Legacy of Luna*, as well as Justin Berton, "Catching Up with Julia Butterfly Hill," on the SFGate Web site of the *San Francisco Chronicle* (April 16, 2009; available at: http://www.sfgate.com/cgi-bin/article.cgi?f=/c/a/2009/04/16/DDPQ16TJPC.DTL&type=printable), circleoflife.org, and whatsyourtree.org.

260 *Talia Lehman, an eighth-grader* Nicholas Kristof, "Talia for President," *The New York Times* (Nov. 16, 2008), and the Reuters Business Wire (May 5, 2008). Kristof also wrote about Rachel Rosenfeld in "Saving the World in Study Hall," *The New York Times* (May 11, 2008).

261 *Wendy Kopp was a senior* Information about Teach for America comes from the organization's Web site, www.TeachForAmerica.org; Sam Dillion, "Teach for America Sees Surge in Popularity," *The New York Times* (May 14, 2008), and Mathematica Policy Research, "The Effects of Teach for America on Students: Findings from a National Evaluation" (June 9, 2004; available at: http://www.mathematica-mpr.com/publications/pdfs/teach.pdf).

261 *the American Diner Museum* Pam Belluck, "Youthful Offenders Restoring Luster to Diners of Old," *The New York Times* (July 14, 2008).

262 *Each year Jim Keane* Details come from a column by David Broder, published on the *Washington Post* Writers' Group Web site (Sept. 24, 2007); unfortunately the *Post* currently only maintains Broder's columns from 2009 online.

262 *great-granddaughter of Mountain Chief* Interviews with Eloise Cobell were supplemented by "Cobell *v.* Kempthorne" from the Indian Trust Web site (www.indiantrust.com); David Dudley, "I Just Want Justice," *AARP The Magazine* (Jan./Feb. 2007); and an editorial, "The Verdict: It's Broken" in *The New York Times* (Feb. 1, 2008).

263 *the new president of Ripon College* Interview with David Joyce. Details on other schools' programs come from Katie Zezima, "With Free Bikes, Challenging Car Culture on Campus," *The New York Times* (Oct. 20, 2008).

263 *Gerald Chertavian served* See Sridevi Raghavan, "Closing the Opportunity Divide for Young Adults" in *The Harbus*, the independent weekly at Harvard Business School (Feb. 26, 2007). Year Up is mentioned by David Brooks in "Thoroughly Modern Do-Gooders," *The New York Times* (Mar. 21, 2008).

264 *the Imagination Library* Seet the Library's Web site, www.dollysimagi nationlibrary.com, and Chris Bohjalian, "The Book Is in the Mail," *The Burlington Free Press* (Nov. 16, 2008).

265 *Mary Louise Hartpence* Information on this authentic patriot comes form the Oklahoma Commission for Human Services.

Chapter 15: Element Five: Everyone an Authentic Patriot

272 *42 million Americans who cannot read* This statistic comes from the National Right to Read Foundation and www.education-portal.com.

Bibliography

Bailyn, Bernard. *The Ideological Origins of the American Revolution*. Cambridge, Mass.: Harvard University Press, 1967.

Bennet, James, ed. *The Future of the American Idea. The Atlantic*, 150th anniversary issue, November 2007.

Brown, Stuart Gerry, ed. *We Hold These Truths: Documents of American Democracy*. New York: Harper & Bros., 1941.

Douglass, Frederick. *Narrative of the Life of Frederick Douglass, an American Slave*. New York: Anchor Books, 1973.

Eaton, Susan. *The Children in Room E4: American Education on Trial*. Chapel Hill, N. Car.: Algonquin Books, 2006.

Estess, Jenifer, as told to Valerie Estess. *Tales from the Bed: On Living, Dying, and Having It All*. New York: Atria Books, 2004.

Flint, Anthony. *Wrestling with Moses: How Jane Jacobs Took on New York's Master Builder and Transformed the American City*. New York: Random House, 2009.

Friedman, Thomas. *Hot, Flat, and Crowded*. New York: Farrar, Straus and Giroux, 2008.

Gore, Al. *The Assault on Reason*. New York: Penguin Press, 2007.

Greenleaf, Robert K. *Servant Leadership: A Journey Into the Nature of Legitimate Power and Greatness*, 25th anniversary edition. New York: Paulist Press, 2002.

Griffin, Susan. *Wrestling with the Angel of Democracy*. Boston: Trumpeter Books, 2008.

Hawken, Paul. *Blessed Unrest: How the Largest Social Movement in History Is Restoring Grace, Justice, and Beauty to the World*. New York: Penguin, 2007.

Hill, Julia Butterfly. *The Legacy of Luna: The Story of a Tree, a Woman, and the Struggle to Save the Redwoods*. San Francisco: Harper, 2000.

Kennedy, Caroline. *A Patriot's Handbook: Songs, Poems, Stories, and Speeches Celebrating the Land We Love*. New York: Hyperion, 2003.

Ketchum, Richard. *Victory at Yorktown: The Campaign That Won the Revolution*. New York: Henry Holt, 2004.

Kowalski, Gary. *Revolutionary Spirits: The Enlightened Faith of America's Founding Fathers*. New York: Bluebridge, 2008.

Liu, Eric, and Nick Hanauer. *The True Patriot*. Seattle: Sasquatch Books, 2007.

McCullough, David. *1776*. New York: Simon & Schuster, 2005.

———. *John Adams*. New York: Simon & Schuster, 2001.

McPhee, John. *Uncommon Carriers*. New York: Farrar, Straus and Giroux, 2007.

National Urban League; Stephanie J. Jones, ed. *The State of Black America 2007: Portrait of the Black Male*. Silver Spring, Md.: Beckham Publications Group, 2007.

Ray, Paul, and Sherry Ruth Anderson. *The Cultural Creatives: How 50 Million People Are Changing the World*. New York: Three Rivers Press, 2000.

Redford, James, producer; Maro Chermayeff, dir. *The Kindness of Strangers*. (Documentary film, 1998).

Rohatyn, Felix. *Bold Endeavors: How Our Government Built America, and Why It Must Rebuild Now*. New York: Simon & Schuster, 2009.

Schama, Simon. *The American Future*. New York: HarperCollins, 2009.

Scheck, Barry, with Peter Neufeld and Jim Dwyer. *Actual Innocence: When Justice Goes Wrong and How to Make It Right.* New York: New American Library, 2003.

Shore, Bill. *The Cathedral Within: Transforming Your Life by Giving Something Back.* New York: Random House, 2001.

Weisman, Alan. *The World Without Us.* New York: Thomas Dunne, 2007.

Wolf, Naomi. *The End of America: Letter of Warning to a Young Patriot, A Citizen's Call to Action.* White River Junction, Vt.: Chelsea Green, 2007.

Wood, Gordon S. *The Radicalism of the American Revolution.* New York: Vintage Books, 1993.

Acknowledgments

ON A FRIGID NIGHT in January 2007 I sat in a Montreal steak house with my creative friend Kate Palmer, complaining that I couldn't decide which of three ideas should be my next writing project. She listened, sipped her wine, then suggested a way to combine all three. This book was literally her idea.

That night was only the beginning of the tremendous help I received over nearly three years. Linda Loewenthal, my agent and friend, was an essential and trusted ally, as ever. George Witte believed in authentic patriotism from the beginning, and hugely improved the manuscript along the way. He is as insightful and patient an editor as any writer could imagine.

In early drafts I relied on valuable feedback from Chris Bohjalian, Dana Yeaton, Justin Cronin, and my brother Mike Kiernan, M.D. Asa Hyde was a huge help with the Internet side of this project, especially the B1 campaign. My buddy Roberta MacDonald and the farm families who own the Cabot cheese cooperative enabled me to pursue this project without interrupting my cherished work in end-of-life care. I truly appreciate their support.

For introducing me to scholars of the 1700s, my thanks go to Jim Ralph, Ph.D., former classmate and now history professor at Middlebury College. I met Harold Freeman, M.D., through my brother Peter Kiernan III, who generously arranged for me to attend the Robin Hood Foundation Heroes' Breakfast in 2007 (and who is an authentic patriot himself). I learned of the Estess sisters through my friend Martha McCully, whose eulogy about Jenifer's sense of beauty was an incredible gift. Pat Harrington guided me through Project ALS with patience and humor. Davin Pelle made my experience with the Chicago Children's Choir harmonious from first to last. Susan Kelley opened the first doors for me at the Volunteers in Medicine Institute. Eric Ferrero deserves a medal for his patience with my digging in and around the Innocence Project. Marsha Gordon was an excellent guide of the South Bronx and Sustainable South Bronx, with multiple visits coordinated by her and Linda Cronin-Gross (including one on the remarkable day a plane went down in the Hudson River but no one died). Mike Noble of Fletcher Allen Health Care connected me with organ donation experts—especially Jeff Reese, M.D., who years ago took generous amounts of time to teach me the ethics of transplanting. Thanks to all.

When you meet people who are changing the world, it is a continually humbling experience. But eventually it becomes an inspiring one. The more time I spent with the authentic patriots this book portrays—people who said that the problems they saw simply should not be happening in America—the more I found my faith in this nation and its founding principles vigorously restored. That is an incomparable gift. To the many people their generosity has already helped, I must add my own deep gratitude.

Index

THE POWERFUL, GROUNDBREAKING INVESTIGATION OF
THE END OF LIFE: ITS PROFOUND OPPORTUNITIES AND
OUR HEALTH-CARE SYSTEM'S MISPLACED PRIORITIES

"A superb resource for boomers dealing with their parents' final
days and anxious to exert more control over their own rites
of passage, as well as for health-care professionals who need
to hear this story from the other side."

—*KIRKUS REVIEWS* (STARRED REVIEW)

 St. Martin's Griffin
www.stmartins.com

Are You Looking for a Speaker?

STEPHEN KIERNAN has won a national reputation for delivering compelling, fascinating, and funny talks before all kinds of audiences—colleges and universities, civic groups, fraternal organizations, social entrepreneur conferences, and more.

Using data that makes a convincing case for civic involvement, and telling stories about people from all walks of life who have accomplished incredible things, Stephen motivates, educates, and illuminates.

Bring the inspiring message of *Authentic Patriotism* to your group by contacting Stephen through www.stephenpkiernan.com.